BULLYING PREVENTION

BULLYING PREVENTION

*Creating a Positive School
Climate and Developing
Social Competence*

PAMELA ORPINAS

ARTHUR M. HORNE

American Psychological Association
Washington, DC

Published by
American Psychological Association
750 First Street, NE
Washington, DC 20002
www.apa.org

To order
APA Order Department
P.O. Box 92984
Washington, DC 20090-2984
Tel: (800) 374-2721; Direct: (202) 336-5510
Fax: (202) 336-5502; TDD/TTY: (202) 336-6123
Online: www.apa.org/books/
E-mail: order@apa.org

In the U.K., Europe, Africa, and the Middle East, copies may be ordered from
American Psychological Association
3 Henrietta Street
Covent Garden, London
WC2E 8LU England

Typeset in Goudy by Stephen McDougal, Mechanicsville, MD

Printer: Edwards Brothers, Inc., Ann Arbor, MI
Cover Designer: Go! Creative, Kensington, MD
Technical/Production Editor: Genevieve Gill

The opinions and statements published are the responsibility of the authors, and such opinions and statements do not necessarily represent the policies of the American Psychological Association.

Library of Congress Cataloging-in-Publication Data

Orpinas, Pamela.
  Bullying prevention : creating a positive school climate and developing social competence / Pamela Orpinas, Arthur M. Horne.
     p. cm.
  Includes bibliographical references and index.
  ISBN 1-59147-282-2
  1. Bullying in schools—Prevention. 2. School environment.
3. Aggressiveness in children. I. Horne, Arthur M., 1942- II. Title.

  LB3013.3O77 2006
  371.5'8—dc22   2005009557

British Library Cataloguing-in-Publication Data
A CIP record is available from the British Library.

Printed in the United States of America
First Edition

CONTENTS

LIST OF TABLES, FIGURES, EXHIBITS, AND BOXES

TABLES

FIGURES

EXHIBITS

BOXES

ACKNOWLEDGMENTS

The content of this book not only represents our own work with children, families, and schools but also reflects the contributions of numerous researchers, scholars, program developers, and practitioners from the United States and other parts of the world. These professionals have committed their energy and skills to reduce the problem of bullying in schools and communities and to help children and adults develop positive relationships. Specifically, we acknowledge the work of Dorothy Espelage, Susan Swearer, Susan Limber, Richard Hazler, John Hoover, William Quinn, Alfred McAlister, Guy Parcel, Steven Kelder, Nancy Murray, Lileana Escobar, Andrew Sprigner, Kris Bosworth, Aleta Meyer, Franklin Gay, Rebecca Stern, Stuart Twemlow, William Porter, David Jolliff, Nicki Crick, Gilbert Kliman, Shelley Hymel, Deborah Staniszewski, and others who have shared freely their ideas and programs with us. We also acknowledge, with gratitude, the work of Dan Olweus, the person most responsible for the development of the research and intervention processes in the field of bullying over the past three-decade period. We appreciate the many contributions to bullying and violence prevention and to school health promotion made by all these significant contributors to our work. We have incorporated many of their ideas and much of their work, and we have attempted to acknowledge their contributions throughout this text. We thank them for their excellent work. If we have failed to acknowledge a specific activity of one of our colleagues, we offer our apologies.

We have had tremendous support for our work from our colleagues at the University of Georgia, and we appreciate all they have done to help bring this project to fruition. We would like to acknowledge members of several research teams. The ACT Early Project, over an 8-year period, included Jean Baker, Randy Kamphaus, and Ann Winsor, who contributed ideas and interventions for more effective teacher–student engagement. As part of the I–CARE and the Multisite Violence Prevention Project, Tracy Elder was engaged throughout the process of writing this book and shared her practical expertise with us on multiple occasions. Additionally, Kat Raczynski, Kate Lindsey, Jenny VanOverbeke Curtis, Ashley Carpenter Wells, Natasha Howard, and Nick Elzey all contributed with their reviews, recommendations, suggestions, and helpful participation. For several years, a bully intervention research team at the University of Georgia has greatly influenced our work. Dawn Newman-Carson, Christie Bartolomucci, Jennifer Stoddard, Christopher Bell, and Natasha Howard worked on the bully project and contributed ideas and program suggestions that influenced the current book in positive and exciting ways.

The faculty and staff members of our departments provided support that helped us stay the course and finish this project. In the Department of Health Promotion and Behavior, we especially recognize Mark Wilson, Stu Fors, and Betty Blum. In the Department of Counseling and Human Development Services, we appreciate all who have contributed to the task, including Diane Cooper, John Dagley, Brian Glaser, Georgia Calhoun, Mary Cash, and Jacquee Rosumny.

Most important, we would like to thank the many principals, counselors, psychologists, teachers, and students who have shared their experiences with us during the past decade. Their contributions have been invaluable to the development of this book. During the many teacher training workshops we have conducted throughout the years, teachers have shared with us their best practices, their most successful interventions, and their lessons learned on what to avoid. We thank them all.

We especially recognize the work of Lindsay Della, who read and edited the book from start to finish. She provided valuable recommendations for revisions, additions, and changes. She was prompt in identifying gaps in our creative thinking, recognizing missing links, and making us aware of redundancies. We also thank Susan Reynolds, Susan Herman, and Genevieve Gill of the American Psychological Association for their conscientious review of our work and for their encouragement; they have been a delight to work with.

Finally, we thank our families, who supported us during the many hours of writing and editing.

BULLYING PREVENTION

INTRODUCTION

Take sides. Neutrality helps the oppressor, never the victim. Silence encourages the tormentor, never the tormented.
—Elie Wiesel, 1986, Nobel Peace Prize acceptance speech

This book presents an approach to understanding and treating child and adolescent behavioral problems that goes far beyond the prevention of bullying. We strongly believe that all children should be able to learn and grow up in a safe and caring environment. The absence of illness is not equivalent to good health. Likewise, the reduction of bullying by itself does not translate to a healthy and inviting community. Beyond the reduction of aggression, parents, psychologists, and school professionals need to increase the positive qualities of the environments in which children live and learn. In addition to and within that positive environment, adults also need to provide opportunities for children to learn social skills that will help them establish both positive relationships with peers and adults and the academic skills they need to succeed in school. This book emphasizes these two components of reducing bullying and aggression: the need to create a positive, caring environment and the need to develop children's social competence skills for engaging in healthy relationships. Both components are summarized in the School Social Competence Development and Bullying Prevention Model, a holistic approach introduced in this book that can be used to bring systemic change to the classroom, the school, and the family.

Throughout the book, we examine state-of-the-art knowledge from bullying and aggression literature and discuss methods for reducing the problem of bullying in schools and families. We have reviewed many programs, but in this book we focus on those labeled "evidence based"—that is, programs for which research has provided some evidence of efficacy. Schools and community programs are in great need of programs that have shown a verifiable impact.

We also review the current literature related to improving the quality of learning and living experiences for children and adolescents. Research has supported the importance of approaching the problems of aggression in schools and families from a holistic, systemic orientation. Although specific strategies may be effective for changing an individual incident, it is more important to create a culture that supports healthy ways of interacting and problem solving. We believe that this book explains a process for accomplishing this lofty goal.

We bring to this book our extensive experience with the process of reducing bullying and improving quality of life for students and families. Each of us has worked with schools for more than two decades. We have had wonderful opportunities to be engaged in a wide range of situations, including helping individual children who have been victimized by bullies, helping bullies develop alternatives to aggression, and working with entire school systems to achieve a positive and inviting atmosphere in the school. We are strong advocates of working with individuals to address their specific problems; we are even stronger advocates of creating inclusive and safe environments that prevent those problems from occurring.

No child or adult should approach a school as he or she would a prison. A school should not be a place of fear and threat, where safety is challenged and where respect and care are absent. Instead, schools should be inviting, exciting, and inclusive places where all who enter celebrate individual differences and understand and value all members of the community. On the basis of our experience working with schools, this goal is not an impossible dream or idle fantasy. The culture of the school is determined by all members of the school community. We have watched as teachers and students created schools that represented their choices rather than accommodating or surrendering to an unacceptable environment. In an inviting school, teachers and administrators take it on themselves not only to reduce aggression but also to create a positive environment that builds on the strengths of students, teachers, and the school community. A healthy school is one in which students not only refrain from fighting or verbally hurting each other but also develop positive relationships.

This book has a strong focus on prevention and early intervention. We propose a proactive approach in which students, faculty, administrators, and parents take the time to define the school of their choice—the school they deserve—and then identify the steps necessary to bring it about. Educators know that it is much easier and less expensive to treat a problem before it develops rather than to resolve a full-blown problem. In a similar way, regarding bullying, it is far better to prevent aggression through effective social competence skills and a caring environment than it is to transform teachers into disciplinarians who must handle bullying and misbehavior as it occurs.

Although prevention is important, we recognize that even the best of programs designed to improve school quality will not remove all problems with bullying and aggression. Thus, the final three chapters of this book address the problem of persistent bullies, or those who need personalized help. These children require early intervention before the problem behaviors are so ingrained that it is difficult or impossible to change them. Providing effective interventions for bullies and aggressors will allow them to establish the emotional, social, and academic skills they need to succeed in school and in life.

As we wrote the book, we used male and female characters in our examples without any intentional implications about gender. Bullying and aggressive behavior are found in both sexes, in all racial and ethnic groups, in different cultures, and in all income and social status groups. Bullies and aggression may be referred to as "equal opportunity" offenders and offenses. We attempted to provide examples that reflect the broad panoply of situations we have experienced. For ease of writing, we frequently use the terms "bullies" and "victims" rather than "children who have committed bullying acts" and "children who have been the targets of bullying behaviors," respectively. However, we do not mean to label children, nor do we assume that these children have immutable personality characteristics. The problem is the behavior and the context where that behavior occurs, not the children.

ORGANIZATION OF THE BOOK

Our goal in writing this book is to provide applied and practical strategies, but not to provide prescriptions, as in a manual. We recognize that schools can address the problem of bullying using many diverse strategies that meet their needs. We therefore hope that the content of this book will be useful for a variety of settings and circumstances. The book is composed of three sections: understanding the problem (chaps. 1–3), universal interventions for addressing the problem (chaps. 4–7), and targeted interventions for persistent bullies (chaps. 8–10). In addition, the appendix provides numerous resources for bullying prevention.

Chapter 1 provides a common nomenclature for the problem of childhood and adolescent bullying and aggression and examines the magnitude of the problem. After distinguishing among the concepts of violence, aggression, and bullying, chapter 1 expands on the concept of bullying and discusses three types of bullies (aggressive, follower, and relational), three types of victims (passive, provocative, and relational), and two types of bystanders (those who are part of the problem and those who are part of the solution). The chapter also examines common classifications of violent, aggressive, and bullying behaviors, highlighting three schemes: (a) instrumental or reactive; (b) physical, verbal, relational, and sexual; and (c) overt or covert. Finally, the chapter reports on the prevalence and consequences of bullying, concluding that the prevalence is high and that the consequences can be serious.

Chapter 2 summarizes the current literature on risk and protective factors for childhood aggression and bullying that are important to recognize and evaluate when developing effective programs to reduce bullying and aggression. Although isolated risk factors may not necessarily be a major concern, the additive effect of multiple risk factors can significantly increase the probability of aggression; conversely, the additive effect of protective factors can reduce the odds. It is important for schools and families to be aware of the potential risk and protective factors affecting children and to take steps to provide circumstances that lead to healthier interactions. Chapter 2 discusses the multiple risk and protective factors based on their source (e.g., child, family, peers, school, and larger community), but based on the ecological model, these levels influence each other and cannot be considered as independent of one another.

Chapter 3 discusses why theories are important for understanding the development of aggression and bullying in children and highlights several theories and models: attribution theory, the social information–processing model, social–cognitive theory, attachment theory, family systems theory, the social interactional model, the developmental pathways to violence, and the ecological model. This is by no means a complete list of theories and models that have been used to explain aggression, but they are currently the most frequently used. Each model has strengths that illuminate the causes of school bullying and point toward solutions to the problem, giving credence to Lewin's (1951, p. 169) statement, "There is nothing as practical as a good theory." A theory should undergird the development of any bullying prevention and intervention program and provide the framework for its evaluation.

Chapters 4 and 5 define and explain the two components of the School Social Competence Development and Bullying Prevention Model: the development of a positive school climate and the enhancement of students' social competence skills. Chapter 4 describes a positive school climate as consisting of those characteristics of a school that enhance learning and nurture an individual's best qualities. A positive school climate is essential for preventing bullying and aggression, as well as for promoting academic excellence. This chapter details eight components of a positive school climate: excellence in teaching, school values, awareness of strengths and problems, policies and accountability, caring and respect, positive expectations, support for teachers, and the physical environment.

Chapter 5 discusses students' *social competence skills*, defined as age-appropriate knowledge and skills for functioning peacefully and creatively in one's community or social environment. This chapter identifies and explains the six components of social competence delineated in the School Social Competence Development and Bullying Prevention Model: awareness, emotions, cognitions, character, social skills, and mental health and learning abilities. These components overlap and influence each other, and it may be difficult to develop a prevention program that addresses one element over another. The six components of social competence should be used as a frame of reference when choosing curricula or when selecting activities that teachers can practice with their students.

Chapter 6 addresses two often overlooked components of bullying prevention programs: the needs assessment and the program evaluation. The needs assessment is essential to ensure that the problem has been accurately identified and quantified and to provide the basis for selecting the best program. The chapter details the steps involved in measuring the problem, selecting a program that is consistent with the evaluation of the problem, defining the methods to evaluate the efficacy of the program, implementing the intervention, evaluating the implementation and the outcomes, and refining the process. Evaluation is a core element of the intervention process and is an essential step in providing decision makers with an accurate assessment of the outcome of the resources being used. Further, the purpose of a program evaluation is not to determine whether a program "passes" or "fails" but, rather, to examine the extent to which the problem has been alleviated and a more positive environment has been created, to offer direction for future intervention plans, and to refine future implementation of the current intervention.

Chapter 7 examines the selection and implementation of universal bullying prevention programs. Researchers and experts in the field of violence prevention have used two strategies to identify promising programs for reducing and preventing aggression: meta-analyses and panels of experts. This chapter asserts that to select the best prevention programs for their schools, educators need to weigh a variety of criteria (e.g., goals of the program, prior evidence of success, cultural relevance of activities). Chapter 7 also cites several programs that seem to be successful in preventing and reducing aggression, with the caveat that success may vary depending on the characteristics of the school environment and the quality of the program's implementation. This chapter provides suggestions to reduce a common, but certainly correctable, flaw of prevention programs—the lack of generalization of behaviors to new environments.

Chapter 8 examines counseling interventions for persistent bullies—that is, the few children who continue to bully despite positive changes in the school environment and classroom. When working with persistent bullies, counselors, psychologists, social workers, school administrators, and other mental health professionals must develop a thorough understanding of the nature and extent of the problem. Because other problems frequently co-occur with persistent bullies, counselors must also be aware of any other diagnoses (e.g., anxiety, depression, hyperactivity) that might adversely influence a child's behavior. In addition, counselors' evaluations of persistent bullies should be comprehensive, taking into consideration the child's family and community. Throughout, the chapter emphasizes the need for counselors to develop a therapeutic relationship with the bully, use a solution-focused approach, and unearth factors that might be perpetuating the inappropriate or aggressive behaviors. Finally, successful counseling interventions emphasize skill development, behavioral change, academic success, and involvement of the child's teachers and parents. To exemplify these strategies, we describe two counseling interventions.

Chapter 9 examines family interventions designed to reduce aggression among children who need more help than positive schoolwide interventions can provide. The first part of this chapter describes the history and the successes of family interventions. This history is then followed by a discussion of seven core elements of effective parenting programs and 10 skills for working with the families of bullies, including skills for connecting with the family and skills for structuring the sessions and intervening. The final section examines six components of an intervention for working with bullies and their families and details specific strategies for each. An annotated bibliography at the end presents sources that can help counselors and parents address their children's bullying behavior.

Chapter 10 provides strategies to help children who are the targets of bullying. The chapter discusses how factors that maintain bullying behaviors vary by type of victim and how adults need to assess whether the victim's own behavior may be contributing to the problem. This chapter also differentiates between dangerous bullying and annoying bullying and provides examples of strategies to handle each type. The chapter concludes by stressing that educators and parents need to recognize the signs of bullying and to use a solution-focused approach to help solve the problem.

The appendix lists organizations and Web sites that can help mental health professionals, educators, children, and families locate materials relevant to reducing bullying and aggression and improving the quality of the school climate. The resource material begins with a table that indicates the intended audience of the Web site. Additional information about specific Web sites is also provided. Although information on the Web may become dated and URLs may change, we have found the materials described to be helpful and easily available for schools and parents.

Martin Luther King famously observed, "In the end, we will remember not the words of our enemies, but the silence of our friends." We hope that other adults will join us in speaking up for children and providing for them the safe environment they deserve.

I

UNDERSTANDING
THE PROBLEM

1

BULLIES:
THE PROBLEM AND ITS IMPACT

Bullies! Bullies! Bullies! Everywhere in this school there are bullies. One of these days I'm going to get big, and then we'll see who the biggest bully is!

—Sixth grader

This chapter develops a common nomenclature for the problem of childhood and adolescent bullying and aggression and examines the prevalence and consequences of the problem. The chapter is composed of three sections. The first defines key terms, delineating the differences among *violence*, *aggression*, and *bullying* through an examination of four forms of aggression. In this section, we also differentiate types of bullies, victims, and bystanders. The second section describes the epidemiology of bullying: how big the problem is, who is more likely to be involved, where bullying happens, and how it has changed over time. The final section examines the consequences of being the target of aggression and bullying.

DEFINITIONS OF KEY TERMS

Bullies are a prevalent problem in schools and one of the biggest difficulties for students, teachers, and administrators. There is a lot of discussion about the problem of bullying, but there has been surprisingly little action. In this book, we hope to encourage educators, counselors, psychologists, parents, and concerned citizens to move from talking about bullying to doing something about it. To accomplish this task, though, it is important to know what bullying is, the extent of this problem, and how it affects students and the school climate.

Violence, Aggression, and Bullying

The terms *violence*, *aggression*, and *bullying* are frequently used interchangeably. However, in the violence prevention field, clear distinctions are made among these terms. The focus of this book is interpersonal aggression and bullying, and specifically aggression and bullying in childhood and adolescence. Examples of violence, aggression, and bullying are presented in Box 1.1.

BOX 1.1. EXAMPLES OF VIOLENCE, AGGRESSION, AND BULLYING

Violence: Nick and Jake

Nick and Jake attended Mr. Hinson's history class at Madison Middle School. Neither boy was very popular with his peers, and both had been overheard making derisive comments about their classmates. As a result, some of their peers responded with direct disparaging taunts, whereas others, more provoked, sometimes responded by bumping into Nick and Jake. Because Nick and Jake frequently caused commotions in the classroom, Mr. Hinson regularly reprimanded them and even sent them to the office after highly disruptive incidents.

Toward the end of the school year, several classmates reported to the school principal that they had heard the two boys threaten to "get even" with those who teased them by seeking revenge for being humiliated and for being sent to the office by Mr. Hinson. Worried by Nick's and Jake's threats of violent revenge, the principal decided to call the police and request an investigation. At the boys' homes, police found that Nick and Jake had stockpiled weapons, obtained floor plans of the school, and developed detailed plans to kill Mr. Hinson on the last day of school, along with any student who interfered with the execution of their plan.

Aggression: Naomi and Jacquee

Naomi had a "short fuse"; she got angry very easily. When she lost her temper, she would strike out at whomever was around.

One morning she could not find her schoolbooks when she had to leave for school. As a result, she arrived late to her first class and was scolded for being tardy. As she left the classroom, she shoved Jacquee, the student nearest to her, against the wall. Upset after being pushed, Jacquee asked, "Why'd you do that?" Naomi retorted, "Just because you were there and because you are ugly," and then walked away.

Bullying: Naomi and Saundra

Later, reflecting on pushing Jacquee, Naomi decided that she probably should not have shoved her because Jacquee had friends who might help her fight back. Still, Naomi was angry and decided that someone had to pay. Instead of tormenting Jacquee, Naomi began calling Saundra names because she irritated Naomi a great deal. Saundra's face was covered with pimples, she had a squeaky voice, and, besides, no one liked her. Naomi tormented Saundra for several days until Saundra started crying whenever she saw Naomi approaching. Finally, Naomi felt satisfied.

The World Health Organization (WHO; Krug, Mercy, Dahlberg, & Zwi, 2002) has defined *violence* as

the intentional use of physical force or power, threatened or actual, against oneself, another person, or against a group or community, that either results in or has a high likelihood of resulting in injury, death, psychological harm, maldevelopment or deprivation. (p. 5)

In the WHO report, violence is classified as interpersonal, intrapersonal, or collective. *Interpersonal violence* pits one individual against another and can be committed against strangers, acquaintances, family members, or intimate partners. It includes extreme behaviors such as homicide, rape, and aggravated assault. *Intrapersonal violence*, however, refers to violence against oneself, such as suicide and suicide attempts. *Collective violence* refers to social, political, or economic violence committed by groups of people, by governments, or by institutions. Collective violence includes gang violence, human rights abuses, or intentional acts that disrupt the economy for many by benefiting a few.

The concept of *aggression* does not preclude physical acts of hostility, but it generally refers to less extreme intentional behaviors that may cause psychological or physical harm to others. Aggression can be dangerous, but its effects are generally milder than those associated with hostile physical violence. Hitting, pushing, isolating a peer on purpose, and name-calling all constitute examples of aggressive behaviors.

Bullying may be considered a subset of aggression. Characterized by what is sometimes referred to as "double I R" (**I**mbalance of power, **I**ntentional acts, and **R**epeated over time), the bully is more powerful than the victim and commits aggressive behaviors intentionally and repeatedly over time (Newman, Horne, & Bartolomucci, 2000). For example, in the Harry Potter books by J. K. Rowling, one of the villainous characters, Draco Malfoy, engages in aggressive behaviors directed at Harry Potter. These behaviors would probably fall into the category of aggression, not bullying, because both students have a similar level of power (although some Harry Potter fans may disagree!). However, the aggressive behaviors by Draco Malfoy directed at Neville Longbottom, another character in the books, are clearly bullying, because Neville does not have the same level of skills to defend himself (at least not in the first books).

Differences in height, weight, physical stamina, and even intelligence may make it easy to determine who is the bully and who is the victim. Frequently, however, this distinction is not obvious. Children, especially, may appear matched in ability, but a bully may use threats and implied aggression as a means of intimidating the other child. On occasion, the strength of a bully comes not from his or her individual characteristics, but from the power of belonging to a clique, gang, or other social group. Also, the power differential may be a function of the children's belief systems. One child may be taught to believe that aggression is an appropriate problem-solving strategy, whereas another may be taught to resolve conflict peacefully. As a result, the child who believes in aggression has the power of using physical threats that the other child does not have, does not know how to use, or does not wish to use.

Not everyone accepts these distinctions among violence, aggression, and bullying, and these terms are frequently used as synonyms. For educators, school psychologists, and counselors, distinct lines of demarcation may not be that important. Clearly, all intentional acts that may hurt others should be prevented. In addition, among children at least, bullying and aggression are often closely linked. For example, a large U.S. study revealed that bullies are significantly more likely to carry weapons to school and to be involved in fights than nonbullies (Nansel, Overpeck, Haynie, Ruan, & Scheidt, 2003). Strategies to prevent bullying and aggression, however, may vary as a function of the power differential between a bully and his or her victim and because a bully's aggression is not random, but targeted to those less able to defend themselves.

All people experience some level of aggression, but most do not live with the anticipatory fear of pain and humiliation caused by the repeated aggression that characterizes bullying. Examples of everyday aggression are multiple: A person may cut off another driver while speeding on the freeway, or a person may rudely bump into another shopper in a grocery store aisle. Nearly everyone sees or experiences this kind of day-to-day aggression, but they generally do not experience repetitive harassment by a person or a group of people. Repeated acts of aggression generate a deeper level of fear and intimidation than an isolated event.

The concept of intention is a key element in definitions of violence, aggression, and bullying. That is, violence, aggression, and bullying are all intentional acts with the potential for hurting others. For example, if a boy is hit and gets hurt as a consequence of rough-and-tumble play, in which there was no intention to hurt him, that act could not be considered an act of aggression. Such injuries often occur during pickup athletic games, competitive sports, and playground activities. However, if a child throws a ball at the face of another child with the intention to hurt him or her but misses, it would be considered an act of aggression, even if it did not have immediate consequences.

Unfortunately, even an objective observer cannot easily determine another's intent. In schools, children's rough-and-tumble play frequently escalates from playing to aggression, and the point at which this transition occurs is not always clear. Indeed, the turning point may not even be the same for each child involved. Similarly, one child's "friendly" teasing may end in tears when the taunting goes too far and hurts the other child's feelings. In an effort to explain this transition, Horne, Bartolomucci, and Newman-Carlson (2003) proposed a continuum of play (e.g., rough-and-tumble play, joking, sports activities, playful teasing), bullying (e.g., physical, verbal, relational, and sexually aggressive or bullying acts), and delinquency (e.g., weapon carrying, assaults, serious threats, rape, theft, property damage) that require different intervention strategies by teachers and school administrators. Additional distinctions between rough playing and bullying are presented in Box 1.2. To complicate the issue further, although aggression is, by definition, intentional, the possible severe consequences of the behavior are frequently unintentional. For example, girls may find it funny to tease and isolate another girl, or others may think that it is okay to taunt a boy because of his effeminate behaviors. These bullies do not consider the potential for their teasing to harm the targeted child's self-esteem to the point that he or she may consider suicide. Thus, intent to bully another person may be different from intent to injure someone.

A final aspect of the WHO definition of violence is the use of power (Krug et al., 2002). Violent acts not only involve the manifestation of physical force but also may include the use of threats and intimidation to coerce people to comply with certain behaviors. The abuse of power may be seen at multiple levels. For instance, the former South African government's institution of apartheid, which segregated neighborhoods and workplaces on the basis of race, exemplified the political abuse of power. A jealous husband who forces his wife to quit her job typifies intimate partner abuse of power. And a clique of kids who threaten to hit a girl if she does not agree to give them her lunch money is an example of abuse of power in the form of bullying. Bullying frequently occurs in the form of threats and in-

BOX 1.2. *IS IT ROUGH PLAYING OR BULLYING?*

It is not always easy to distinguish rough playing from bullying. When does playing cross the line and become bullying? The following are three ways to differentiate between rough play and bullying:

1. When playing stops being fun and starts hurting, it is time for the "playing" to stop; it has crossed the line. Each child has a different level of tolerance for rough-and-tumble play, gauging his or her experience against culture, stress, and level of friendship. Because the level of tolerance may also change from one day to another, this general rule must apply: If it hurts, it must stop.
2. Adults may ask themselves, "Are the play roles interchangeable?" If the answer is no, the behavior is more likely to be bullying. For example, Ringo and George liked to play cowboys. Ringo was the sheriff, and George was a thief who was running away from the law. Ringo would run after George, catch him, and drag him to jail. The adult should ask him- or herself, "Is Ringo always the sheriff who is chasing, dragging, and putting others in jail, and is George always the bad guy?" If the answer is yes, the adult should suspect bullying.
3. Is the playing so rough that it is disrupting other students or bothering the teachers? The students may not be bullying each other, but their rough play may be a form of bullying others. At a minimum, it is disrupting others and therefore is not appropriate at that time.

timidation, and it thrives in the silence of the victim and the acquiescence of observers.

Bullies, Victims, and Bystanders

Although not always true, bullying is most likely to occur in social situations when peers are present. Thus, students may take one or more roles in the "bullying process" (Atlas & Pepler, 1998; Salmivalli, Lappalainen, & Lagerspetz, 1998; Sutton, Smith, & Swettenham, 1999b). These roles are not always stable; children do not necessarily always take the same role. Students may be bullies or victims in varying degrees across different situations. In addition, a growing body of literature suggests that some students who act as bullies may also be victims in other instances. This issue and others are explored as we describe the most common roles of bullies, victims, and bystanders in this section (Box 1.3 lists their key characteristics).

BOX 1.3. *TYPES OF BULLIES, VICTIMS, AND BYSTANDERS*

Bullies	Aggressive
	Follower
	Relational
Victims	Passive
	Provocative
	Relational
Bystanders	Part of the problem
	Instigate
	Watch
	Are scared
	Are ashamed or feel guilty for not helping
	Part of the solution
	Ask for help
	Help defuse the problem

Bullies

We distinguish three types of bullies: the aggressive bully, the follower, and the relational bully (Box 1.4 gives examples of each). The aggressive bully, the role most recognized by teachers and peers, initiates the aggression. An aggressive bully tends to use overt aggression, either physical or verbal, as well as threats and intimidation, to achieve his or her goals. Whether bullies are skilled manipulators or socially inept is debatable; the issue is complicated by the fact that there are several types of aggressive bullies, including some who are quite popular and others who are shunned by classmates. Some bullies' behaviors have been reinforced through repeated payoffs, teaching them that aggression typically helps them get what they want. Bullying for these individuals becomes an instrument for achieving their goals. For example, a bully may use physical force or threats to be first in line for lunch, to coerce other children into doing things for him, or to use the playground equipment longer than others. Another bully may use aggression because she is socially unskilled and angry, and consequently her classmates reject her because of her aggressive and inappropriate behaviors.

BOX 1.4. EXAMPLES OF BULLIES: AGGRESSIVE, FOLLOWER, AND RELATIONAL

Aggressive Bully: Elijah

Elijah and Brock were in the same sixth class period. Elijah was the class star athlete and loved to play any kind of sport, although basketball was his favorite. Brock, too, loved to play basketball and was almost as good as Elijah. During free play on Fridays, Elijah would always get a group together to play a basketball game. When Brock tried to join the game, Elijah would tell him that he could not play unless a teacher was watching. If a teacher was watching, then Elijah would let Brock play. During the games, when Brock got to play, Elijah would constantly make mean gestures toward him, calling Brock names and tripping him as he ran down the court. When Brock complained to his teachers about Elijah's sportsmanship, the teachers believed Elijah's behavior to be in good fun and part of the spirit of the game, rather than to be inappropriate and too aggressive. (In this case, the teacher's behavior is helping to maintain the problem.)

Follower: Doug

Doug attended the same school as Elijah and Brock. He had few friends and was usually not included in social gatherings. He would have liked to be more popular at school, but he didn't know how to be liked by others. One day, he saw Elijah taunting Brock on the basketball court. Allying himself with Elijah, Doug began taunting Brock as well, even though Brock was considerably bigger. Over the next few days, Doug's taunting intensified, and he even began to get physically aggressive with Brock. Other students noticed Doug's behavior and laughed about what he was doing to Brock. As the conflict escalated, Brock lost his temper and became very angry with Elijah and Doug. After several incidents, Brock yelled that he wouldn't take it any more. When the school principal learned of the conflict, Doug and Brock were reprimanded. Brock was embarrassed by the principal's reprimand. Doug, however, was proud of the fact that he was gaining popularity. He was being noticed by other students and by the principal, he had showed his influence by getting Brock in trouble, and he had allied himself with Elijah.

Relational Bully: Kamieka, Tosha, and Lexi

Kamieka, Tosha, Lexi, and Reanah were best friends who did everything together. One year for math, however, Reanah was placed in a higher level math class than the others. Reanah missed being with her other friends, but she liked her class and even got to be good friends with Lola, whom she previously did not know very well. When Reanah told her best friends about Lola and suggested that they invite her to go to the mall with them on Saturday, her friends became furious that she had made another friend without them. Kamieka, Tosha, and Lexi decided that they were so mad at Reanah for being a traitor that they were not going to go to the mall on Saturday with her, but instead would have a sleepover without her. When Monday came and Reanah tried to talk with her friends about the weekend, Lexi informed her that they were no longer friends and huffed off. As the week progressed, Reanah's friends grew increasingly cold toward her, and she even overheard them talking meanly about her in the bathroom.

Because these individuals are frequently unaware of their classmates' negative feelings toward them, it is difficult for them to improve their social relations. Classmates may be afraid to communicate their resentment, or they may not care enough about the bully to explain the motives behind their rejection. Thus, it is often very difficult for bullies to improve their social relations. Aggressive bullies may also be rejected because they tend to attribute aggression to others' behavior; that is, they tend to believe that they are being attacked or victimized when they are not (Dodge & Frame, 1982; Olweus, 1994a; Ross, 1996). They respond with aggression to perceived or real attacks, which creates more hostility among peers and reinforces their reputation as bullies. For example, a bully may perceive a nonintentional push in the hallway as aggression and will react accordingly. In addition, these individuals are likely to blame others, rather than themselves, for their own behaviors ("She made me do it") and for their negative consequences ("It's his fault; he made me so mad that I had to hit him").

Contrary to popularly held assumptions that bullies' aggressive behaviors are manifestations of feelings of inferiority and poor self-concept, some studies have shown that bullies sometimes have high levels of self-esteem (e.g., O'Moore & Kirkham, 2001). However, Staub (1999) referred to it as "fake" high self-esteem because they frequently maintain their self-esteem through dubious methods such as denigrating others, manipulating peers, and exerting power through threats and physical superiority. Most bullies do not have access to authentic sources of self-esteem, such as positive friendships and good academic performance, and so they rely on aggression to heighten their esteem.

The followers (they also have been called "passive bullies") are less common than the aggressive bullies. They are less likely to start the bullying but will follow the aggressive bully if the bullying behavior is rewarded. Olweus (1991) described these children as anxious, insecure, and attention seeking.

They may seek to bolster their self-esteem by joining the bullies, acting as either "assistants" who help the bully or "reinforcers" who encourage the bully by cheering or simply laughing (Salmivalli, 1999).

The final form of bullying is relational. The relational bully uses covert or indirect forms of aggression, such as intentionally isolating another student, excluding peers from a group, threatening to withdraw friendship, or spreading negative rumors or lies about a child. Relational bullies inflict harm by damaging friendships and personal relationships. As such, relational bullying can be particularly damaging to a child's self-esteem.

Because schools are an important venue for social development—children establish friendships, foster close relationships, and seek acceptance from peers while at school—it is important for teachers and counselors to recognize relational bullying in addition to other, more overt bullying behaviors. It is regrettable that most relational bullying research, which is comparatively new in the field of violence prevention, has focused on describing the prevalence of the problem and the demographic characteristics of the perpetrators and victims. Fewer studies have addressed behavioral, psychological, or social determinants of relational bullying. A number of studies have assessed whether the perpetration of relational bullying differs by gender. The results, however, have been inconclusive. Some studies show that girls report more instances of relational bullying than boys (e.g., Crick & Grotpeter, 1995), others indicate no gender differences (Prinstein, Boergers, & Vernberg, 2001), and still others show that boys report more relational aggression than girls (Tomada & Schneider, 1997). These variations among study findings suggest that relational aggression may be influenced by other factors besides gender, such as the culture of the local school and community. In our studies of elementary and middle school students, we have found as much relational aggression among boys as girls. However, teachers have more frequently communicated to us that they observe relational aggression among girls more than boys.

Victims

The victim is the person who is systematically and repeatedly harassed or abused by the bully. Stein and colleagues suggested that the term *victim* may not be the most appropriate, because it connotes powerlessness. Instead, they supported use of the term *target of aggression*, and we agree (Stein, Gaberman, & Sjostrom, 1996). Sometimes, however, the word *victim* is easier to use, particularly because it is a common expression that is familiar to teachers and parents. Still, many in this same audience probably would feel more comfortable with the expression *target of aggression*. We use both terms interchangeably in this book.

We distinguish three types of victim: passive, provocative, and relational (Box 1.5 gives examples of each). Passive victims are children who are singled out without provocation (Olweus, 1993a). They may exhibit some characteristics that make them easier targets of aggression: having few friends or no lasting friendships, having fewer verbal skills to respond to verbal taunting, or appearing shy and anxious. Sometimes just being different (e.g., having an accent, being unusually tall, or dressing against the mainstream) may be enough to increase the likelihood of being the target of bullying. Passive victims are the children to whom most people would assign the label *victim of bullying*.

BOX 1.5. EXAMPLES OF VICTIMS: PASSIVE, PROVOCATIVE, AND RELATIONAL

Passive: Macarena

Macarena was new to her school and felt very uncomfortable because she was overweight, knew none of the other students, and was quiet and shy. Her attempts to make friends were unsuccessful because most of her peers already knew each other, and opportunities to enter into their friendship groups were few. One of the girls at school, Corinne, began taunting Macarena, calling her names like "fatso" or "tubby." Other students heard the name-calling, but they didn't want to get on the wrong side of Corinne, who they all knew had a mean temper. Classmates laughed, walked away, or ignored the taunting. After a few days, Macarena felt paralyzed when Corinne came near and became desperate when Corinne threatened to beat her up if she complained to the teacher.

Provocative: Mike

Mike was an unpopular fifth grader. Other students usually ignored Mike or made derogatory remarks when they did speak to him, like "Mikey Nobody" or "jerk." As the school year went by, Mike got angry at being ignored and called names. He responded by taunting several of the popular boys in his class, calling them mean names. A couple of the boys got tired of Mike's name-calling and told him to shut up. As the conflict escalated, one of the popular boys retaliated by shoving Mike. Eventually, the conflict became so physical that Mike was hurt and needed medical attention.

Relational: Tyson

Tyson was not admired, but he was not unpopular either. He felt as if he just "existed" at his middle school, but he wanted to be

---

more involved with his peers and to have lots of friends. As a result, Tyson began inserting comments into conversations at the lunchroom, on the playground, and at other school gatherings in an effort to increase his social participation. Stanley got very angry with Tyson for trying to be part of the crowd without being invited, and so he convinced the other boys in Tyson's class to play a trick on him. For a few days, the boys acted very friendly toward Tyson. They asked Tyson about things that made him happy and the kind of friendships he would like to have. Then, after Tyson shared his personal thoughts and feelings about different things, the boys told Tyson that he didn't belong in the group. They said he wasn't liked and continued to tease Tyson with the information he had shared.

Conversely, provocative victims know the right "buttons to push" to provoke the bully's aggression (Boulton & Smith, 1994; Olweus, 1993a; Schwartz, Dodge, & Coie, 1993). Through inappropriate behaviors, such as teasing and annoying behaviors, they may antagonize not only a bully but also the entire classroom. They often continue their annoying behavior until someone lashes out at them, and then they complain of victimization. As their behavior clearly indicates, these children need skill development in appropriate social and interpersonal interactions. Educators need to pay close attention to provocative victims: Frequently they are the most rejected students of the class, and they may be at increased risk for suicide (Pellegrini, 1998; Perry, Kusel, & Perry, 1988).

Finally, relational victims are the victims of the more subtle, covert relational bullying. Although it is unclear whether boys or girls are more frequently the perpetrators of relational bullying, girls most often become the victims of relational bullying. However, boys can also be victimized. In a large survey conducted by the American Association of University Women (2001), 19% of the boys reported that someone had called them gay. Students who experience relational bullying may be left out of groups, experience exclusion by cliques of students at lunch or in games, and be the target of rumors spread about them.

It is unclear how bullies decide to exert relational aggression against another student, but explanations may include being jealous of the victim and wanting to exclude him or her, desiring to show power or to retaliate, or desiring to gain attention and recognition from others by controlling what happens to the victim. The targets of relational bullying may lack specific characteristics, but they may be caught in relationships they have little control over. For example, they may be new to a school, they may be the object of contempt or anger from a powerful person in a group, or they may lack the skills or resources that an in-group person may have.

Bystanders

Bystanders—those who witness the aggression—can broadly be categorized in two groups: those who are part of the problem and those who are part of the solution. Bystanders who are part of the problem encourage bullies to continue fighting or to retaliate. As students gather around other students who are fighting, they may shout at the aggressor to "keep on" or shout at the victim, "Are you going to put up with that?" They may even push a fleeing victim back into the fight. Bystanders who witness a bullying incident and choose to do nothing to stop it or, even worse, are entertained by it silently condone violence (Slaby, Wilson-Brewer, & Dash, 1994). Bystanders who are part of the solution are those who try to help solve or defuse the problem. They may choose to ask for help from an adult, say or do something to de-escalate the tension (e.g., say, "Come on, it's not worth a fight; let's do something else"), or invite a student who is a frequent target of aggression to join their group. Some bystanders may not have the skills or the knowledge to stop the bullying and may feel guilty for not doing anything to stop it. These bystanders may become secondary victims of the bullying process (Newman et al., 2000).

Types of Violent, Aggressive, and Bullying Behaviors

We have discussed the similarities and differences among violence, aggression, and bullying, with bullying being a subset of aggression. In addition to understanding these concepts, it is also important to examine how the behaviors are classified. The process of classifying violent, aggressive, and bullying behaviors is an imperfect one and frequently does not achieve widespread acceptance. The following caveats are appropriate: Categories are frequently not exhaustive or exclusive, certain behaviors may be included in more than one category, and an aggressive incident often includes acts from several categories. Still, attempting to classify violent, aggressive, and bullying behaviors can help increase one's awareness of the types of problems that need to be assessed and evaluated.

One popular taxonomy used for classifying aggressive behaviors separates behaviors on the basis of the purpose of aggression (i.e., instrumental or reactive). *Instrumental aggression* refers to an aggressive behavior that is used to obtain valued goods such as money, objects, or respect from others; it is not the result of provocation. Conversely, *reactive aggression* refers to an aggressive behavior that is in retaliation for a perceived or real prior aggression or threat of aggression (Box 1.6 gives examples of both types). Although this distinction between instrumental and reactive aggression may seem academic, it has important implications for prevention. When evaluating the problem of violence in a community or school, it is necessary to understand the motivations behind the aggression to develop an adequate prevention plan.

BOX 1.6. AN EXAMPLE INVOLVING INSTRUMENTAL AND REACTIVE AGGRESSION

As soon as Fred and Barney reached the playground at recess, they made a mad dash for the only remaining swing. Barney, being the faster of the two boys, got there first.

Instrumental Aggression: Fred

Fred, being stronger, pushed Barney off the swing so that he could use it himself.

Reactive Aggression: Barney

Very disappointed, Barney walked off. Fred yelled at him, "If you weren't such a wimp, you could have gotten the swing." Barney felt his anger rise. He turned around, picked up a handful of sand, and threw it at Fred.

A second, and the most common, taxonomy of aggression is based on the nature of the acts; they may be *physical, verbal, relational,* or *sexual* (Table 1.1 lists definitions and examples). Most schools have policies that prohibit physical aggression, and teachers are likely to stop it. However, the same school policies frequently do not address verbal and relational aggression because teachers, counselors, and administrators may be unaware of the problem or lack the skills to handle it. Verbal and relational aggression, in many cases, warrant as much attention as physical aggression because they perpetuate negative learning environments for victims and may serve as precursors of physical fights.

Bullying in the form of *sexual harassment* can be physical, verbal, or relational. Sexual harassment, in legal terms, refers to unwelcome and unsolicited sexual advances, requests for sexual favors, or verbal or physical conduct of a sexual nature imposed on a person who reasonably perceives it as offensive. A behavior constitutes sexual harassment when such behavior

- becomes a term or condition of employment, status in a classroom, or participation in an activity; or
- affects decisions about that person (like a grade in a class or participation on a team); or
- is so severe, persistent, or invasive that it interferes with an individual's work, educational performance, or otherwise; or
- creates an intimidating, hostile, or offensive working or learning environment.

TABLE 1.1
Types of Aggression

Type of aggression	Definition	Examples
Physical	The intentional use of physical force with the potential to cause death, disability, injury, or harm	Homicide, fighting with weapons, hitting, punching, slapping, biting, pulling hair, kicking, poking, burning, shoving, pushing, choking, throwing objects, and damaging property
Verbal	The intentional use of words with the potential to cause psychological or emotional harm	Threatening to use a weapon, threatening to physically harm, yelling, blackmailing, coercing, putting down, insulting, name-calling, teasing, hassling, and encouraging others to fight
Relational	Behaviors that harm others through hurting peer relationships	Excluding someone from a group, leaving a student out of an activity, spreading rumors, gossiping, withdrawing friendship, keeping others from liking a student, isolating a student during lunch or sports, disclosing personal information, and sending negative notes about someone
Sexual	Any unwelcome and unsolicited words or conducts of a sexual nature	Rape; attempted rape; being forced to do something sexual; spreading sexual rumors; being spied on while getting dressed or in the shower; being forced to kiss or touch someone; being the target of sexual graffiti; and being the target of any unwanted or unsolicited sexual comments, sexual propositions, suggestive gestures, suggestive facial expressions, touching, pinching, grabbing, or pulling at clothes

In the adult world, the concept of consent frames any discussion of sexual harassment. However, behaviors of a sexual nature are never appropriate in a K–12 school setting and should not be tolerated, regardless of whether the behaviors are consensual. Some students may not be familiar with the term sexual harassment; the term *bullying* or *sexual bullying* may be easier for them to understand.

The final classification discriminates between overt and covert aggression. *Overt aggression* is any form of direct physical, verbal, or sexual aggression, and *covert aggression* is any form of indirect aggression, such as relational aggression.

EPIDEMIOLOGY OF BULLYING AND AGGRESSION

A number of studies have attempted to answer the question of how frequently and how intensely children are bullied at school and in the community. Unfortunately, efforts to measure the extent of the problem have not converged on standard protocols for which questions to ask, what response categories to use, and what time frame participants should be asked to recall (e.g., ever, past year, past month, past week, today). All of these factors limit cross-study comparisons. Some researchers ask general questions, such as "How frequently have you been bullied?" This broad question is likely to yield a lower prevalence than asking about specific behaviors, such as "How many times has another child pushed you?" In addition, a positive response to either of these questions indicates how frequently the child was bullied or pushed, but it does not indicate how intense the bullying or pushing was or how damaging, physically or psychologically, the consequences were.

Prevalence of bullying may also be underestimated if the respondent is not aware of the problem and considers bullying a "normal" part of growing up. Moreover, asking about bullying requires children to indicate that one of their peers is stronger or more powerful than they are, a distinction that is frequently in the eyes of the beholder. The targeted child may not want to admit that he or she is less powerful or weaker than a peer, making interpretation of survey responses more difficult. Prevalence estimates for bullying vary greatly depending on whom the researcher uses as a respondent: children, teachers, or parents. Generally, the prevalence of aggression is much higher in students' self-reports of bullying than in teachers' or parents' reports (Stockdale, Hangaduambo, Duys, Larson, & Sarvela, 2002).

Tables 1.2 and 1.3 present data on the prevalence of aggression, bullying, and victimization. Consistently, boys are more likely than girls to be both the perpetrators and the victims of physical and verbal aggression, and most studies indicate that girls are more likely to be the victims of relational and sexual aggression. Bullying and aggression tend to increase from elementary to middle school, generally peaking in sixth grade. In high school, fighting, incidences of carrying weapons, and injuries due to fights decline from 9th grade to 12th grade, although the reason for this decline is not clear. A hopeful explanation would link this decline to an increase in social competence and overall maturation between 9th and 12th grades. In a more pessimistic view, the decline could also be influenced by the high dropout rate or even incarceration of aggressive adolescents. The lower victimization rate may also be a result of victimized children leaving school as soon as they are legally allowed. In our counseling, teaching, and consulting experience, we have found that many adults did not complete their education because they found school threatening. However, the explanation of a higher dropout rate for aggressive adolescents is not consistent with the prevalence of criminal incidents (rape, thefts, larceny, physical attacks with and without weapons, robbery and vandalism), which increases with grade level and peaks in high school (DeVoe et al., 2002).

The prevalence of violent crime and theft in schools has decreased during the past decade. However, the prevalence of bullying has increased (DeVoe

TABLE 1.2

Prevalence of Aggression and Bullying

Author	Behavior	Time frame	Sample	Prevalence
Grunbaum et al. (2004): Youth Risk Behavior Surveillance	Specific serious aggressive behaviors (self-report)	12 months preceding the survey	Representative U.S. sample of 15,240 students in Grades 9–12, 2003	In a physical fight: boys, 41%; girls, 25% In a physical fight on school property: boys, 17%; girls, 8% Carried a weapon on school property: boys, 9%; girls, 3% Were threatened or injured with a weapon on school property: boys, 12%; girls, 7%
Nansel et al. (2001): WHO Bullying Survey	Bullying (self-report)	Current term	Representative U.S. sample of 15,686 students in Grades 6–10	Some bullying: total, 44%; boys, 53%; girls, 37%; 6th grade, 46%; 10th grade, 36% Weekly bullying: total, 9%; boys, 12%; girls, 5%; 6th grade, 10%; 10th grade, 7%
Orpinas et al. (2000): Students for Peace	Specific aggressive behaviors (self-report)	Prior week	9,377 students in Grades 6–8 from 8 inner-city public schools in Texas, 1996 (63% Latino, 19% Black, 5% White)	At least once in prior week: Called others bad names, 60% Made fun of someone, 55% Pushed someone, 44% Kicked or slapped someone, 39% Threatened to hurt or hit someone, 36%
Crick and Grotpeter (1995)	Overt and relational aggression (peer nomination)	No time frame	491 students in Grades 3–6 from 4 public schools in a Midwestern town (60% White, 37% Black)	Students reported on specific behaviors that were combined into scales; 1 SD above the mean was defined as aggressive group Percentage of students in each category: Boys: overt aggression, 16% Boys: relational aggression, 2% Boys: overt and relational, 9% Girls: overt aggression, <1% Girls: relational aggression, 17% Girls: overt and relational, 4%
Silvernail, Thompson, Yang, and Kopp (2000)	Specific aggressive behaviors (self-report)	No time frame	4,496 students in Grade 3 from 127 public schools in Maine, 1999	At least once a month: Said mean things, 18% Teased others, 14% Called others names, 14% Hit, kicked, or pushed, 14%

TABLE 1.3
Prevalence of Victimization

Author	Behavior	Time frame	Sample	Prevalence
Grunbaum et al. (2004): Youth Risk Behavior Surveillance	Feeling unsafe; sexual victimization (self-report)	12 months preceding the survey	Representative U.S. sample of 15,240 students in Grades 9–12, 2003	Felt too unsafe to go to school: boys, 6%; girls, 5% Forced to have sexual intercourse: boys, 6%; girls, 12%
Nansel et al. (2001): WHO Bullying Survey	Being bullied (self-report)	Current term	Representative U.S. sample of 15,686 students in Grades 6–10	Some victimization: total, 41%; boys, 47%; girls, 36%; 6th grade, 50%; 10th grade, 28% Weekly bullying: total, 8%; boys, 11%; girls, 6%; 6th grade, 13%; 10th grade, 5%
American Association of University Women (2001)	Being sexually harassed at school by other students (self-report)	Ever, at school	Representative U.S. sample of 2,064 students in Grades 8–11 (1,559 surveyed in school, 505 surveyed online), 2000	Sexual comments, jokes, gestures, or looks: boys, 34%; girls, 48% Were touched, grabbed, or pinched in a sexual way: boys, 20%; girls, 29% Had sexual rumors spread about them: boys, 14%; girls, 21% Experienced sexual harassment often: boys, 24%; girls, 30%
Orpinas et al. (2000): Students for Peace	Specific victimization behaviors (self-report)	Prior week	9,377 students in Grades 6–8 from 8 inner-city public schools in Texas, 1996 (63% Latino, 19% Black, 5% White)	At least once in prior week: Were called a bad name, 49% Were pushed, 43% Were kicked or slapped, 21% Had feelings hurt, 23%
DeVoe et al. (2002): National Crime Victimization Survey	Being bullied at school (self-report during household survey)	Past 6 months	8,374 students, aged 12–18 years, 2001	Total, 8% 6th graders, 14%; 12th graders, 2% Boys, 9%; girls, 7% White, 9%; Black, 6%; Hispanic, 8%

Study	Measure	Time frame	Sample	Results
Silvernail et al. (2000)	Specific victimization behaviors (self-report)	Current term	4,496 students in Grade 3 from 127 public schools in Maine, 1999	At least once a month: Teased in a mean way, 41%; Called hurtful names, 40%; Left out on purpose, 34%; Threatened, 23%; Hit, kicked, or pushed, 38%
Silvernail et al. (2000)	Specific victimization behaviors (self-report)	Current term	4,496 students in Grade 3 from 127 public schools in Maine, 1999	At least once a month: Teased in a mean way, 41%; Called hurtful names, 40%; Left out on purpose, 34%; Threatened, 23%; Hit, kicked, or pushed, 38%
Crick and Bigbee (1998)	Overt and relational victimization (self-report)	No time frame	383 students in Grades 4 and 5 from 4 public schools from Illinois (90% White, 9% African American)	Students reported on specific behaviors that were combined into scales; 1 SD above the mean was defined as victimization group. Percentage of students in each category: Boys: overt victimization, 9%; relational victimization, 4%; overt and relational, 12%. Girls: overt victimization, 1%; relational victimization, 12%; overt and relational, 4%
Kochenderfer and Ladd (1996)	Specific victimization behaviors (self-report during interview)	Ever, in their classroom	200 kindergarten children in the Midwestern United States (74% White, 20% African American)	Sometimes or a lot: Picked on, 51%; Had mean things said to you, 54%; Had bad things said about you to other kids, 42%; Been hit, 43%

et al., 2002). Although it is possible that instances of bullying have truly escalated since 1995, it is also possible that the number of bullying instances has remained static and that increased awareness of the problem has led to higher levels of reporting. In general, the prevalence of aggression and bullying is high and deserves attention.

Teachers have also been victims of student aggression. In a national survey conducted by the U.S. Department of Education in the 1999–2000 academic year, almost 10% of public schoolteachers reported that a student had threatened them with injury during the year prior to the survey. Although 10% may not seem significant, it represents almost 311,000 teachers a year. In addition, 4% of the teachers surveyed indicated that within the past year they had experienced an attack by one of their students. African American teachers, secondary teachers, and teachers in public schools were more likely to be victimized than White, primary, or private school teachers, respectively (Gruber, Wiley, Broughman, Strizek, & Burian-Fitzgerald, 2002). Fortunately, victimization of teachers has decreased over the past 6 years. The number of teachers who reported that they had been threatened with injury decreased by 25% from 1993 to 2000 (DeVoe et al., 2002).

Finally, from an epidemiologic standpoint, it is important for teachers to know when and where bullying occurs. The simple answer is, where adults are not present or when adults are not looking. Unsupervised areas—bathrooms, playgrounds, lunchrooms, and school corridors—are the preferred locations for perpetrators to bully a victim (Glover, Gough, Johnson, & Cartwright, 2000). In general, supervision of these areas may significantly reduce acts of physical aggression. Relational and verbal aggression might be more difficult to spot than physical aggression because children engaged in this type of bullying may look as though they are simply talking in a group. In the American Association of University Women (2001) study, even older students (i.e., those in Grades 8–11) reported that sexual harassment could occur anywhere in the school, but most frequently it happened in the classroom, hallways, and gym or play area.

CONSEQUENCES OF BULLYING

It is not surprising that victims of bullying report depression and low self-esteem as well as other problems related to stress like headaches and stomachaches, difficulty sleeping well, and bed wetting (Hawker & Boulton, 2000; O'Moore & Kirkham, 2001; Williams, Chamgers, Logan, & Robinson, 1996; Wolke, Woods, Bloomfield, & Karstadt, 2001). Students who are the target of bullying are also likely to avoid going to school because they fear for their safety (Berthold & Hoover, 2000). They report having few good friends and thus feel lonely at school (Boulton & Underwood, 1992). Moreover, the fact that they have few friends makes them an easier target of aggression.

Other children may not want to be their friend for fear of being the next target of the bullies. All of these consequences are likely to be detrimental to personal and academic life, which may result in victims receiving lower grades, disliking school, and even dropping out of school.

Victimization in the form of sexual harassment affects girls more than boys. In a recent study, more girls (66%) than boys (28%) reported feeling somewhat or very upset after being sexually harassed in school. Victims felt self-conscious, embarrassed, and afraid. One fourth of the girls reported that they doubted that they could have a happy romantic relationship, and some students even questioned whether they could graduate from school (American Association of University Women, 2001).

Suicide and homicide are relatively rare consequences of bullying, but they highlight the reality that bullying may be followed by tragic events. In 2002 in Edinburgh, Scotland, a 12-year-old girl was found dead, hanging in her bedroom. Her grandparents said that she had been the victim of vicious verbal and physical abuse by her school peers. A similar tragic event occurred in Detroit a year earlier. Repeated bullying can also lead to extreme forms of retaliation. For example, in Northampton, Massachusetts, a 15-year-old student whose peers constantly harassed him, calling him "faggot" and "homo," broke down and stabbed the leader of the bullies to death. Recently, the U.S. Secret Service and the U.S. Department of Education examined characteristics of children who have been the perpetrators of school shootings. They found that almost three fourths of the school shooting incidents by students against other students had in common the acting out of anger or revenge for having been the victims of bullying at school (Vossekuil, Fein, Reddy, Borum, & Modzeleski, 2002).

In conclusion, we emphasize that bullying and aggression are unacceptable and should not be tolerated, not only because of their serious consequences but because it is wrong! Just as adults have the right to go to work without fear of physical or emotional harm, children should not be afraid to go to school and should not have to defend themselves. Unlike work for adults, school attendance by children is required by law; it is the role of parents and teachers to protect children and provide them with a safe environment. In interviews we conducted with children, they frequently commented that they wanted to come to school to learn and to be with their friends. Learning, growing, and building friendships should constitute the essence of going to school. It follows, then, that schools need to provide a safe and positive environment so that children can maximize their intellectual and social capacities.

2

RISK AND PROTECTIVE FACTORS
FOR BULLYING AND AGGRESSION

I was in a lot of trouble: failing in school, getting into fights, starting with drugs. . . . My father disappeared a long time ago, and my mom blamed me for her troubles; she didn't care about me. If it hadn't been for my grandma, I think I would now be in jail.

—Ninth grader

The literature focusing specifically on bullying has increased dramatically during the past decade, but it is still relatively sparse when compared with the abundant literature on risk factors for student aggression. This chapter describes the current literature on risk and protective factors for childhood aggression and bullying. We first discuss the concepts of risk and protection related to aggression. Following this general discussion, we examine specific risk and protective factors in four levels using an ecological model: individual, family and other close relationships, school, and community and culture.

WHY DO PEOPLE ENGAGE IN BULLYING AND AGGRESSION?

In the aftermath of tragic events, such as the school shooting at Columbine High School in Littleton, Colorado, in 1999, in which two students killed 12 classmates and a teacher, or the most recent school shooting in Red Lake, Minnesota, in 2005, in which a student killed a teacher, a security guard, and five students before killing himself, people ask, "Why did this happen?" There is generally no shortage of explanations. Although people know that violence and aggression are complex problems, most expect a simple answer. Such answers, although easy to give, are most frequently incomplete or incorrect.

The root cause of youth aggression is the subject of much debate, and the destruction of family values, exposure to violent media, poverty, easy access to weapons, and drug abuse have all been assigned blame at one time or another. In seeking a root cause to which to assign blame, most analyses miss the mark. First, all of the identified "causes" are risk factors, not causes. Risk factors are characteristics of an individual or an environment that increase the likelihood that the individual will behave in a certain way. In the case of aggression and bullying, risk factors are those factors that predispose a person to behave aggressively. However, risk factors, in and of themselves, do not make a person behave aggressively. Second, the cumulative impact of several risk factors on an individual is a much stronger predictor of aggressive behavior than the presence of one discrete factor (Garmezy, 1993). For example, eating unhealthy food increases the risk of heart disease. However, this risk is greatly increased if, in addition, an individual smokes, avoids exercise, and has a family history of heart problems. Similarly, the accumulation or synergy of several risk factors for aggression dramatically increases the likelihood that an individual will act out through aggression and bullying.

Protective factors, however, are characteristics of an individual or an environment that help diminish the possibility that the individual will engage in detrimental behavior or help reduce the likelihood of disease and injury. Factors such as participation in organized extracurricular activities and positive parent–child relationships decrease the likelihood that an individual will display aggressive behavior.

During the past 50 years, studies on child and adolescent aggressive behavior, violence, and delinquency have focused primarily on risk factors. The resulting literature on risk factors—what is missing or what went wrong— is abundant. Ideally, however, intervention programs also need to examine the other side of the coin. Not only do these programs need to fix what is broken, they also need to capitalize on means to develop positive, nurturing environments that bring out the best in children. Only recently has the interest of educators and researchers begun to shift to include evaluations of the protective factors or assets that have the potential to improve the well-being of youths and to reduce aggression. Describing protective factors, however, can be a challenge. Researchers have yet to reach a consensus on whether risk and protective factors are two extremes of one continuum or whether protective factors are independent and totally distinguishable from risk factors. For example, parental monitoring could be considered a continuum in which the likelihood of aggression increases as parental monitoring decreases. But does the likelihood of caring behaviors increase with increased parental supervision? Some may argue that the protective factor goes beyond parental supervision to providing a positive presence in the life of the child. An example of a protective factor that is independent of risk factors is when the child has a special skill, like playing the piano or participating in athletics or martial arts, that bolster the child's self-esteem and positive peer support. The identification of risk and protective factors can be used to develop interventions to prevent and reduce bullying, as exemplified in the public health model (Box 2.1 provides further detail).

BOX 2.1. *THE APPLICATION OF RISK AND PROTECTIVE FACTORS TO INTERVENTION DEVELOPMENT USING THE PUBLIC HEALTH MODEL*

Identifying risk and protective factors related to aggression is a key step in the public health model for preventing violence and aggression (Mercy, Rosenberg, Powell, Broome, & Roper, 1993). Researchers studying the bullying phenomenon can use this four-step model to reduce and prevent bullying. The public health model assumes that the majority of aggression does not occur by chance and, therefore, is preventable. The search for an explanation of the causes of violence can be useful when it reveals risk factors that are changeable and protective factors that can be enhanced, as well as when it promotes an understanding of how these factors vary among different populations and locales. These steps involve answering the following four questions:

1. *What is the problem?* The first step, clearly defining the problem, can be difficult because individual definitions of aggression and bullying may vary. To define the problem, one needs answers to the following questions: Who are the victims and who are the perpetrators? When and where does aggression happen? How frequently does aggression occur? How intense or serious is the aggression? Which type of violence, aggression, or bullying is taking place? (Chaps. 1 and 6 discuss definition and evaluation, respectively, of the problem.)

2. *What factors increase and decrease the probability that aggression will occur?* The second step is to identify risk and protective factors that are potentially modifiable and that can serve as the basis for prevention. Frequently, teachers identify factors that are not modifiable (e.g., gender or socioeconomic level) or that are beyond their control (e.g., family

---

dynamics), which enhances a sense of hopelessness. The emphasis must be on evaluating factors that are within the realm of influence. For instance, does the perpetrator possess any assets that can be enhanced to deter the bullying behaviors?

3. *What interventions work to prevent and reduce aggression?* The third step is to develop and evaluate interventions on the basis of the information gathered. Numerous programs to reduce aggression and bullying and to increase social skills have been implemented. As a result, the number of promising practices for violence prevention is increasing. (Chap. 7 provides further information on existing programs.)

4. *How can effective interventions be disseminated?* The fourth step is to apply proved strategies to the whole community and to develop effective dissemination strategies. The definition of *whole community* depends on the stage of development of the intervention. For example, a school counselor might test a new curriculum in two classes of sixth graders and, after finding that it increased positive communication skills among students, test it with all the sixth graders in that school. If successful once again, the concept of community would be expanded to all sixth graders in the school district and then eventually, in a widening "ripple effect," to all sixth graders in the state. As the definition of community grows, practitioners should begin to formalize dissemination strategies. For instance, key elements of the intervention should be compiled into a manual that addresses techniques for adapting the intervention to different cultural realities, methods for managing unexpected results, and processes for training facilitators.

To sort out the factors that increase the likelihood of a child acting as a bully or behaving aggressively from those that reduce the odds, we have structured risk and protective factors using the ecological model (outlined in Exhibit 2.1), which is described in detail in chapter 3. To summarize, an ecological model, as applied in public health, posits that a variety of personal and environmental factors influence individuals' behaviors. An ecological framework assesses influences from multiple perspectives, typically beginning with research at the individual or intrapersonal level and subsequently expanding to include other levels (family, friends, schools, community, and culture). The model grows more complex, however, when one considers that these levels are not independent of each other.

As a general framework for the remainder of this discussion, we first describe intrapersonal risk and protective factors at the level of the individual child. We then discuss the influence of individuals who have close relationships with the child, namely family and peers. Next, we review risk and protective factors in the school environment, and finally, we delineate positive and negative influences found at the community level, including cultural factors and media effects.

INTRAPERSONAL RISK AND PROTECTIVE FACTORS

Intrapersonal risk and protective factors for bullying and victimization are numerous. The next section organizes risk factors into four large categories: gender, biological and behavioral factors, school performance, and psychological factors.

Risk Factors

Being male is a risk factor for aggression. A school administrator asked, "Do you know which is the most important risk factor for aggression?" Without waiting for an answer, she continued, "Testosterone!" Men and boys across cultures engage in more violence, aggression, and bullying than women and girls. Decades of research has shown that, in general, boys display more aggression than girls (Grunbaum et al., 2004; Hyde, 1984; Maccoby & Jacklin, 1974). It is not clear, however, whether the culprit is solely testosterone. Not all boys are aggressive, so the socialization process must also be entered into the equation. As discussed in chapter 1, some studies indicate that girls may simply exhibit aggression less overtly. Although boys tend to show aggression in physical and verbal ways, girls tend to hurt others by damaging their relationships (e.g., spreading rumors or isolating peers; Crick & Grotpeter, 1995). However, these gender differences in relational aggression are still under discussion.

The bulk of epidemiological evidence supports the notion that boys, when compared with girls, are more frequently the perpetrators of aggression. Boys are also more frequently the victims of aggression in all areas except in instances of sexual violence or extreme physical violence in intimate relationships. To help monitor health risk behaviors among adolescents, the Centers for Disease Control and Prevention conduct the Youth Risk Behavior Survey every other year in a nationally representative sample of high school students. In 2003, close to twice as many boys (41%) as girls (25%)

EXHIBIT 2.1
Risk and Protective Factors for Aggression

Risk factors	Protective factors
Intrapersonal factors	

The child
- is male;
- receives low academic grades;
- has high self-efficacy for aggression;
- expects success when using aggression, as well as no negative consequences;
- values the outcomes of aggression;
- holds beliefs that support violence;
- attributes aggression to others where there is none;
- lacks problem-solving skills;
- shows other high-risk behaviors (e.g., alcohol or drug use, weapon carrying, gang membership); and
- has a diagnosis of hyperactivity disorder or learning disability.

The child
- is female;
- receives good academic grades, is committed to learning and motivated at school, reads for pleasure;
- is connected to school and participates in school activities;
- displays positive values such as honesty, friendship, peace, and respect;
- is socially competent (e.g., uses problem-solving skills, has a goal orientation, makes friends);
- is culturally competent;
- has a positive identity, including high self-esteem, a sense of purpose in life, a positive view of the future; and
- uses time constructively.

Close relationships: Family and peers

The child's parents or caregivers
- have a negative relationship with the child;
- have poor communication with the child;
- do not supervise the child;
- do not set limits and consequences for negative behaviors;
- display high levels of aggression, including intimate partner violence, child abuse, harsh discipline, and delinquency;
- support violence; and
- reject the child.

The child's friends
- are delinquent or aggressive; and
- use tobacco, alcohol, or drugs.

The child's parents or caregivers
- are loving and caring;
- communicate positively with the child;
- provide active supervision;
- have clear rules and consequences;
- are role models of conflict resolution, restraint, and control;
- are involved in the child's school and overall life; and
- share activities.

The child's friends
- are positive and caring; and
- enjoy academic work.

School environment

The school
- has a negative climate;
- does not encourage positive relationships between teachers and students;
- lacks supervision;
- has no policies against bullying;

The school
- has a positive climate;
- encourages positive relationships between teachers and students;
- provides high levels of supervision;
- has clear policies against bullying;
- fosters excellence in teaching;

• allows bullying behaviors by adults toward students; and • has a punitive discipline system.	• provides opportunities for children who need academic help; • provides opportunities for meaningful participation in school activities; and • has high expectations of all students.
Community, culture, and media	

The community has high levels of violence.
  • The culture supports violence.
  • The media portray high levels of violence.
  • Access to firearms is easy.
  • Access to the Internet is unsupervised.
	The community values young people, education, and the peaceful resolution of conflict.
	  • The community provides supervised activities for children and youths.
	  • The community's police force has a problem-solving orientation.
	  • The culture celebrates diversity.
	  • The media are educational.

reported having been in a physical fight during the year prior to the survey. Even more worrisome, 17% of the boys and 8% of the girls reported having been in a physical fight at school during the year prior to the survey, and 9% of the boys and 3% of the girls reported having carried a weapon—defined as a club, stick, bat, knife, or firearm—on school property during the month prior to the survey (Grunbaum et al., 2004). As alarming as these frequencies are, these figures are the lowest in the past decade.

Notably, romantic relationships change the balance between male and female aggression. In the 2003 survey (Grunbaum et al., 2004), infliction of deliberate physical harm by a boyfriend or girlfriend did not vary by gender (9%). However, girls (12%) were more likely to report being forced to have sexual intercourse than boys (6%). Consistent with these results, most observational and experimental studies using different types of instruments and indicators (ratings, questionnaires, or projective measures) have found that boys are more aggressive than girls (Eagly & Steffen, 1986; Hyde, 1984; Maccoby & Jacklin, 1974). Others have found that boys are more aggressive than girls not only in their behaviors but also in their fantasies and dreams (May, 1980; Munroe et al., 1989; Pollak & Gilligan, 1982). Again, this phenomenon has not been sorted out to identify the extent to which biology versus socialization influences the outcome.

Biological and behavioral characteristics of children can also increase their risk for violence. Children who suffer from attention-deficit/ hyperactivity disorder (ADHD) are at risk for aggression and victimization. Children with ADHD have difficulty completing tasks, sitting still, thinking before they act, and planning ahead. Using a system of rewards and punishments is less effective with them than with other children. Their behaviors can be unpredictable, confusing, and frustrating to the people around them. To function in a world of fast-paced technology that has a strong focus on academic achievement, they may need medication and specialized support from an educational or behavioral therapist, as well as skilled parents and teachers. Not all children with ADHD have this kind of support, and many are diagnosed later in their academic life, after years of struggling in school. A life of academic failure and frustrating relationships with adults can be a risk factor for violence. Further, these children may find support in the wrong kind of peers (low academic achievers, rule breakers, or bullies), which adds another risk factor for violence (Tripp & Alsop, 1999, 2001). In addition to ADHD, children who have poor motor skills, who have learning disabilities, and who have suffered perinatal complications and head injuries may be more prone to violence and delinquency (Buka & Earls, 1993).

School failure is a strong predictor of teenage and adult violence, as well as of male delinquency (Busch, Zagar, Hughes, Arbit, & Bussell, 1990; Farrington, 1989; Huesmann & Eron, 1984; Loeber & Dishion, 1983). How are aggression and academic achievement intertwined? Aggressive children are more likely to be depressed and anxious and to have less social support than nonaggressive peers (Kashani, Deuser, & Reid, 1991; Kashani & Shepperd, 1990; Ney, Colbert, Newman, & Young, 1986). Any child's poor academic performance generally results in fewer positive behavioral reinforcements. Moreover, aggressive children experience deterioration in their relationships with teachers and other students. Teachers give aggressive children more negative and less sustaining feedback (Fry, 1983). Academic achievement is also important because those who drop out of school are more prone to live in the midst of violence (e.g., physical and sexual assaults, drug use, weapon confrontations; Chavez, Edwards, & Oetting, 1989).

Numerous psychological characteristics are associated with an increased risk for violence. A large number of studies have evaluated the psychological characteristics of aggressive children. Much of the research has been conducted in schools with young children, most frequently with boys; thus, the results need to be evaluated with some caution. Some individual characteristics may vary by the degree of provocation and by the gender of the aggressor and the victim. The psychological characteristics most frequently studied include the following:

- perceived self-efficacy: judgment of one's capabilities to perform a certain behavior correctly ("I'm confident that I can hit him . . .");
- outcome expectations: judgment of the likely consequence that a behavior will produce (". . . and, as a result, he will respect me . . .");
- outcome values: degree to which an individual attaches importance to, or cares about, an outcome (". . . and I really like being respected");
- beliefs that support violence ("It is okay to hit others");

- aggressive attributional bias: attributing or imagining aggressive intentions from peers where there are none ("He tripped me in the hallway on purpose"); and
- level of ability to effectively apply problem-solving skills ("There is nothing I can do but hit him").

As expected, aggressive children tend to be confident that they can use aggression to achieve goals and that they will be successful (Perry, Perry, & Rasmussen, 1986). Unfortunately, they are probably correct. Why wouldn't they use aggression to obtain prestige among peers, extra money for lunch, or more time on the playground if it has worked in the past? A basic social learning principle is that people tend to maintain behaviors for which they receive rewards and from which they escape punishment. When supervising adults do not stop children's aggression or do not provide negative consequences for it, children learn that they can continue using aggression to get what they want. These children are also more likely to expect rewards when they behave aggressively and to believe that their unacceptable behavior does not warrant negative repercussions (Perry, Williard, & Perry, 1990). An even more serious problem is when highly aggressive children do not care about the negative consequences of their behavior for others (Guerra & Slaby, 1989). Teachers frequently report that such children do not respond to any classroom management strategy. Aggressive students are also more likely to believe that their aggression is a justifiable behavioral response, that their aggression increases their sense of self-esteem, and that their aggression is harmless to others (Slaby & Guerra, 1988).

The problem-solving skills of aggressive children are limited. Some studies have drawn attention to the specific components of problem solving that are amiss among these children: Aggressive children are motivated by hostile intentions, they hold beliefs that support violence, they foresee few consequences for aggressive behavior, they choose fewer nonaggressive alternatives to solve problems, they lack confidence in using nonviolent strategies, and they generate ineffective solutions (Bosworth, Espelage, & Simon, 1999; Guerra & Slaby, 1989; Joffe, Dobson, Fine, Marriage, & Haley, 1990; Neel, Jenkins, & Meadows, 1990; Slaby & Guerra, 1988). (Conflict resolution steps are discussed at length in chap. 5.) Aggression is rarely the only problem behavior that an aggressive child exhibits. Aggressive children may also use alcohol and drugs, use tobacco, carry weapons, belong to gangs, and start sexual activity early (Orpinas, Basen-Engquist, Grunbaum, & Parcel, 1995).

Finally, there has been a long-standing debate about whether children who bully lack social competence skills (like the mean and intellectually backwards Dudley Dursley in the Harry Potter series) or whether they possess specific social competencies that they use to bully others (like Draco Malfoy in the same series; Arsenio & Lemerise, 2001). Proponents of both arguments may be accurate, given that the definition of social competence varies among researchers. Some researchers define social competence as skills that lead to positive social adjustment. By that definition, children who bully lack social competence. Others characterize social competence as neutral skills that can be used to promote social relations or to manipulate others. From this perspective, children who bully have competence—such as knowledge of others' weak spots—and use it for antisocial purposes.

Protective Factors

Protective factors, also called *developmental assets*, include the opposite of many of the risk factors previously described, but they also encompass other positive phenomena. Scales and Leffert (1999), from the Search Institute (http://www.search-institute.org/), defined *developmental assets* as "positive relationships, opportunities, competencies, values, and self-perceptions that youth need to succeed" (p. 1). The Search Institute, in a large study with an aggregate sample of almost 100,000 middle and high school students from 213 communities in the United States, identified 20 internal developmental assets, categorizing them under four main subheadings: commitment to learning, positive values, social competence, and positive identity.

Given poor academic achievement as a risk factor, its converse—good academic achievement—is equally recognized as a protective factor against the development of aggressive behavior. *Commitment to learning*, however, encompasses more than just grades; children who are motivated to do well in school also read for pleasure, feel connected to school, participate in school activities, and complete their homework. Several of these assets could be classified as school characteristics as well as individual characteristics. It is the synergy that is created among the school, the family, and the child that motivates the child to stay connected and do well in school. The net effect of these factors is that a child is less likely to be involved in aggression and delinquency (Fors, Crepaz, & Hayes, 1999; Scales & Leffert, 1999).

Of primary importance in *positive values* is an attitude that supports the use of peaceful means of conflict resolution, but there is an array of other positive values that deserve mention as protective factors. Positive values include caring for others; being empathic and understanding of others' circumstances; promoting equality and social justice; standing up for one's own beliefs; being honest and responsible; and practicing self-restraint in relation to alcohol, drugs, and sexual activity.

Social competence refers to skills used to make positive decisions, solve conflicts without violence, plan for the future, resist negative peer pressure, make friends, and enjoy being around people from different cultures. Children who are socially competent are also more likely to have positive academic achievement (Welsh, Parke, Widaman, & O'Neil, 2001).

Positive identity includes assets such as having high self-esteem, a sense of purpose in life, a positive view of the future, and a feeling of control over the future. In a study on self-esteem and bullying, students who defended the victims of bullying were more likely to have positive self-esteem, whereas bullies and their followers were more likely to have "defensive" self-esteem, that is, self-esteem that was ill founded and inflated (Salmivalli, Kaukiainen, Kaistaniemi, & Lagerspetz, 1999); victims were also likely to report low self-esteem (O'Moore, 2000).

RISK AND PROTECTIVE FACTORS INVOLVING FAMILY AND PEERS

The family is a primary source of support and learning, and it is through family experiences that risk and protective factors become evident. Almost all children are born into a family unit, and with the birth experience come strong influences from the development of risk and protection for future functioning. As children grow, friends and peers also play important roles in the child's life.

Risk Factors

Parental and familial risk factors can be organized into three groups: common parental practices, prevalence of violence within the family, and the degree of neglect present in the home. Responsibility is a core precept of good parenting. Parents need to show love to their children, talk with them (not only *to* them), discuss their values and be consistent in modeling those values, spend time with their children having fun and doing chores, know where their children are, meet their children's friends and their friends' parents, help their children with homework, help them negotiate friendships and relational problems, and so forth. All parents handle these responsibilities differently. For some, successful parenting is a natural and fun process. For others, however, it is a hard road to success because they are ill equipped for the task. These parents may not have been raised in an encouraging environment themselves and may possess limited social skills to assemble a network of social support to deal with the pragmatics of being a parent. Economic circumstances, especially in the case of single parents who are the sole breadwinners, may isolate them from a social support system. The needs of an emotionally or physically handicapped child may overwhelm an ill-prepared parent. Understanding the conditions that lead to poor parenting skills and knowing the causes of the problem will shed light on possible remedies to help parents and children. For example, parents working multiple jobs to meet basic expenses spend little time with their children for entirely different reasons than parents who are financially comfortable but indifferent toward parenting. These two types of family require different intervention approaches, each tailored to both the risk factor and the reasons that the risk factor exists.

The three parenting practices most frequently studied in relation to childhood bullying and aggression are parent–child communication, the parent–child relationship, and parental supervision. When parents develop a poor relationship with their children, do not communicate well with them, and do not set limits or supervise whom they spend time with and where they are, children are more likely to engage in multiple high-risk behaviors (e.g., antisocial behavior, delinquency, alcohol and drug abuse, tobacco use, and early sexual activity; Biglan, Duncan, Ary, & Smolkowski, 1995; Cohen, Farley, Taylor, Martin, & Schuster, 2002; Ledoux, Miller, Choquet, & Plant, 2002; Metzler, Noell, Biglan, Ary, & Smolkowski, 1994; Patterson, DeBaryshe, & Ramsey, 1989; Patterson & Stouthamer-Loeber, 1984; L. Steinberg, Fletcher, & Darling, 1994).

Parents can have considerable influence, both positive and negative, on their children through what they communicate and how they communicate about these high-risk behaviors (Herrenkohl et al., 2001). For example, some parents praise their children for acting tough. In one large study of middle school children conducted in Texas, parental support for fighting was the strongest predictor of students' aggressive behavior, fighting, and weapon carrying (Orpinas, Murray, & Kelder, 1999). When parents believe that "the best defense is a good offense," schools and other agencies face a tougher challenge in trying to influence children to engage in nonaggressive behaviors. In essence, schools and communities become entrenched in a tug-of-war with familial values, and influencing children to engage in nonaggressive behaviors is much more difficult. Frequently, parents who tell their children to fight back if someone hits them have a good intention—they do not want their children to be the victims of bullies. Moreover, these same parents often do not know of any other solution to the problem, and many lack verbal problem-solving skills. It is difficult for parents to teach and model skills or values they do not have.

The parent–child relationship has a strong influence on the child's aggression. Aggressive behaviors steadily and systematically increase as a child's relationship with his or her parents declines (Orpinas et al., 1999). Consistently across studies, parents of bullies lack warmth, use authoritarian parenting styles (i.e., expect unquestioning obedience to their authority), and are not supportive of their children (Baldry & Farrington, 1998; Ladd, 1992).

Lack of parental monitoring, high levels of permissiveness, and a lack of limits facilitate children's and adolescents' exposure to peers who exhibit high-risk behaviors. Escaping parental supervision not only puts the child at risk for peer influences that may encourage violence and other health-compromising behaviors (such as drug use) but also may send a message that the parents do not care. In our work, we have encountered adolescents who have expressed a desire for their parents to be more involved and committed, which is contrary to the general belief that teenagers want to be left alone by parents. An anecdote supports this point: A high school student—a smart and friendly teenager with a good relationship with his parents—was invited to a party where alcohol was served. The "big bully" of the school threatened him by saying, "When I drink, everyone drinks." The student responded, "But when you drink, you don't have to deal with my mom." The bully was taken by surprise, paused for a moment, and then responded, "I wish I had a mom who cared."

The second group of family risk factors is parental aggression. Parental or family child abuse, intimate partner violence, corporal punishment, and abusive discipline are all risk factors for children's aggression (Widom, 1989a, 1989b). Children who observe violence between their parents or between their parents and other children learn how to be aggressive, and they learn that violence is the best—or at least their family's—way to manage conflict. Most important, violence toward children destroys the trust and respect that should exist between parents and their children. When children lose the sense of bonding with their parents, they are more likely to follow a path of antisocial behavior (Straus, 1994; Straus, Sugarman, & GilesSims, 1997). Even after controlling for the effects of parental abuse, children exposed to violence between parents have been found to be at increased risk for bullying at school (Baldry, 2003). Children of abusive parents are also more likely to suffer from depression and other mental health problems, as well as poorer health overall, than nonabused children (Walker et al., 1999).

The third group of family risk factors is parental rejection. Eron (1987) found that the less nurturing and accepting the parents were toward their children, the more the child was punished at home, and the less the child identified with either or both parents, the more aggressive the child was in school. In addition, the child's lack of identification with the parent was a potent predictor of aggression in a 10-year follow-up. In a 22-year follow-up study, more positive levels of adult development were exhibited by those whose parents' child-rearing styles were characterized by acceptance, a nonauthoritarian approach to punishment, and identification of the parent with the child (Dubow, Huesmann, & Eron, 1987).

Family risk factors increase the likelihood of aggression not only directly but also indirectly by having a negative effect on the selection of peers. Children who come from families where there is little supervision and caring are more likely to choose deviant peer groups that reinforce aggression and to engage in other high-risk behaviors such as drug use or early sexual activity (Pettit, Bates, Dodge, & Meece, 1999).

Protective Factors

Thousands of interviews and millions of dollars spent on research have repeatedly proved that the quality of parenting matters (e.g., Resnick et al.,

1997). The greatest protective factor against drug use, violence, delinquency, early sexual activity, smoking, and suicide attempts is a set of loving parents who spend time and energy in parenting. Parents need to be present when their children need them: when they wake up, when they come home from school, while they are doing their homework, at dinnertime, and at bedtime. Parents are important not only for young children but also for adolescents. Parents frequently believe that their teenagers are looking for ways to gain independence, but even though kids may complain, the benefits of parental presence are amplified when parents are proactive. In general, successful parents are those who

- share activities with their children and maintain family rituals (e.g., eating dinner together),
- communicate with their children (e.g., discuss their values regarding violence, sex, and drugs),
- convey high expectations regarding high school and college attendance and grades, and
- express interest in their children's activities and share the ups and downs of daily life.

Parents' positive communication helps their sons and daughters feel confident to ask for help and advice when new situations arise (Magen, 1998).

As role models for their children, parents teach children how to (or how not to, in the case of aggressive families) solve conflicts, manage anger and other emotions, and express love (Bandura, 1986; Scales & Leffert, 1999). Children learn self-control, an important tool for managing conflicts, from their parents. Scales and Leffert (1999) suggested that effective parents also set limits on their children's behavior by keeping track of where their children are, knowing their children's friends, and communicating with the parents of their children's friends. They encouraged parents to support their child or their teenager's participation in organized activities at school and in the community. Such participation serves as a constructive use of time, another protective factor for aggression. Finally, parents should be involved in school meetings and activities, because their involvement not only conveys the message that school is important but also increases their awareness of when their child has engaged in bullying or has been a victim of bullying. Chapters 9 and 10 address strategies parents can use if they learn that their child is bullying others or has been a victim of peer aggression.

Children also develop close relationships with peers and friends. As students move to upper grades and enter the teenage years, they spend less time with their family and more time either alone or with their friends (Larson & Richards, 1991). Studies conducted in the 1950s and 1960s contended that parents were losing their influence on their adolescent children as peers became the strongest influence. However, studies conducted during the past 15 years have shown that parents can have an extensive influence on their adolescent child by monitoring their child's friends and whereabouts, maintaining a positive parent–child relationship, discouraging drug use and violent behaviors, and supporting academic achievement (L. Steinberg & Morris, 2001).

Although peer pressure to conform is stronger during the teenage years, the school environment is composed of a number of subgroups or cliques with which children can identify, most of which are not antisocial groups. Children are not "pulled" and do not "fall" by chance into a group with values and behaviors that conflict with their existing personal values or tendencies. Rather, children are most likely to choose a group of friends on the basis of personal dispositions (e.g., academic achievement vs. drug use), and these dispositions are strongly influenced by parenting practices (Brown, Mounts, Lamborn, & Steinberg, 1993).

Raising children in a warm and caring environment—one in which parents make themselves available when their children need them, involve their children in family decision making, espouse clear values that do not support aggression or drug use, and give love and praise freely—will have two important effects on children's peer relationships. First, children will be less likely to be influenced by their peers (Bogenschneider, Wu, Raffaelli, & Tsay, 1998). Second, children will be more likely to establish positive, close relationships with friends (Lieberman, Doyle, & Markiewicz, 1999).

RISK AND PROTECTIVE FACTORS IN THE SCHOOL ENVIRONMENT

Many risk and protective factors for school violence parallel those factors for family violence. Common factors to the family and the school include what types of behaviors adults model, what kind of communication adults establish with children, how warm or antagonistic is the relationship adults and children establish, how well adults supervise children's whereabouts, and how adults solve conflicts. In this section, we describe risk and protective factors that are unique to the school environment.

Risk Factors

Risk factors that are unique to the school environment include teachers' lack of classroom management skills, poor teaching abilities, low expectations of student success, and an inefficient discipline system (Bear, 1998; Hyman & Perone, 1998; Olweus & Limber, 2002; Sugai & Horner, 2002).

From the identified list of risk factors, a school's discipline plan is widely recognized as important but is also a subject of much debate. To reduce episodes of violence, some schools have responded with zero tolerance policies, hiring security personnel, installing surveillance systems, and establishing harsher punishments for violent behavior (e.g., suspensions and expulsions). These strategies are designed to reduce and eliminate school violence and drug use by severely punishing certain offenses. So far, no evidence indicates that zero tolerance policies improve school safety or that that they contribute to creating a positive school climate. Moreover, the policies have been controversial in terms of the fairness of their application (Skiba, 2000; Sugai & Horner, 2002). Although zero tolerance policies send a powerful message to students and parents that violence is unacceptable, they ironically communicate that students will not be heard and that teachers' professional judgment is irrelevant to solving discipline problems (Curwin & Mendler, 1997). Aside from their powerful statements about violence, zero tolerance policies may be more problematic than beneficial. They react to disciplinary problems, rather than seeking to prevent them. They seek a solution to the problems of disruption and violence with a cookie-cutter, single-answer approach, rather than using an array of strategies to solve these complex problems. The other side of this debate is that the lack of official school policies against bullying communicates that bullying is accepted, or at least tolerated. Clearly stated and consistently reinforced school policies against bullying reflect a schoolwide commitment to reduce bullying and aggression and highlight them as unacceptable. As described in chapter 4, the best discipline policies focus on finding a solution to bullying problems, rather than merely on punishing the perpetrators.

Another well-known school violence risk factor is lack of adult supervision. Not unexpectedly, bullying is most likely to occur in locations where teachers are not present: bathrooms, hallways, playgrounds, and other out-of-the-way locations (Glover, Gough, Johnson, & Cartwright, 2000).

Finally, aggressive and bullying behaviors by adults toward students is a risk factor that not only creates a negative school environment but makes teachers models of the bullying behaviors they are trying to prevent. Unpublished results from the Texas Students for Peace (described in Orpinas et al., 2000) project indicate that over half of the teachers queried reported witnessing another teacher put down a student in the month prior to the survey (reported in Orpinas et al., 2000). Classrooms in which teachers ignore bullying, respond capriciously or unfairly, shout at students, distrust what students say, show favoritism, or exhibit dislike for students foster a negative classroom environment. This type of classroom atmosphere is likely to lead to increased conflict among students, disrespect for teachers, and low academic engagement. Pianta's (1999) extensive review of the literature on the importance of the student–teacher relationship confirmed a direct association between a negative teacher–student relationship and higher rates of classroom aggression, lower academic achievement, and negative student attitudes toward school. His findings were consistent with Aspy and Roebuck's (1977) work. Almost three decades ago, Aspy and Roebuck reported that when teachers showed little positive interest in students, students were more likely to have poorer academic achievement, to miss school more often, and to engage in more school vandalism and aggression. School personnel who bully others should be held accountable for their behavior.

Protective Factors

Although many schools have accepted bullying and class disruptions as an inevitable part of school life, others have significantly reduced or even eliminated the problem. During an interview with an elementary school principal and several teachers at a very successful low-income public school, they summarized their strategies to promote a positive school climate in five areas:

1. Teachers developed positive relationships with all students, a process that, by one teacher's admission, had been a long one. This teacher admitted to initially using an authoritarian style but said that children had always found ways to bypass the rules. Next, she had moved into a laissez-faire style, but discipline in her classroom had deteriorated even further. She finally realized that she needed to develop a positive relationship with all her students. She developed a genuine sense of care for her students, and in return, her students loved her. (Chap. 4 provides more details on developing a positive school climate and caring and respect for students.) Students would try their best to keep this positive relationship, and thus they would strive to comply with classroom rules.

2. Teachers worked very hard to make their program of studies interesting. Their curriculum contained clear objectives to be accomplished every week, and content was integrated across disciplines. Children were more interested in learning and had less time to be bored.

3. The school established different intervention strategies for children who needed extra academic help, such as a mentoring program and after-school activities. Teachers maintained high academic expectations of all students and would not let children fall behind.

4. The school adopted definitive policies against bullying. The administration understood that school personnel could inadvertently reinforce aggression when they failed to intervene against bullying and that the perpetrators could perceive such failure as approval of negative behaviors (Hoover, Oliver, & Hazler, 1992). The school also established clear policies for teachers that prohibited shouting at children or ridiculing them.

5. The school supported a strong arts program, especially music and dance. Good grades were a prerequisite for student participation in these programs, and despite the fact that several of these programs were offered only after school, students were eager to participate. They worked very hard to maintain good grades. Parent participation had dramatically increased during recent years; more than 300 parents attended every parent meeting after teachers combined children performances and meetings with teachers in the same session.

A similar experience was reported by Hein (2004), who followed two extraordinary middle school teachers for a semester. She observed that aggression and bullying were practically nonexistent in their classrooms. Children who were constantly sent to the office for disruption in other classes were working on task and had positive interactions with their peers in these teachers' rooms. She concluded that the most important factor that influenced students' behavior was the creation of a positive classroom environment, one in which students felt respected and cared for. Other researchers have also found that a positive classroom and school climate reduces aggression (Kasen, Berenson, Cohen, & Johnson, 2004; Pianta, 1999; Somersalo, Solantaus, & Almqvist, 2002).

In *Protective Schools: Linking Drug Abuse Prevention With Student Success* (http://www.drugstats.org), Bosworth (2000) proposed 10 steps to create a positive school climate and prevent drug abuse. Because drug abuse and aggression tend to coexist, these same strategies are applicable to preventing violence and aggression. The steps are forging a vision of success, building a protective school culture, increasing leadership commitment, supporting a strong academic program, implementing a research-based prevention program, providing a continuum of services, providing ongoing professional development, strengthening home–school–community relationships, leveraging funding and resources, and using data to guide decision making.

Henderson and Milstein (2003) described six school characteristics that help develop *student resiliency*—that is, the ability to succeed in spite of adversity. These characteristics are similar to those described earlier in this section: increased connectedness of students to school; clear, consistent boundaries; instruction in life skills; a caring and supportive environment; high expectations; and opportunities for meaningful participation. The Search Institute pinpointed similar school assets that reduce aggression: a caring school climate in which clear rules and consequences make students feel safe; an environment in which students are encouraged to do their best academically by teachers and other adults, who set high expectations; and an atmosphere in which participation in other school and creative activities is encouraged (Scales & Leffert, 1999). These characteristics will be extensively discussed in chapter 4.

RISK AND PROTECTIVE FACTORS
IN THE COMMUNITY, CULTURE, AND MEDIA

Each child lives in a neighborhood, a community, and a subculture, all of which influence his or her behavior. In the following sections, we describe the risks and protective factors of these areas of influence.

Risk Factors

Living in an unsafe community with high levels of aggression provides opportunities for learning new aggressive behaviors, reinforcing existing negative behaviors, and joining delinquent peers (Bandura, 1986; Pettit et al., 1999). Unfortunately, some children are exposed to an enormous amount of violence in their communities. In a Texas study, almost 9,000 middle school students were asked how frequently they had observed certain violent behaviors in their community, not on television or in movies, during the past year. Reports of violence were surprisingly high: 80% reported seeing someone arrested or being beaten in their community, 66% related observing gang activity in their neighborhood, 50% recounted seeing drug deals, and 33% described watching a community member pull a gun out and point it at another person (Orpinas et al., 2000). Easy access to guns at home, at friends' houses, or elsewhere in the community can be another risk factor not only for interpersonal violence but also for suicide. In the Texas study, almost half of the students surveyed had access to a gun at home. Frequently, the cultural attitudes that support violence directly relate to the prevalence of violence a community experiences (Orpinas, 1999).

In addition to the community, traditional media venues (e.g., television, movies, music lyrics) and the Internet can also have a powerful influence on behavior. In developed countries, television is a particular concern to attentive parents and educators, because most families have a television set at home, and some children and adolescents spend more time watching television than they spend in school. An average 18-year-old has spent the equivalent of over 2 years of his or her life in front of a TV (Van Evra, 1990). After an extensive review of the literature, the position statement of the American Psychological Association (APA) is that media violence does, in fact, increase the risk of aggression among viewers (APA Council of Representatives, 1999). Likewise, several researchers have found that children are exposed to an enormous amount of violence via their daily television watching activities (Donnerstein, Slaby, & Eron, 1996; Huesmann & Malamuth, 1986; Price, Merrill, & Clause, 1992; Rule & Ferguson, 1986; Thomas, Horton, Lippincott, & Drabman, 1977). Psychologists assert that repeated exposure to aggressive behaviors in the media can change an individual's attitudes toward violence and teach aggressive behaviors (Anderson et al., 2003). Media violence can convey the message that using aggression is appropriate in a large number of situations.

From television, children can learn more strategies to retaliate with aggression than strategies to solve problems peacefully. Violence in the media provides a moral evaluation regarding whether aggression is appropriate, and children may become convinced that solving a problem with aggression is acceptable. In movies, for example, the good guys display just as much violence as the bad guys, but the good guys' use of violence is praised and rewarded. Thus, viewers may come to believe that their own aggression is permissible as long as it can be justified. Finally, psychologists contend that observing violence in the media can change an individual's normal emotional response to violence. Audiences become desensitized to violence portrayed in the media because, in many instances, the characters who use violence do not suffer repercussions. Further, the media's portrayal of violence seldom depicts the pain experienced by the victim, the victim's family, and the victim's friends. Viewing violence repeatedly may numb people's reactions when they are faced with real-life aggression.

A relatively new cultural influence is access to the Internet. The Internet is increasingly becoming a source of concern as more families and public libraries have computers and Internet access. Although the Internet can be a fabulous source of knowledge (the appendix to this book lists Internet resources for bullying prevention) and help in the understanding of cultures, it can also be dangerous for children and adolescents. The Internet provides information on how to build a bomb and how to commit suicide. It provides access to sexually explicit material and can be a portal for sexual predators through e-mail and chat rooms. The Federal Bureau of Investigation's *A Parent's*

BOX 2.2. INTERNET WARNING SIGNS FOR PARENTS AND CAREGIVERS

- The child spends a lot of time on the Internet, especially at night.
- The child receives calls or gifts from people the parents do not know.
- The child turns off the computer or changes the screen when a parent enters the room.
- The child becomes withdrawn from the family.
- The child uses an account that belongs to someone else.
- The parent finds pornography on the child's computer.

Note. From *A Parent's Guide to Internet Safety*, by Federal Bureau of Investigation, n.d., Washington, DC: Author. Retrieved February 20, 2005, from http://www.fbi.gov/publications/pguide/pguidee.htm

Guide to Internet Safety (available online at http://www.fbi.gov/publications/pguide/pguidee.htm) lists warning signs that indicate that children are accessing inappropriate material while using the Internet (Box 2.2 lists these signs). As a general rule, computers with Internet access should be located in an open family room, not in the child's bedroom, and parents need to maintain open communication with their children about possible Internet dangers.

Protective Factors

Communities that care for and value young people protect children from engaging in violence (Scales & Leffert, 1999). Often this caring becomes manifest in the development of extracurricular or supervised after-school activities for young people. In addition, positive communities—in which children see adults solve conflicts peacefully, perceive that adults value educational achievement, and witness the police modeling a community and problem-solving orientation—will protect them from viewing violence as an effective means to an end. Finally, communities that respect differences among individuals and celebrate cultural diversity are more likely to protect children from violence.

3

THEORETICAL PERSPECTIVES ON BULLYING AND AGGRESSION

There is nothing as practical as a good theory.
  —Kurt Lewin, *Field Theory in Social Science: Selected Theoretical Papers*

This chapter discusses the role of theory in bullying prevention, and it comprises two main sections. The first section examines why it is important to establish theoretical frameworks when developing and evaluating interventions. The second section summarizes commonly used theories and models in the field of prevention of bullying and aggression: attribution theory, the social information-processing model, social–cognitive theory, attachment theory, family systems theory, the social interactional model, the developmental pathways to violence, and the ecological model.

WHY SHOULD THEORY GUIDE PRACTICE?

Social psychologist Kurt Lewin's (1951, p. 169) famous pronouncement, "There is nothing as practical as a good theory," may hold truth for academicians, but many practitioners perceive theory as an intellectual exercise rather than as a useful tool for intervention development. Health educators, counselors, school psychologists, teachers, social workers, and other professionals who work to prevent and reduce bullying among young people define themselves more often as practitioners than as researchers or theoreticians. In other words, they see a problem and do something to solve it, usually without theoretical consideration for that plan of action. Because these practitioners constantly struggle with deadlines, budgets, and administrative or public pressures, they frequently view theory and theoretical frameworks as extraneous and as interfering with addressing the real issues at hand. Given this mindset, it is not surprising that most of the practice of violence prevention, and even some of the research, is atheoretical.

Theory—a systematic explanation of reality—helps to explain and predict events and to untangle the complexities of human behavior. Researchers hold defined theories about human behavior from their respective fields, but most laypeople also possess general theories about the problems they face. In fact, their theories are the explanations people use to describe why things happen as they do. Often, researchers simply place a formalized and standardized structure around such ideas. For example, we have asked many teachers why certain children bully other children. Their most frequent explanation is the influence of the children's parents. For instance, some teachers say that the bully has parents who have not established a positive relationship with him or her (attachment theory) or who treat their child aggressively (modeling, as described in social–cognitive theory). Other teachers might say that deviant peers influenced him or her to act aggressively (social interactional model). And still others, holding a more comprehensive view of the problem, might contend that intrapersonal, family, peer, school, and community issues negatively affected the bully (ecological model). These teachers' theories are not very dissimilar from those held by violence prevention researchers.

Theories play a fundamental role in clarifying how and why a program is successful. The lack of explicit theoretical models in bullying prevention practice has made it difficult to advance the field for three main reasons: Theories often are not used to develop or select the prevention programs, the program evaluation does not assess the key constructs of the theory, and the theoretical explanation of the problem does not match the selection of the program.

Bullying prevention programs are frequently selected by school personnel on the basis of circumstantial evidence (e.g., the program "seems right") or because they are easily available. Theories are generally not used to guide the process of selection and evaluation of the program. When school principals deem a violence prevention program necessary for their school, they may seek out programs with prior success. However, even if identified programs were originally developed from a theoretical perspective, it is unlikely that the principals will scrutinize that theoretical basis. Unfortunately, such an informal process of program selection leaves many critical questions unanswered. Teachers or administrators often seek to replicate a successful program without knowing or understanding the key elements responsible for the initial success. For example, a teacher implements a series of lessons on social skills to prevent bullying among her middle school students. A survey of the students conducted before and after the lessons indicates that the students' self-reported frequency of bullying declined. However, the following questions remain unanswered: Did the students learn to communicate more effectively from the lessons targeted at improving social skills? If they did improve their social skills, is that improvement related to the reduction of bullying? Perhaps the decline in bullying can be explained by other factors. Did the teacher make better connections with her students, in essence developing a more positive classroom climate, which lessened aggressive behaviors? Did new classroom rules and consequences for bullying deter students from acting aggressively? Did bystanders who previously had remained uninvolved now intervene to support victims? Or maybe the program actually had no effect at all, and the reason behind the decline was that the bullies moved to another school.

Without adequate evaluation and theory, school professionals will never be able to answer these questions. When programs fail, the problem is even more complicated. Practitioners, not privy to the underlying elements responsible for the program's failure, may continue a frustrating, unending search for an ideal program rather than remedying the one or two elements that stood in the way of desirable results.

Even when an intervention has been developed from a theoretical perspective, evaluations of the intervention often neglect to examine the constructs or key concepts of the theory. Because many theories are designed to influence variables related to the theory's constructs (e.g., communication skills) in addition to an ultimate outcome (e.g., bullying and victimization), effective evaluations should use instruments that measure both the theoretical constructs and the outcome. For example, Mr. Jones was concerned with the problem of bullying in his class. He believed that the bullies lacked empathy toward their peers, and consequently he developed a series of lessons intended to increase empathy, with the ultimate goal of reducing bullying. After finishing the lessons, Mr. Jones observed that the frequency of bullying had not changed. Because he did not measure possible changes in empathy, he could not be sure of what had happened. If Mr. Jones were certain that empathy had increased, he could hypothesize (a) that the link between bullying and empathy does not exist or (b) that in addition to empathy, he needed to increase other social assets for the program to be effective. If he knew that empathy had not increased, Mr. Jones could conclude that the program was not strong enough to increase empathy and, therefore, could not affect the bullying. Because Mr. Jones did not support his experience and good intentions with an evaluated theoretical approach, he had no guidance in interpreting how the program had failed or how it might be improved.

Finally, when practitioners design a program, they frequently neglect their own theoretical explanations about why the problem exists and simply develop a program to target different determinants of aggression. For example, if educators hold a theory about student aggression that links aggressive behaviors to parental influences and economic deprivation, developing a program designed to increase children's social skills has no connection to their theory. Clearly relating the constructs of the theories that professionals think should be addressed (e.g., increased school connectedness, improved social skills, enhanced empathy) to the program activities that are actually developed should augment intervention effectiveness.

In addition to formal theories, other sources of information are important when developing an intervention, including prior research on the program's success record and the experiences of students, parents, teachers, and administrators with bullying. Securing this information may require formal or informal interviews or observations. The process of identifying the relevant theories and constructs, as well as identifying the best strategies for intervention, will require an exchange of information between researchers or educators and the members of the target population. Students, parents, and teachers can give valuable information for identifying which constructs and theories are key, how those constructs are to be evaluated, and which interventions are the most relevant. The researchers, in an iterative process, gather information from theories, the relevant research studies, and the target population (Bartholomew, Parcel, Kok, & Gottlieb, 2001; Murray, Kelder, Parcel, & Orpinas, 1998).

For instance, bullies, victims, and bystanders may have different definitions of bullying and may identify other risk factors than those proposed in a given theory. The researchers would not necessarily reject the theory, but rather, on the basis of the information gathered from the target population, they might test new constructs that are theoretically consistent with the original model. Thus, interventions need a strong theoretical base, but that theory may be expanded to reflect the characteristics of the target population to develop a meaningful and successful intervention. As Lewin observed, a good theory is very practical, and theories are developed to be examined, refined, and extended. This process can occur only if intervention developers understand the theory, as well as their population and settings. Researchers and educators need to challenge their hypotheses, be willing to change them on the basis of the data and their experience, and be open to and curious about the complexity of their work.

Most often, no single theory can explain the complexity of human behavior. It may be necessary to string together several theories, or constructs from different theories, to develop a model that provides a comprehensive understanding of people's behaviors in certain situations. Models in the social sciences share some similarities with the scale models that architects use. Architects develop models to help their clients visualize what the completed building will look like. Social science models attempt to explain the realities of human behavior. Models not only help people identify certain components of reality but also indicate the relationships among those components. In bullying prevention, models help delineate the relationship between interpersonal issues and social influences.

As an additional complication, evaluators may need to use different theories when attempting to change the behaviors of different populations. Not all bullies and victims are alike. Some bullies are never victimized, whereas others may be victims as much as they are bullies. Some bullies may act aggressively because they lack the cognitive and social skills to interact positively with their peers, and other bullies may expertly manipulate social interactions to attack their peers' insecurities.

In sum, the failure to use theory in selecting, developing, and evaluating programs prevents advancements in the field of bullying prevention. The process of incorporating theory into bullying prevention programming must be adjusted according to the nuances of different types of perpetrators, bystanders, and victims. Having a theoretical model as a guide in working with bullying provides needed direction for measuring the problem and developing a successful intervention. When program developers use theory, rather than being guided by wishful thinking and hope, the intervention is guided by research on how and why changes in bullying behavior occur.

THEORIES THAT ARE APPLICABLE
TO BULLYING AND AGGRESSION

While making the argument that bullying prevention would benefit from increased use of theory, this section reviews some of the theories that have been used in the area of bullying and aggression prevention. Some of these theories provide explanations for why children engage in aggressive behavior at the individual level (i.e., attribution theories, the social information-processing model). Other theories provide interpersonal and developmental explanations (i.e., social–cognitive theory, attachment theory, family systems theory, the social interactional model, developmental pathways to violence). Some of these theories examine the importance of the family and other close relationships in the development of aggression; others explain the evolution of violence from birth to adolescence. Finally, the ecological model provides a macro framework to understanding violence, aggression, and bullying. Exhibit 3.1 summarizes the theories and models that are applicable to aggression and bullying.

Attribution Theories

Attribution refers to causal explanations that individuals generate to explain their own behaviors and the behaviors of those around them. Attribution theories help explain two processes: what these causal explanations

EXHIBIT 3.1
Theories and Models That Are Applicable to Aggression and Bullying

Level	Theory and models
Intrapersonal	Attribution theories
	Social information-processing model
Interpersonal	Social–cognitive theory
	Attachment theory
Developmental	Family systems theory
	Social interactional model
	Developmental pathways to violence
Macro	Ecological model

are and what the emotional and behavioral ramifications of those explanations might be. In general, people make either internal attributions (i.e., another person's behavior is the result of something I did) or external attributions (i.e., the person's behavior was influenced by something aside from me).

In the area of aggression, the attribution of intention is very important. The following scenario illustrates how important the attribution of intentions can be: Sean borrowed a book from Jamie but failed to return it. Jamie might ask, "Why did Sean forget to return my book?" If Jamie attributed Sean's delay to the fact that Sean had been very worried because his mother was sick and had most likely forgotten about the book, the lender would probably feel sorry for him. If Jamie's attribution was that Sean was a thief and intended to steal the book, then Jamie might become very upset with Sean. The latter attribution would be more likely to lead to aggressive behavior.

A number of studies have been conducted to research *aggressive attributional bias*, which refers to attributing aggressive intentions when they do not exist (e.g., Dodge, 1980; Dodge & Newman, 1981; Nasby, Hayden, & Depaulo, 1980; M. S. Steinberg & Dodge, 1983). Dodge (1980) developed a study in which he manipulated children's perceptions of one of their peers. In this study, Dodge asked both aggressive and nonaggressive children to complete a classroom task. During the break from their task, the students learned that an unknown peer (who was actually working for the researcher) had destroyed their work. The researchers, when informing the students that their work had been destroyed, led some students to believe that the peer destroyed their work on purpose (hostile intent). He led other students to believe that the peer had tried to help them with their work but had accidentally destroyed it in the process (benign intent). Finally, he told some students only that the peer had destroyed their work; they were not given a reason for why their peer behaved this way (ambiguous intent). Both aggressive and nonaggressive children responded with aggression when the actions of their peer were thought to be intentional, hostile behavior. Likewise, both types of students responded without aggression when they thought their peer was trying to help them. In the ambiguous situation, however, nonaggressive students responded benignly, whereas aggressive students responded with aggression.

Through additional questioning, Dodge (1980) found that in the ambiguous situation, aggressive boys were more likely to attribute the peer's behavior to hostile intentions, to expect continued hostility from the peer, and to distrust the peer. In general, the students' attributions about the peer's intentions were highly predictive of the students' behavioral responses. When boys attributed the behavior to a hostile intention, they were more likely to retaliate than when they attributed the behavior to a benign intention. Other studies have also shown that the level of aggression is related to the strength of the attributional bias (Dodge, Price, Bachorowski, & Newman, 1990; Slaby & Guerra, 1988) and that boys make hostile attributions more frequently than girls (M. S. Steinberg & Dodge, 1983).

Most teachers have heard from bullies "It's her fault" or "He made me do it." Why do children blame others inappropriately? Several studies have tried to answer this question by examining attributions. Dodge, in his 1980 study, found that aggressive children tended to selectively recall hostile cues and to fabricate new cues (i.e., they remembered seeing things that never happened). In addition, aggressive and nonaggressive children tend to attribute aggressive intentions to peers with an aggressive reputation. Consequently, most children are more likely to respond with aggression toward peers with aggressive reputations, even if the situation does not warrant an aggressive response. Thus, aggressive children are not only the perpetrators of aggression but often the victims as well (Dodge, 1980; Dodge & Frame, 1982).

Social Information–Processing Model

The social information–processing model provides a cognitive explanation of children's social adjustment using a series of steps, not necessarily linear, that children progress through when interpreting and responding to social situations (Crick & Dodge, 1994; Dodge & Coie, 1987). According to the social information–processing model, children first encode internal and external cues from a social situation. Then, in the second step of the model, they interpret these cues. During the first two phases of the model, the selective choice of cues and the attributions of hostile intent play a key role in the enactment of aggression.

After interpreting the situation, children select a goal—the third step of the social information–processing model. For example, the goal of a nonaggressive child may be to stay out of trouble or to maintain a friendship, whereas the goal of an aggressive child may be to get even with the other child, save face among observing peers, or obtain what he or she wants at any cost. In the fourth step of the model, children contemplate their possible responses to the issues at hand, playing out future scenarios on the basis of results of similar situations in the past and the observations of relevant peers. In novel situations, a child may develop a new behavioral response. Because of exposure to deviant peers, an aggressive child tends to maintain a larger repertoire of aggressive responses and a smaller collection of friendly responses than a nonaggressive child. How children address the fifth step of the model—deciding what to do—depends on their evaluation of the outcomes of potential courses of action and the strength of their belief that they can obtain the desired outcome using particular behaviors. Not surprisingly, an aggressive child is likely to expect that aggression will render favorable results and to feel confident that he or she can obtain what he or she wants using aggression. Finally, in the last step of the model, children enact their selected responses (Crick & Dodge, 1994).

The benefit of a process or stage model such as the social information–processing model is that it allows interventionists to develop programs targeted at specific stages in the process. Although numerous studies have supported the cognitive failures of aggressive children, as discussed in chapter 2, not all researchers believe that bullies act aggressively because they fail to make realistic judgments of decision outcomes because they have misunderstood or misinterpreted social clues (Arsenio & Lemerise, 2001; Sutton, Smith, & Swettenham, 1999a).

Social–Cognitive Theory

Social–cognitive theory is a complex and encompassing theory that addresses multiple social and personal influences on behavior (Bandura, 1973, 1986). This section examines some of the theory's main constructs and components that relate to the development of aggression: reciprocal determinism, social learning of aggression, rewards and punishment, the social environment, and personal cognitions.

Reciprocal Determinism

According to social–cognitive theory, a person's cognitive characteristics, the environment that surrounds the person, and the person's behaviors are in continuous interaction. This interaction is called *reciprocal determinism*. Thus, although children's behavior is influenced by their personal characteristics and by the environment (family, peers, school, subculture, neighborhood), the quality of the environment and of their personal cognitions will also influence the children's behaviors. The construct of reciprocal determinism has important implications for practice: To change a child's behavior, one can influence personal cognitions or change the characteristics of the environment, or both. Social–cognitive theory has been used extensively in addressing the problems of aggressive children in the family and at school (Orpinas, Horne, & Multisite Violence Prevention Project, 2004; Reid, Patterson, & Snyder, 2002).

Social Learning of Aggression

Social learning is the process of learning how to relate to other people by observing, interacting, and engaging in social relationships. According to social–cognitive theory, aggressive behaviors can be socially learned the same way as any other behavior. The processes regulating the acquisition of any behavior are simple: People learn from the consequences of their own behavior and from observing other people's behaviors and the consequences of those behaviors. Thus, in addition to their own experience, children and adolescents also learn from observing how others behave and from watching which behaviors are rewarded, ignored, or punished. These observed outcomes influence behavior as much as any personal consequence experienced directly.

Through observation and modeling, people learn not only behaviors but also the emotions and rationalizations associated with those behaviors. Through their behaviors and emotions, parents, teachers, and other authority figures demonstrate how to justify aggressive and peaceful actions, how to act in a manner consistent with values and beliefs, and how to practice self-control and anger management.

Rewards and Punishment

A general rule is that reinforced behaviors tend to recur, whereas behaviors that are punished tend to cease. At school, children's aggressive behaviors may be reinforced by enjoying the laughter of their peers, getting money from their victims, being first in line by pushing, or having extra time to use the playground equipment. Reinforcement of aggression may be especially important for gang members, who often gain status by behaving aggressively (Porche-Burke & Fulton, 1992). Families teach children about appropriate and inappropriate behaviors by reinforcing or rewarding good behavior (e.g., giving praise, encouragement, and hugs) or punishing bad behavior (e.g., providing scoldings, criticism, or spankings).

The definition of *reinforcement* or *reward* is somewhat tautological: A reward is something that increases the frequency of the behavior. Consequently, rewards are not universal: A punishment for one child (e.g., being sent to the school principal) may be perceived as a reward by another child (e.g., an opportunity to be out of class). Thus, teachers may inadvertently reward some students' behavior by sending them to the hallway or the main office. To the extent that bullying goes unpunished, observers may believe that the behavior is allowed or that at least it does not hold negative consequences. As a result, other children may begin to imitate the bullies as they learn that aggression reaps many rewards with few repercussions. Through the same process, children may learn positive behaviors when those behaviors are rewarded. Unfortunately, adults tend to take good behaviors for granted and forget to reinforce them.

The effectiveness of punishment in deterring aggressive behavior is determined by a number of factors:

- the value of the reward achieved by the aggressive behavior;
- the availability of alternative means of securing goals;
- the likelihood of punishment;
- the nature, severity, and duration of the punishment;
- the time elapsed between the aggression and the consequence;
- the level of instigation to aggression; and
- the characteristics of the person who inflicts or determines the punishment (Bandura, 1973).

Given the number of variables that can influence the effectiveness of a punishment, using punishment to reduce aggression sometimes creates more problems than it solves. Some issues that punishment can create include the following:

1. When the reward outweighs the occasional punishment, aggression may persist (e.g., the reward of gaining status by making others laugh at the expense of a classmate vs. the punishment of a checkmark on the board).
2. When an adult punishes a child with aggression, the adult teaches the child that aggression should be answered with aggression, essentially modeling the behaviors that the adult wants to discourage. Espelage, Bosworth, and Simon (2000) found that the use of physical discipline at home was associated with bullying at school.
3. Punishment inhibits aggression only when the person who punishes is present. When the punisher is not present, the child will likely revert to using aggression. Because adults cannot observe a child all the time, encouraging self-control rather than obedience would be a better solution to the problem of aggression. (Chap. 4 discusses the difference between a model based on obedience and a model based on responsibility.)
4. When a child is punished, he or she is not provided information about appropriate behaviors to solve conflicts.

In addition, the effectiveness of a punishment may depend on the relationship between the child and the punisher. In a longitudinal study, Eron (1987) found that punishment inhibited aggressive behavior only for children who closely identified with their fathers. Thus, when children did not have a positive relationship with their parents, as the punishment increased, the child's aggression both at school and at home increased.

The Social Environment: Families, Peers, and School

Children model their behavior after what they observe. Many social skills, aggressive or otherwise, are developed through familial interactions in early childhood. Later interactions with peers and other adults help people hone those skills (Horne & Sayger, 2000; Patterson, 1982). In families in which coercion and aggression are the primary means of solving problems and managing social interactions, children learn to use aggression to accomplish their goals at home and at school. Schwartz and his colleagues noted that children who had been raised in aggressive home environments, in which they had witnessed marital violence and physical abuse, were likely to be bully–victims (i.e., to bully others but also to be victims of other bullies) by the time they reached third or fourth grade; they proposed that bullying behavior is a function of repeating aggressive behaviors observed at home (Schwartz, Dodge, Pettit, & Bates, 1997). Patterson (1982) and Olweus (1994b) also reported that physically abused children were more likely to be aggressive toward their peers. This modeling process is consistent with the research of Howes and Eldredge (1985), who found that abused children tended to respond to aggression with aggression. Even more worrisome, abused children responded with aggression to other children in distress.

As part of the social learning process, children also learn to escalate their aggressive interactions to obtain what they want. In a familiar example, a father is too tired to pay attention to his son after returning home from work. To gain notice, his son intensifies his request for attention from talking to making noise to throwing a tantrum. Eventually, the annoyed father attends to the child, rewarding his son's negative behavior with his attention. The father has taught his son to use escalating adverse behaviors in the future. This scenario exemplifies a concept researchers term *coercive reciprocity*, which refers to a goal-oriented escalation of aggression until the more powerful (e.g., teacher, parent) or more aggressive (e.g., bully) person wins. In many families and schools, children have effective role models and problem solvers; in others, children are exposed to a learning process that leads to continued and escalating aggression. In the prior example, the father, upset with his son, is coerced by the son's behavior into reciprocating attention. The father's response, however, may take the form of negative attention (i.e., punishment).

Personal Cognitions

Personal cognitions and other constructs from social–cognitive theory that are particularly important for intervention development are self-efficacy, outcome expectations, expectancies, emotional coping responses, and self-control. These constructs are defined and examples are provided in Table 3.1.

TABLE 3.1

Social–Cognitive Constructs Applied to the
Prevention of Students' Aggression at School

Social–cognitive constructs	Definition	Examples of applications
Behavioral capability	Students' knowledge and skills to prevent aggression, handle conflict, and be friendly and prosocial toward others	Teach conflict resolution and communication skills
Self-efficacy	Students' confidence in their ability to respond in nonaggressive and friendly ways, to avoid or ignore situations or persons that may lead to aggression, to report aggressive acts, to help victims, and to ask for help	Use role-plays to rehearse how to respond to conflict, divide complex behaviors into small steps, provide clear instructions about how to report and ask for help, and reinforce positive behaviors
Outcome expectations	Students' expectations of the consequences of behaving aggressively	Provide clear consequences for aggressive behaviors that are known to all students and that are applied systematically
Expectancies	The value that students give to behaving aggressively and to behaving prosocially	Provide clear statements of school values and teach goal setting and value clarification
Emotional coping responses	Strategies used by students to manage their emotions	Provide anger and stress management training and teach empathy skills
Self-control	Students' ability to control their own behavior	Provide opportunities to students to make their own decisions, to establish goals, and to compare the outcomes of their behaviors with their goals
Reinforcements	Responses from teachers and peers that increase the likelihood of positive behaviors and reduce the likelihood of aggressive behaviors	Increase awareness among teachers and students of how they may be reinforcing negative behaviors inadvertently; provide positive consequences for prosocial behavior and negative consequences for aggressive behaviors

In violence prevention, the cognitive mechanisms used to justify reprehensible conduct are particularly important. These mechanisms are moral justification, labeling, displacement of responsibility, diffusion of responsibility, distortion of consequences, dehumanization of the victim, and attribution of blame (Bandura, 1973, 1986). These mechanisms are not used on every occasion or by every person, but they shed light on how "normal" people can do terrible things.

Moral justification neutralizes or ameliorates self-condemnation for aggressive behaviors by justifying these behaviors in terms of higher moral values. Moral justification is not an unconscious defense mechanism operating to protect the aggressors, but rather a "conscious offense mechanism" (Bandura, 1986, p. 377). People may engage in hostile or aggressive acts and then justify their behavior on religious or moral grounds. For example, some groups condemn gay lifestyles and become violent toward innocent people who are different, justifying their acts with religious or historical precedents. In other words, people consciously justify their aggressive acts by claiming that they were performed in the name of religious principles, moral values, or national ideologies. Children who bully their peers may also justify their aggression in the name of values (e.g., fairness and respect), saying, "It wasn't fair" or "They had it coming." These children believe that because someone has been treated with special favors or in an undeserving manner, their aggressive actions toward that individual are morally justified. We experienced such a situation when a child started a fight with a Muslim student. When asked about the clash, the aggressor explained, "He deserved it, because they shouldn't have done what they did in New York." The aggressor felt morally justified in picking the fight because of the actions of terrorists totally unrelated to the victim.

Labeling, also termed *euphemistic labeling,* uses positive or neutral language to refer to reprehensible behaviors, reframing the context in which one thinks about an inappropriate behavior. Pornographic movies are called "adult movies." Films with extreme acts of brutality are called "action movies." Killing stray dogs is referred to as "euthanasia." Bandura (1986) contended that people can act more aggressively when they label their action a "game" rather than aggression. In the classroom, bullies often justify their actions by saying they were "just playing" or "just teasing." As Bandura indicated, generally unacceptable behaviors can even become a source of pride when labeled in a supportive manner.

Displacement of responsibility occurs when individuals justify reprehensible acts on the basis of hierarchy—that is, the aggressive acts were ordered by a legitimate authority willing to assume responsibility for the behavior. Soldiers frequently justify atrocities committed during wars by claiming obedience to a higher authority. Gang members defend aggressive and delinquent acts committed as part of gang initiation rites by saying they followed orders from the gang leader. In a less violent example, a bully's clique at school may act aggressively because the main bully promotes engaging in inappropriate behaviors. For example, a student may say, "Brian told me to hit Kent because he lost us our break time by goofing off." By shifting the responsibility to Brian, the follower of the bully displaces his own responsibility and justifies hitting Kent.

Diffusion of responsibility through division of labor, group decision making, or collective action helps individuals avoid personal responsibility for a reprehensible act. Members of a clique, gang, or sports team diffuse their responsibility for ostracizing, physically attacking, or verbally berating another individual when the group acts collectively. At school, bullies, and even bystanders when part of a crowd, may harass their peers in ways that they would never do on their own. When members of an exclusive clique at school decide to be cruel to others by excluding or taunting them, each member of the group can attribute the cruelty to the group as a whole rather than take personal responsibility.

Distortion of consequences occurs when individuals minimize the painful consequences of a reprehensible act or selectively recall the benefits of the act while forgetting its harmful consequences. Often bullies make light of their actions, countering, "It didn't hurt" or "It wasn't that bad." They may also insist that if it had happened to them, "It would not be a big deal." It is even easier for bullies to distort the consequences of their inappropriate behaviors when these behaviors have no visible consequences (e.g., excluding, teasing, and taunting). Although victims may be severely hurt by relational and verbal aggression, many bullies make light of their actions because there is no physical evidence of damage. Some bullies distort the situation to convince themselves that their victims actually enjoyed being bullied, saying, "You know he likes it. He isn't stupid, so if he didn't like it, he'd quit acting queer, and then we wouldn't pick on him."

Dehumanization of the victim is the process by which an aggressor removes the human qualities of the victim. Aggressors assign subhuman qualities to their victims in an effort to reduce the dissonance between two inconsistent cognitions: "I am a good person, but I know that I am doing bad things" (Festinger, 1962). Feshbach (1971) noted that most people have difficulty purposely inflicting pain on another human being unless they can find a way to dehumanize the victim. Historically, dehumanization or denigration to subhuman forms has been based on race, ethnicity, religion, and gender. In the past, African Americans, Jews, American Indians, and Gypsies have been labeled as "inferior" races. Depersonalization and dehumanization still occur. When individuals use derogatory references and epithets (e.g., "pigs," "fags," "gooks"), they frame these groups of people as inferior or inadequate and therefore feel little empathy toward them or concern about mistreating them. Bandura (1986) indicated that when adequate institutional safeguards are instated (e.g., commitment to equality, respect, and support for minority groups), dehumanization and the subsequent mistreatment of others will not occur. Conversely, institutional abuse of power may lead to increased dehumanization and aggression. Anonymous and impersonal school or community environments may result in a greater dehumanization and concomitant mistreatment of less powerful members of the group. When schools lack social supports for students who are different, bullies are more likely to find peers who support their inappropriate behaviors (e.g., treating students who are new or different with contempt).

Attribution of blame suggests that the victims, because of their character or behavior, brought the suffering on themselves (victim blaming) or that the situation warranted aggressive behavior. When aggressors and bullies attribute blame to others or to extenuating circumstances, they usually see themselves as essentially good people forced into aggression by these factors. Thus, bullies can excuse their behavior—and even find it righteous—by blaming their victim (e.g., "He deserved it" or "He asked for it"). Unfortunately, attributing blame to the victim or the situation can mislead bystanders into believing that the victim deserves to be blamed. In these situations, those who observe the aggression begin to think that that there must be some justification for bullying the victim, that the victim may be partially responsible for what is happening, and that the harassment would not be transpiring if the victim did not deserve it.

Attachment Theory

Whereas social–cognitive theory emphasizes the influence of the family through modeling, rewards, and punishments, attachment theory provides a very different perspective on aggression. It addresses the importance of the quality of the relationship between the child and the mother or main caregiver during infancy and early childhood (Shaw & Bell, 1993). The early family environment establishes the foundation for future relationships, because the child expects other adults to follow patterns consistent with those of early primary caregivers (Bowlby, 1982). Ainsworth and Bowlby (1991) suggested that a child develops an internal image of himself or herself on the basis of this primary relationship. As the infant grows up, this original relationship strongly influences how the child relates to others. Parents who are helpful, responsive, and caring foster a secure attachment with their children. These children find it easier to develop positive, caring relationships with peers and adults and are able to trust and depend on others. They develop the ability to manage new relationships securely, with self-assurance and confidence, and do not need to constantly depend on others to feel good about themselves. Conversely, parents who are inconsistent in their response to their infants, who are slow in responding, or who are cold and unloving foster an insecure or anxious attachment with their children. These children find it difficult to depend on others or to have healthy, close emotional relationships. They respond to new relationships with discomfort, fear, and general distress.

According to attachment theory, aggression emerges through several mechanisms. First, aggression can be a reaction to an unsatisfactory and frustrating relationship with the mother or main caregiver. Second, children may develop disruptive behaviors in an effort to attract the attention of neglectful parents or caregivers. Third, children who develop an anxious or insecure attachment find it difficult to develop positive relationships with peers and other adults. They may also use aggression to drive away unknown adults, whom they perceive as a threat. In a school environment, their relationships, characterized by lack of trust, anger, and insecurity, can easily turn violent (Greenberg, Speltz, & DeKlyen, 1993).

The association between insecure attachment and aggression has been supported by a considerable amount of research. For example, Volling and Belsky (1992) found that poor infant–mother attachment was related to later aggression with siblings. Ladd (1992), in an extensive review of the literature related to child and family relationship development, reported that preschool children with secure attachments behaved more positively and had fewer behavior problems than children with insecure attachments. Preschoolers with positive attachments to their caregivers demonstrated more cooperative and socially appropriate interactions with other children. Troy and Sroufe (1987) reported that children described as having insecure attachments at 18 months were, at age 5, much more likely to bully others than securely attached children.

On the basis of attachment theory, the most effective interventions provide early support and education to parents who are at high risk for developing an unattached relationship with their infants. Such parents would include single parents, women who have unplanned pregnancies, or parents who themselves lacked a positive parental role model. Ideally, the support should start during pregnancy or even earlier, through educating new couples on effective communication. Other intervention programs (e.g., Big Brothers/Big Sisters of America), in which mentors act as a substitute parent to provide the positive connection that the child lacks, have been successful in reducing aggression and drug use and in increasing academic achievement. Teachers who recognize that a child's aggressive behavior may be a response to an unfulfilling family relationship may adopt a more supportive disciplinary approach to the problem, rather than focusing only on punishment for the child's actions.

Family Systems Theory

Family systems theory emphasizes the complex interrelations among members of the family, describing the family as a whole in terms of the subsystems operating within it (e.g., the parental subsystem, the marital subsystem, the offspring subsystem). The family is seen as a unit composed of many interconnecting relationships (Bowen, 1985). Conflict within one subsystem of the family affects all the other subsystems and the entire family. In this theoretical framework, when a child is identified as a bully or as an aggressive child, his or her behavior is branded a symptom of a dysfunctional relationship within the family unit. The behavior reflects problems within the larger context of the family, rather than being an isolated behavioral incident by the child. Consequently, interventions must be designed to help the family as a whole. Ingoldsby, Shaw, and García (2001) examined the interplay of family systems and conflict. They reported that if only one family subsystem was under stress, that problem alone did not cause the child to behave aggressively at school. The likelihood of conflict with teachers and peers in schools increased, however, when several subsystems were problematic, especially the parental subsystem and the parent–child subsystem.

Interventions for families with dysfunctional family systems are generally beyond the scope of services provided by schools. Such programs are available through other resources in the community, including mental health services, private practice family therapists, church and other religious organizations, and medical professionals. Chapter 9 describes a family intervention model to reduce bullying behaviors that may be provided through schools or other agencies.

Social Interactional Model

Horne, Norsworthy, Forehand, and Frame (cited in Horne, 1991) integrated many of the risk factors discussed in chapter 2 into the social interactional model, which defines a pathway for the development of aggression and delinquency in children and adolescents. As illustrated in Figure 3.1, the model has three components: The upper half of the model highlights key areas in the development of aggression, the center provides a developmental timeline from birth to adolescence, and the lower half represents the family and community influences on the child in the development of aggression.

Children are born with characteristics such as temperament, intellectual abilities, and physical attributes that influence their development. A child who has a difficult temperament (e.g., shows high impulsivity, adapts slowly to new situations, or exhibits negative emotionality, such as a tendency to cry or to get angry or upset) is likely to make the parenting process harder. Rearing a difficult child can lead to adversarial parent–child interactions and a poor level of bonding, an issue described in attachment theory.

When the parent–child bond is weak and the relationship is adverse, childhood conduct problems, power struggles, and aggressive acting out are more likely to occur. These problem behaviors may be reflective of children who have been rewarded for acting out and who have achieved little success through being compliant. As a result, according to this model, aggressive children do not develop effective social competence skills. Because of their poor social skills, aggressive children may be rejected by peers, who feel intimidated or simply fail to connect with them.

Concurrent with the failure to develop effective social skills, an aggressive child may fall behind in the academic work as a result of being sent out

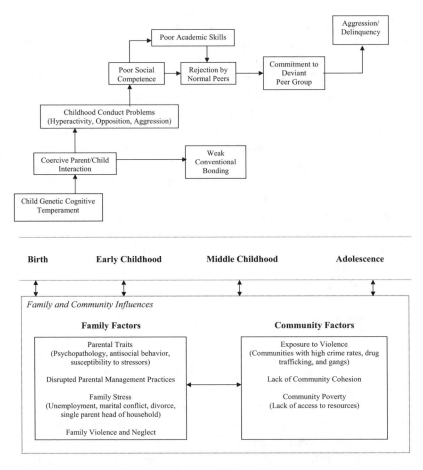

Figure 3.1. The Social Interactional Model: A Conceptual Framework for the Development of Aggression in Children. From *Family Counseling and Therapy* (2nd ed., p. 464), edited by A. M. Horne and J. L. Passmore, 1991, Itasca, IL: F. E. Peacock. Copyright 1991 by F. E. Peacock. Adapted with permission.

of the classroom because of discipline problems or not being able to work with other children in the classroom. When children experience rejection by peers and failure in academic areas, they are likely to turn to peers who are experiencing similar troubles. They may establish a commitment to a deviant peer group, leading to a self-perpetuating culture of greater aggression and possible delinquency.

As illustrated in the bottom half of the conceptual model presented in Figure 3.1, family and community factors, in continual interaction with the child, may enhance or ease the development of aggression. For example, parents who behave antisocially not only model aggressive and delinquent behaviors to their children but also frequently fail to maintain a caring relationship with them. Beyond the problem of individual parental traits, high levels of stress (due to unemployment, conflicted marital relationships, lack of support from a partner, insufficient resources, divorce, or poor parenting skills), family violence, and parental neglect are all family characteristics that pave the road toward aggression and delinquency in children.

Finally, beyond parental characteristics and family functioning, the community in which the family lives may pose additional risk factors for the development of aggression and delinquency. The social interactional model highlights exposure to violence, lack of community cohesion, and community poverty as risk factors for violence. Although poverty does not cause violence, opportunities for exposure to aggression and delinquency are greater in low-income neighborhoods. The family and community factors highlighted in the bottom part of the model in Figure 3.1 continuously influence the developmental process described in the top part of the model.

According to the social interactional model, an intervention may alleviate the negative influences the child is experiencing at each point along the process of the development of aggression. Teaching the child specific social skills (e.g., anger management, problem solving) may increase acceptance by peers. Providing effective tutoring and academic support programs may increase academic success. In addition, effective parenting programs may lead to better attachment and bonding. Parent training opportunities can eliminate or reduce the development of coercive parental interactions and provide parents with the opportunity to learn effective parenting skills. Finally, community empowerment and development can lead to better organized and more cohesive communities.

Developmental Pathways to Violence

In the United States, a number of studies have followed children into adolescence and even into adulthood, such as the 25-year ongoing National Youth Survey Family Study (Hewitt et al., 2003), the Pittsburgh Youth Study (Kelley, Loeber, Keenan, & DeLamatre, 1997), the Denver Youth Survey (Loeber, Kalb, & Huizinga, 2001), the Rochester Youth Development Study (Kelley, Thornberry, & Smith, 1997), the Seattle Social Development Project (Herrenkohl et al., 2001), the Child Development Project (Pettit, Bates, Dodge, & Meece, 1999), and the Kauai Study (Werner, 1989). A few studies have been conducted in Canada (Brame, Nagin, & Tremblay, 2001; Lacourse, Nagin, Tremblay, Vitaro, & Claes, 2003), New Zealand (Fergusson & Horwood, 1995; Moffitt, Caspi, Harrington, & Milne, 2002), and England (Farrington, 1989). In spite of the tremendous scientific contributions of these studies, many questions still remain regarding the developmental paths to aggression.

Several studies have indicated that the development of youth violence follows two distinct trajectories: the early-onset group and the late-onset group. Members of the early-onset group display multiple behavior problems during their whole childhood and commit their first violent offense before puberty.

They are likely to commit more crimes in general and more serious violent crimes, as well as to continue their violent career into adulthood. Characteristically, members of the late-onset group, statistically the larger of the two groups, commit their first offense in adolescence. Frequently, this group of adolescents exhibits no behavioral problems or signs of violence earlier in their lives. Their offenses are more limited in time; they start later in life and frequently do not continue past their teenage years (Moffitt, 1993; U.S. Department of Health and Human Services, 2001).

Although widely recognized, some researchers question the accuracy and comprehensiveness of the two-pathway model. Loeber and Stouthamer-Loeber (1998), for example, expanded on Moffit's (1993) prior work and proposed three pathways: life-course, late-onset, and limited-duration groups. The life-course group includes children who display aggression in early childhood and whose aggression persists and worsens through adolescence. The late-onset group comprises a small number of people without a history of violence who start displaying violence as adults. The limited-duration group includes children who start displaying aggression early in life but whose aggression desists either in elementary school or in late adolescence. Loeber and Stouthamer-Loeber's characterization of the limited-duration pattern questions the generally held assumption that aggression is highly stable over time (e.g., Olweus, 1979). Evidence from research and the experiences of educators support the premise that many children move away from aggression. However, more evidence is needed about turning points and transitions, including how, when, and why children desist in their aggressive behaviors (Loeber & Stouthamer-Loeber, 1998).

Many conclusions about developmental pathways have been based on studies of males only. More recently, researchers have cautioned that these male trajectories cannot be generalized to females. Broidy and colleagues (2003), in an analysis of six longitudinal studies, concluded that early aggression increased the risk for later aggression, but only among boys; no clear associations were found among girls. Fergusson and Horwood (2002) found identical offending trajectories for boys and girls; however, the probabilities of being a member of each trajectory or developmental path varied with gender. It is important to identify and understand gender differences to develop meaningful interventions for boys and girls.

Understanding the developmental pathways to violence has important implications for bullying prevention and intervention. Most important, not all aggressive children are identified as aggressive in childhood. Therefore, programs should be developed to influence children who start displaying aggression early in life, as well as children with a late onset of aggressive tendencies. Educators should be cautious, however, about extrapolating information on developmental pathways to violence and delinquency to bullying. Although bullying, aggression, and violence do have common risk factors, bullying—particularly the nonviolent type—may not follow any of these

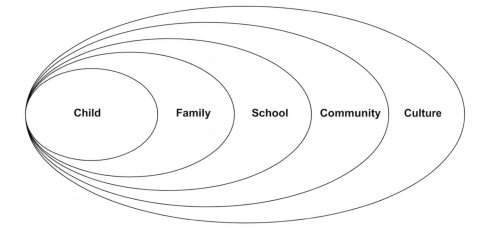

Figure 3.2. The Ecological Model.

pathways. Thus, more research is needed to understand how the developmental pathways of bullying vary from those of violence.

Ecological Model

Often viewed as the most comprehensive model, the ecological model has been increasingly used to describe the interplay of multiple factors that influence whether a person will develop positive social skills or will behave aggressively (Orpinas et al., 2004; Smith, Connell, Wright, Sizer, & Norman, 1997). The ecological model can be visualized as concentric circles that represent different levels of influence indicating where interventions can be implemented, as illustrated in Figure 3.2. The inner circle represents the individual. The second circle represents the family and other close relationships, such as peers and friends. The middle circle represents the school, the work environment, and other organizations that may influence behavior. The two outer circles represent the community and culture in which the individual lives. Theories that address only one of these levels, like personal lifestyles, may be limited in their explanation and prediction of children's behavior (Sallis & Owen, 2002; Stokols, 1996). The ecological model does not devalue the usefulness of individual and family theories to explain certain aspects of behavior and to develop interventions; it expands the areas of influence and intervention to include the physical and social environment.

Proponents of the ecological model contend that understanding the multiple levels of influence is important for comprehending the problem and selecting interventions to reduce aggression. In addition to appreciating the big picture (i.e., the interplay of multiple levels of influence), the model creates an awareness of spheres of influence. For example, teachers may not be able to influence how much television a child watches at home, but they may be able to increase the child's self-efficacy for distinguishing between fiction and reality in television shows. Likewise, educators may not be able to influence how children and parents engage in problem solving at home, but they can model effective conflict resolution methods in the classroom. Thus, in the process of selecting the violence intervention, the motto "Think globally, act locally" is well applied when referencing the ecological model.

The ecological model is particularly important in the prevention of school bullying. Individual interventions—for example, programs designed to increase students' social competence—are less likely to be effective without the support of a positive school climate, as described further in chapter 4. Moreover, particularly with bullies who persist in their aggression in spite of the positive characteristics of the school environment, the involvement of parents and caregivers may be necessary (see chaps. 8 and 9).

II

ADDRESSING THE PROBLEM: UNIVERSAL INTERVENTIONS

4

SCHOOL SOCIAL COMPETENCE DEVELOPMENT AND BULLYING PREVENTION MODEL: THE SCHOOL

You must be new here; we don't do that in our school.
>   —Second grader to a classmate who is pushing the
>   child in front of him while in line for the cafeteria

This chapter examines how to create a positive school climate in which students and faculty feel supported and respected. Chapters 5 and 7 discuss schoolwide programs that can be instituted as an alternative to individually targeted interventions; this chapter emphasizes actions school administrators can take to change a school's general environment and foster a culture that reduces bullying. The chapter is organized into two main sections; the first defines the concept of positive school climate, and the second examines how to develop a positive school climate, highlighting eight critical areas of focus: (a) excellence in teaching, (b) school values, (c) awareness of strengths and problems, (d) policies and accountability, (e) caring and respect, (f) positive expectations, (g) teacher support, and (h) physical environment characteristics.

WHAT IS A POSITIVE SCHOOL CLIMATE?

In life, some people have a gift for bringing out the best in those around them. These individuals somehow help others connect with their most positive emotions and behaviors. Other individuals, unfortunately, can drain the energy of those around them, generally depressing those with whom they interact. Environments, particularly those in which people spend a lot of time (e.g., workplace or school), can similarly affect the psyches of those who occupy them. In essence, environments have "personalities," or climates, that can foster the best or the worst in people. An organization's climate is more than just a building or the individual characteristics of the people who work or go to school there. Climate also encompasses more subjective features of an environment, such as management styles, rules and regulations, ethical practices, and candidness or reticence in communication. From our research experiences, which have been corroborated by the studies of many educators and researchers, we have found that schools with a more positive climate experience fewer incidents of bullying. Indeed, creating a positive school climate appears to go hand in hand with reducing bullying and aggression (Bear, 1998; Orpinas, Horne, & Staniszewski, 2003; Somersalo, Solantaus, & Almqvist, 2002; Sugai & Horner, 2002).

A school with a positive climate is inviting. Typically, students and teachers alike enjoy being at school and feel energized to perform their best. All of the educators we have interviewed in our research on bullying and aggression agree that creating a positive school climate is important not only in reducing aggression but also in promoting positive youth development and academic excellence. Even when a school has successfully fostered a positive climate, however, the process used to achieve this state generally has not been recorded or specified. Thus, the process of attaining a positive school climate is often an enigma. The concept of school climate is frequently discussed, and most educators understand its significance, but few people ever define it. Here is our definition: *Positive school climate* refers to the characteristics of the school—the quality of the interactions among the members of the school community and the influence of the physical and aesthetic qualities of the school building and its surroundings—that enhance learning and nurture an individual's best qualities.

To understand how a positive school climate is achieved, we organized the critical components of school climate into the School Social Competence Development and Bullying Prevention Model. This model, as illustrated in Figure 4.1, is composed of two areas: The outer area reflects the school climate, which is described in the next section of this chapter, and the central area reflects the students of the school and details specific characteristics that warrant attention to reduce and prevent bullying. (Chap. 5 examines the student component of the model.)

COMPONENTS OF A POSITIVE SCHOOL CLIMATE

We identified eight components that are critical ingredients for creating a positive school climate and that result from our definition: (a) excel-

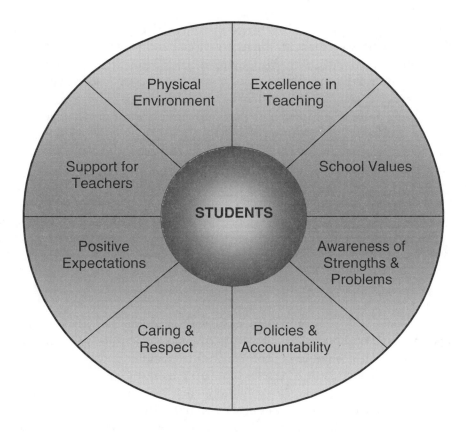

Figure 4.1. School Social Competence Development and Bullying Prevention Model: The School Climate.

lence in teaching, (b) school values, (c) awareness of strengths and problems, (d) policies and accountability, (e) caring and respect, (f) positive expectations, (g) teacher support, and (h) physical environment characteristics. The first seven components reflect the significance of interactions between adults and students within a school, as well as the adults' values and the school policies they create. The last component focuses on the building or facility itself and its impact on school climate.

Excellence in Teaching

The goal of schools is to educate children. To achieve this goal, educators know that there is no substitute for a good teacher and for a motivating academic program. Excellence in teaching includes not only the breadth and depth of subject knowledge but also the mastery of skills in transmitting this knowledge to students, motivating students to learn, and managing other classroom behaviors (see Box 4.1). A teacher who has developed a positive relationship with his or her students but lacks a solid foundation in content and teaching methods will probably be a poor teacher. Conversely, a knowledgeable teacher who lacks strong motivational and relationship skills may also be an ineffective teacher. Although it is outside the scope of this book to expand on how to be a good teacher or how to develop an academic program that motivates students, it is important to recognize that excellence in teaching can help to prevent bullying and that bullying prevention strategies may enhance academic performance.

BOX 4.1. *ELEMENTS OF GOOD TEACHING*

- knowledge of subject
- teaching skills
- motivational skills
- classroom management skills
- relationship skills

Students' academic achievement is, without doubt, the first and most important goal of schools. Frequently, teachers struggle to balance the time needed to teach academic content related to standardized tests—student performance on standardized tests is often an important component of their own professional performance evaluation—and the time needed to teach social skills. However, the dichotomy between these two classroom priorities is somewhat artificial, and in fact they usually interact and overlap with one another. Social competence and academic achievement influence each other, and children need both to succeed academically and socially and, later in life, professionally (Welsh, Parke, Widaman, & O'Neil, 2001). When teachers fail to educate students about appropriate and inappropriate social behaviors, they will probably spend an enormous amount of time managing student misbehavior at the expense of academic content.

The most successful administrators and teachers frequently use a comprehensive approach that promotes both positive behavior and academic performance (Flay, 2002; Flay & Allred, 2003). Research supports this comprehensive approach, indicating that prosocial behavior (e.g., cooperation, assistance, empathy) can have a strong impact on increasing academic achievement (Caprara, Barbaranelli, Pastorelli, Bandura, & Zimbardo, 2000).

Strong teaching and motivational skills reduce behavioral problems in the classroom and promote a positive classroom climate (Hein, 2004; Pianta, 1999; Pierce, 1994). We have found that many students bully their peers when they do not understand classroom content and when they are frustrated because of their lack of academic skills. These bullies often get caught in a downward spiral: bullying others because they are afraid of being called stupid, and then being disciplined in ways that put them further behind academically (e.g., office referrals, detention, suspension). Bullies who are frustrated with learning also tend to be unprepared for class, avoid working in class, challenge school authority, interrupt others in discussions, and display flippant attitudes about learning. Unfortunately, these inappropriate behaviors usually thwart the bully's ability to establish a relationship with the teacher, who is less likely to provide special attention to the bully's academic needs after having his or her authority challenged and class time wasted.

In an extensive review of the literature conducted by the U.S. Department of Health and Human Services (2001), excellence in teaching was identified as a primary method for the prevention of violence. In particular, two teaching strategies were highlighted as successful for increasing academic success: continuous progress programs and cooperative learning. Continuous progress programs present students with a hierarchy of skills; students progress from the beginning level to the advanced level as they master each unit. Cooperative learning groups are composed of students with different skill levels who work cooperatively on academic tasks. The report concluded that cooperative learning can improve academic achievement, race relations, and positive attitudes toward school. Thus, this strategy appears to be promising for helping bullies reduce academic failure and learn skills for working and interacting cooperatively.

In addition to these two strategies to increase academic success, teachers have recommended using diverse teaching strategies to accommodate different learning styles; dividing the solution to a problem into small, achievable steps; providing positive reinforcement for effort and achievement; and providing age-appropriate examples that are interesting to students. Mendler (2000), in his book *Motivating Students Who Don't Care*, discussed numerous techniques to motivate students to learn. Support groups (described later in this chapter) or in-service training can also be used to enhance teaching skills and refine positive discipline management.

School Values

A clear and easily understood school philosophy that promotes a safe and a positive environment is essential for bullying prevention (Sullivan, 2000). As the number of school administrators who define bullying as a problem continues to grow, schools ideally should incorporate bullying prevention into their concept of a safe school and strive to meaningfully implement these philosophies every day (Limber & Small, 2003). To simplify the process of transforming an abstract concept into tangible guidelines, Curwin and Mendler (1997) proposed four steps to creating a positive, violence-free environment: (a) identify the school's core values, (b) create rules and consequences based on these values, (c) model these values, and (d) eliminate interventions that are not congruent with these values. The steps seem easy and straightforward until one begins applying them. With regard to the first step, identifying the school's core values, our work with schools has revealed that many teachers simply did not know their school's values or were only vaguely familiar with them. Teachers' lack of familiarity with their school's core values frequently stemmed from the fact that the schools did not clearly delineate their educational philosophy. In some schools, the values were posted in the main office but served a rhetorical function rather than a pragmatic one; the values had little or no connection to daily happenings.

As school districts strive to create safer learning climates, a close look at the values of the school's decision makers may be warranted. How much time are school administrators willing to dedicate to preventing and reducing bullying? How many resources are school boards willing to invest? (Someone once said, "Values are best reflected on our calendar and in our checkbook!") Bullying prevention does not "just happen." Rather, a serious, concerted effort to prevent bullying needs to be delineated by school leaders and implemented by all school staff. In the worst-case scenario, bullying incidents are handled on a case-by-case basis, and little or no effort is given to prevention. In a slightly better scenario, teachers' participation in the prevention program may be voluntary, but the school may fail to allocate sufficient time and resources to support a more comprehensive program. In our observation of busy teachers working at schools where voluntary prevention programs were available, the teachers rarely found additional time to dedicate to programs extraneous to their daily lessons. We even heard some principals say, "I cannot afford to waste time on bullying prevention." Conversely, those who really appreciated the value of bullying prevention often said, "I cannot afford *not* to have a bullying prevention program."

To generate interest and support, teachers, and ideally all members of the school community, should participate in the process of defining their school's values and mission (Bosworth, 2000). One way to approach incorporating teachers into the value generation process is to hold a values session during in-service training at the beginning of the academic year. In-service training provides the perfect opportunity for teachers to work in small groups to identify basic school values. These values can then be shared and discussed with the whole group, allowing everyone to feel as though they contributed to the process (Orpinas et al., 2003). The values generated should be the basis of the discipline program, as indicated by the next steps proposed by Curwin and Mendler. For example, if one of the school values is respect, a logical rule that follows is that put-downs and name-calling are not acceptable. And to ensure that new teachers can identify with the school's values, as well as to address changing circumstances, a school can repeat the process of discussing and establishing the school values every 3 to 5 years.

Most of our research has been based on three values that support children and educators and discourage any form of aggression and violence (Horne, Orpinas, Newman-Carlson, & Bartolomucci, 2004; Orpinas, Horne, & Multisite Violence Prevention Project, 2004). We believe that these values provide a framework for bullying prevention and promote a positive school climate. (Box 4.2 describes how all three values can be violated in a single incident.) These values, which apply to teachers and students, are described in the following paragraphs.

BOX 4.2. MS. CASTAGLIA VIOLATES SCHOOL VALUES

One morning, while several teachers were talking with the school secretary and receptionist, Ms. Castaglia came storming in, pulling along a child with each hand. She was obviously very upset and irritated. As she headed for the principal's office, she looked at the group and shouted, "Project kids! You know how they are!"

Ms. Castaglia's behavior violated all three proposed values:

1. *All children can learn.* By labeling the children "project kids"—that is, children who live in the nearby housing project—she implied that they have some negative, unchangeable characteristic that impedes their success in school. The label implies that these children are destined to fail.

2. *All people should be treated with respect and dignity.* Criticizing the children, particularly in a public office and in front of strangers, was very disrespectful.

3. *There is no place for violence in the school.* Ms. Castaglia's behavior toward the children was very aggressive. Her language was rude and disrespectful, and her physical handling of the children was excessively rough. She was definitely not managing her anger appropriately.

First, *all children can learn.* All children can learn academic content and behavioral skills to establish positive relationships, including victims of bullying, the bullies themselves, and even persistent bullies (i.e., children who continue to bully in spite of a positive school environment and schoolwide support for learning social competence skills). That is, even children who have been aggressive for a long time can learn new and more effective relationship skills. Most likely these children will need extra help from an adult who provides an encouraging and supportive environment in which the child can explore new ways of fulfilling his or her emotional needs. In our discussions with teachers, when we refer to children who bully and their victims, we never imply that these are fixed characteristics. We use the terms to address behaviors that need to change, but we view a child as a person in transition rather than as a fixed entity. Our years of working with individuals in bullying problems have reaffirmed our belief that bullying behaviors can be changed. We believe that, given the opportunity, most students will elect to not use aggression, but if they have no other resources available, they will do what they know how to do best.

Second, *all people in the school community deserve to be treated with respect and dignity*. Treating people with respect and dignity should be extended to everyone in the school community. Many children who bully, particularly persistent bullies, do not expect to be treated with respect or dignity. They have been labeled, identified, and categorized; they anticipate that they will be treated with disdain, reproach, or anger. Children who are treated without dignity will respond in kind. Adults working with children must realize that if they expect children to be respectful of others, then the children must also be treated with respect. In addition to bullies, victims are frequently treated without respect. After being bullied, these students may need someone to help restore their sense of dignity. Finally, all teachers need to be treated with respect and dignity. Teachers and students often comment that students treat teachers disrespectfully, creating a negative classroom environment. When teachers respond assertively and keep their self-control, they will maintain their self-respect and the respect of their students.

Third, *violence, aggression, and bullying are not acceptable in school*. All schools have clear polices against violence (i.e., fights, assaults, weapon carrying). However, school administrators should extend the principle of violence as unacceptable behavior to all forms of aggression and bullying, including the following forms:

- aggression among students, such as teasing, pushing, fighting, excluding peers, and passing rumors;
- aggression by students toward teachers, such as making derogatory remarks, rolling one's eyes, making threats, and refusing to follow instructions or following them with a sarcastic attitude;
- aggression by teachers toward students, such as making demeaning comments, shouting, threatening, and instituting unfair discipline decisions; and
- aggression among faculty and staff, such as bursting into another teacher's room without knocking on the door or asking for permission, passing rumors, and refusing to cooperate with colleagues.

Awareness of Strengths and Problems

It is impossible to solve a problem when one is unaware of its existence. In particular, it is impossible to solve the problem of school bullying when teachers and administrators are unaware of the problem. No school or community is perfect, and most schools have some problem with bullying. Thus, a fundamental aspect of creating a positive school climate is to recognize areas that need improvement and to build on the strengths. The results of student and teacher surveys, described in chapter 6, can help illuminate the nature and extent of bullying and aggression problems. If bullying is identified as a potential issue that the school needs to address, supplemental information can then be gathered from parents and other members of the school community to clarify the extent of the problem. In teacher and staff meetings, school leaders can often increase problem awareness by simply developing visual displays (i.e., charts and graphs) of the frequency with which bullying and victimization occur in the school and retelling children's stories about what they have observed or suffered.

In the process of examining areas of strength and areas that need improvement, school leaders may also need to examine other areas such as teachers' and administrators' attitudes. Their attitudes may or may not support a bully-free environment and may be at odds with the intervention and implementation strategy that school leaders have decided to use to reduce bullying. Exhibits 4.1 and 4.2 examine common myths about bullying and victimization and about teacher interventions to reduce bullying.

After bullying prevalence statistics, faculty attitudes, and other relevant information have been presented, small group discussions can be used as a tool to facilitate problem resolution dialogues among administrators, support staff, teachers, students, and parents. These small group discussions can be followed by a large group interchange of ideas, during which participants brainstorm areas of strength and areas that need action and develop a draft plan of action. The sample worksheet presented in Figure 4.2 takes a slightly different track; it asks participants to list their "prouds" and "sorries." Another approach to developing awareness of strengths and problems and identifying solutions is to ask stakeholders to prioritize a list of areas that are in need of improvement (e.g., school discipline planning, professional development, student–teacher relationship development, school bus management, student cafeteria behavior, bullying victim services, bullying prevention activity coordination, academic teaching coordination). Schools can then target the top three items on the list for improvement.

Small and large group discussions should be framed within two parameters. First, these discussions should examine only problems that are within the group's realm of influence; blaming parents, the media, or a governor's policies will be fruitless to accomplish immediate goals. However, strategies to change state-level policies or to increase parental awareness regarding the media may be included in long-term planning. School principals can set the tone of the discussion by refusing to blame others for school problems (e.g., a state budget cut) and by focusing on solutions (Whitaker, 1999). Second, these discussions should use a solution-focused approach (Horne, Bartolomucci, & Newman-Carlson, 2003; Murphy, 1997). By focusing on the solution rather than the problem and by concentrating on the future rather than the past, schools can take a positive approach to

EXHIBIT 4.1
Challenges to Erroneous Beliefs About Bullying and Victimization

Erroneous belief about bullying	Challenge to the belief
Bullying is just a normal part of childhood.	Bullying is not a normal part of growing up. Children can and should be socialized to respect and treat others kindly and to know that hurting others is never appropriate.
Bullying is child's play.	Bullying may have long-term consequences and is likely to get worse in middle school. Further, the number of bullies in school may decrease with each grade level, but those who continue are likely to engage in more serious and aggressive behaviors.
Name-calling, spreading rumors, or purposefully embarrassing a student is simply kids being kids.	Name-calling, spreading rumors, and causing embarrassment are all forms of bullying. Relational bullying often leads to isolation of victims or rejection by their peers. Feelings of isolation and rejection can have serious long-term consequences such as school dropout, severe adult psychological problems, and even suicide.
Children will outgrow bullying.	Although aggression and bullying decrease as children mature, unless adults or influential peers take action, bullying is likely to continue and, in some cases, escalates to violence and delinquency.
Only boys bully.	Physical bullying by boys is the most obvious and common form of bullying among schoolchildren. However, physical, verbal, and relational bullying is prevalent among both boys and girls.
Bullying happens on the way to and from school, not during the school day.	Bullying does occur on the way to and from school, especially on the school bus. However, even more bullying occurs during the school day, in the bathrooms, school playground, and classrooms. Bullying increases when adults are not present.
Some children are just born rough.	Bullying behavior is learned and maintained by the social situation (school, classroom, neighborhood), and it can be stopped there as well.
Bullies only pick on kids who are different.	Bullies do target students who are different, but most important, they target peers who appear less powerful than themselves.
Some kids ask to be bullied. They act in unusual ways that attract the bully.	Provocative victims do spark the bullying, but these children are few and in great need of help. Each child is doing the best he or she can, and no child deserves to be victimized. The educators' job is to solve the problem, not to blame the victim.
Bullies help kids who seem weaker by pushing them to learn to stand up for themselves.	Bullies typically have much more power in the form of strength, intellectual abilities, or social clout than victims. Children can learn assertiveness skills to stand up to bullies, but those skills are best learned in an encouraging and supportive setting, not in an interaction founded on fear and intimidation.
Aggressive behaviors of bullies are related to school frustrations.	School is one of the many contexts that can influence the development of bullying behaviors. Children may experience difficulty with their schoolwork for a variety of reasons, but signs of behavior problems may occur before the onset of academic problems.

Note. From *Bullying in American Schools: A Social–Ecological Perspective on Prevention and Intervention* (pp. 309, 315, 317), edited by D. L. Espelage and S. M. Swearer, 2004, Mawhah, NJ: Erlbaum. Copyright 2004 by Erlbaum. Reprinted with permission.

EXHIBIT 4.2
Challenges to Erroneous Beliefs About
Teachers' Interventions to Reduce Bullying

Erroneous belief about teachers' role	Challenge to the belief
Teachers "can't" intervene in bullying situations because they lack adequate training and skills.	Many teachers believe they do not have the knowledge and skills to intervene in bullying situations. However, students trust teachers and rely on them for help when they are in need. Teachers can become experts at managing bully problems and supporting students on a daily basis with adequate training.
Intervening will only add "fuel to the fire" and result in continued or increased bullying.	In fact, the opposite is more accurate. If bullies learn that they can usually get away with their behavior, their behavior will tend to continue or even increase. Conversely, intervention by an adult can result in decreased bullying.
It is best to ignore bullying incidents.	Ignoring bullying sends the message to bullies that they can continue to act as they have and a message to victims that they are on their own and vulnerable to the bullying. Ignoring the problem confirms students' beliefs that teachers are unaware of or insensitive to the problem.
Teachers cannot change the way children are treated at home.	Children may learn to react aggressively at home or in their neighborhood, but they can also learn to be nonaggressive in school. When a child forms meaningful bonds within the school community and perceives the school environment as encouraging and supportive, the child is less likely to respond with aggression.
If the teachers do not see bullying as it takes place, there's nothing they can do about the behavior, because they cannot be sure it really happened.	Bullies are particularly adept at being aggressive in sneaky or private ways, but that does not mean the behavior is not happening. It is the responsibility of the teacher to provide a classroom environment that is safe and supportive.
There isn't enough time during the school day to address bullying incidents or to introduce issues related to bullying into the curriculum.	Bullying and victimization interfere with children's ability to succeed academically. Children who bully or are victimized are not likely to be in an emotional state to succeed academically. Introducing the topic of bullying creates a forum to discuss and solve the problem.
Teachers want to help their students and hope that students will talk to them, but they really don't want to create a situation where everyone is tattling on each other.	Teachers should teach students the difference between tattling and reporting. Initially, the reporting of problems may increase. This is a good sign; it means that students trust that teachers will do something about bullying. As students learn new skills, bullying will decrease, and victims will feel more confident in handling situations independently.
Bullying is not a problem in a particular class or school.	For some teachers and classrooms, it is true that bullying is not a problem. However, out of fear that they will be targeted by the bully, students sometimes adhere to a code of silence. Discussing issues related to bullying may help students to feel more comfortable in speaking up.

Note. From *Bullying in American Schools: A Social–Ecological Perspective on Prevention and Intervention* (pp. 309, 315, 317), edited by D. L. Espelage and S. M. Swearer, 2004, Mawhah, NJ: Erlbaum. Copyright 2004 by Erlbaum. Reprinted with permission.

PROUDS AND SORRIES

The purpose of this activity is to summarize strengths and weaknesses of different aspects of our school, and develop a plan for strengthening certain areas. In small groups, discuss each section, list your "prouds" and "sorries," and then brainstorm constructive ideas for a plan of action.

Prouds	Sorries
School Building	School Building
Administration	Administration
Coordination/support among teachers	Coordination/support among teachers

Plan of action:

Figure 4.2. Example of a Small Group Workshop.

solving problems. A positive approach to problem solving can have a profound impact on participants' attitudes because it produces an optimistic frame of mind when dealing with a school's challenges. Participants are more likely to translate their anger and frustration into the energy and enthusiasm needed to find solutions. If a group gets mired in discussing the problem without seeing any solutions, the group facilitator might try asking for success stories to get the discussion back on track. For example, the facilitator could ask each participant to describe when they or someone else did something that really made a difference in their lives, their students, or the school.

Policies and Accountability

Policies regarding the prevention of bullying, the handling of bullying problems, and the accountability of the offenders are a fundamental aspect of a positive school climate. Beyond having clear policies, however, how those policies are created and implemented will also affect the school climate. When establishing policy and accountability, all members of the school community should be viewed as partners in decision making and policy development that facilitate win–win solutions. When people participate in decision-making processes, they tend to be more committed to the policy's goals, to cooperate with one another, and to implement the plan of action. Most people resent authoritarian environments, which stifle creativity, and typically resent having to work toward objectives that they did not develop. For example, character education programs mandated from "above" may not garner much teacher support, because teachers do not perceive it as part of their role or simply do not have a full understanding of its importance. Consequently, when they are required to discuss "courage" as the "word of the month" in their character education programs, these teachers may write the word on the board and mention it in passing. Although this technically satisfies the requirement, it falls short of contributing to the program's ultimate goal of fostering positive virtues or values. Most likely, policies that require teachers to implement some activity without knowledge or support of the overarching goal will fail. Asking teachers to work toward agreed on goals—and then evaluating them on the basis of how well those goals were achieved—is more effective than asking them to simply implement certain activities. Teachers need the freedom to choose the best strategies to achieve the goals on the basis of their personality, experience, and teaching style.

Another means of obtaining teacher and stakeholder support is to involve them in the process of evaluating the implementation of policies. For example, end-of-the-year teacher evaluations could be based on agreed-on criteria developed cooperatively by teachers and administrators. Similarly, the classroom discipline rules or the student evaluations of a class project can be based on criteria defined jointly between the teacher and students.

To create a positive school climate, schools must have specific antibullying policies based on the school's values or philosophy—these are paramount. If the school values respect, and therefore expects all members of the school community to treat each other with mutual respect and dignity, it clearly follows that pushing, hitting, teasing, and fighting will be considered unacceptable behaviors in this environment. Likewise, teachers who direct condescending and harsh language at students are not modeling positive communication skills, nor are they demonstrating how to show respect. In a school striving for a positive climate, these adult behaviors would also be unacceptable.

Policies, rules, and consequences should be based on the school's values and integrated into written school policies or standards of conduct. Policies should incorporate the following elements:

- school values or philosophy,
- rules and consequences that parallel the school's stated values,
- procedures to prevent bullying from happening,
- procedures for handling bullying incidents, and
- legal requirements.

Handling bullying incidents and consequences for perpetrators is one of the muddier topics in school policy development. Often the policy generation process requires that the whole discourse around punishment be revisited. Most teachers complain that consequences are not tough enough, that they are not applied systematically, and that in spite of the punishment students do not abide by the rules. In actuality, administrators, staff, and teachers frequently view punishment along a continuum, with extreme punishment at one end and permissiveness at the other (i.e., too harsh or too loose). Traditionally, punishment is something done *to* students, who are passive receptors of what adults impose on them. This approach is likely to alienate children, increase their anger, and worsen their relationship with the community. Ultimately, punishment (e.g., scolding, suspension) may worsen bullying problems, rather than solve them.

An alternative approach to punishment involves holding students accountable for their actions. This process requires clear behavioral limits and, at the same time, strong support for and a caring relationship with the student. By establishing policies for accountability, schools do something *with*, rather than *to*, the bully, helping the child recognize the problem and take action to repair the damage. A school's consequences for bullying should work toward solving the problem via actions that increase awareness, promote new skills, or build relationships, rather than merely punishing the perpetrator. In a school with a positive climate, compliance with the rules results from the students' understanding of the effects of their behavior and the adults' commitment to building relationships. Compliance with the rules is not simply a goal in and of itself; rather, administrators, teachers, and students alike recognize that those who commit an offense such as insulting or hitting a classmate are not only attacking their victim but also intimidating other classmates and contributing to an unpleasant, stifling environment. As a result, teachers, parents, and school administrators committed to reducing bullying and creating an enriching school environment should look beyond simply punishing bullies to address the impact bullying has on victims, bystanders, teachers, and the community at large.

Two theoretical models in the literature illustrate the difference between the effects of punishment and the effects of accepting accountability—the obedience model and the responsibility model. Curwin and Mendler (1999) compared the two models. The obedience model strives to cultivate students who obey their teachers and do not break the rules. In this model, the consequences for bullying a peer are "enacted upon the student." Punishments (e.g., threats, scoldings, writing 100 times "I will not bully others," suspensions) are used to enforce the rules. As a result, students learning in an environment that uses an obedience model often report feeling as if they have no control over the situation (i.e., an external locus of control). In this oppressive scenario, students mainly learn that they should avoid being caught.

Nelsen, Lott, and Glenn (2000) pointed out that teachers should reconsider using "logical consequences" as punishments. If, for example, Martha pushes other children around during outdoor playtime, the logical consequence is that she stays in the classroom during playtime. Although this consequence is logical, it does not solve the problem, does not nurture a positive relationship, and does not restore the damage to the victims.

The responsibility model, however, strives to teach students that they are always accountable for their own choices. In this model, when a student makes a poor judgment call or a bad decision, teachers and school administrators help the student to learn from the outcome of that decision. Thus, consequences are based on solving problems, rather than just punishing behaviors. For example, in a school that functions using the responsibility model, Josh, a student caught bullying his peers, might be required to apologize or make a restitution to the victim, to develop a plan for how to behave the next time a similar situation occurs, or to explore alternative behaviors by role-playing them with the teacher. The emphasis is on Josh's learning from the "punishment" and restoring what he has damaged, rather than on paying for what he has done.

The responsibility model approaches the actions of the perpetrator and the comebacks of the victim with the same even-keeled approach. For instance, Ryan was teasing Lisa at lunch. Ryan chose to tease Lisa, but Lisa's response to Ryan's behavior was her choice: She could tease him back or laugh off his taunting. Ultimately, though, Lisa should be held responsible and accountable for her behavior in response to the offense, just as Ryan should be held accountable for his inappropriate actions. The clear expectations, reciprocal respect, and fair treatment experienced in a school using a responsibility model enhance all other efforts a school makes to establish a positive climate.

Unfortunately, models based on responsibility can take more time to plan and implement than an obedience model and may not have as immediate an effect. In addition, shifting from an obedience model (a reactive approach to discipline, demanding compliance with rules and regulations) to a responsibility-based model (a more proactive approach to disciplining bullies) may feel unnatural for teachers and administrators at the onset of the transition. Regrettably, these issues can erode teacher support for and cause teachers to abandon an accountability approach unless they receive considerable help.

Caring and Respect

In an effort to reduce violence, schools frequently adopt "get tough" attitudes that involve developing strict discipline systems. Detailed lists of punishments, metal detectors, police support, and locker searches usually accompany get tough approaches. With this attitude, schools share more features with a prison than with a positive learning climate. Although students should be accountable for their behaviors, the goal of a school's leadership should be to create an environment in which students behave appropriately because they care about each other and because they are engaged in learning, not because they fear being reprimanded. Environments that foster respect and dignity tend to cultivate students who feel less angry and, therefore, are less likely to bully others (Hein, 2004). It is hard to bully those one cares about.

How can teachers promote respect and caring to create a positive school climate? From interviews with teachers, we learned that one of the characteristics most strongly related to promoting respect, caring, and rapport in the classroom is job satisfaction: Teachers need to enjoy their work. Being a teacher can be very stressful, and teachers who do not enjoy their work often have a hard time developing caring and compassion for their students. In addition to enjoying their jobs, other specific strategies exist for teachers to foster caring and respect and consequently a positive classroom climate, including planning activities that increase their connectedness with students, modeling respect with other teachers and with students, mastering positive approaches to discipline, developing ways to celebrate classroom diversity, and teaching students how to solve conflicts without aggression.

Increasing Connectedness and Sense of Belonging

Students need to feel that teachers and peers care about them, and they need to have a strong sense of belonging to their school. Lack of connectedness to peers and the school is a risk factor for aggression (Resnick et al., 1997) and does not promote a positive school climate. To increase students' senses of belonging and connectedness, schools can promote cooperation rather than competition, encourage students to reach out to others who need help, emphasize a democratic decision-making process, and provide opportunities for meaningful participation. Chapter 5 provides examples of exercises teachers can implement to increase bonding and communication among students.

Modeling Respect

We noted in the School Values section earlier in this chapter that the last two steps Curwin and Mendler (1997) proposed for creating a violence-free environment involve modeling positive values and eliminating programs that are incongruent with the school's values. Box 4.3 delineates examples of how teachers can model caring and respect for each other and for students; students need to feel valued and respected, just like adults. For instance, shouting at students should be permitted only in extreme, life-threatening circumstances. During everyday activities, shouting might elicit an immediate response, such as silencing a rowdy class, but it will not create a positive environment or solve the problem of disruptive classroom behaviors.

BOX 4.3. *EXAMPLES OF TEACHER BEHAVIORS THAT SHOW CARING AND RESPECT*

- *Know your students:* Learn their names, ask them about how they feel and what they think (don't "read their minds"), show interest and learn about their lives outside of class, and remember and demonstrate that you remember special things they have told you.
- *Use positive language:* Speak *with* students (avoid speaking *to* them), avoid the "coach attitude" of shouting directions at students, and avoid sarcastic remarks and patronizing language (e.g., say "Thanks for helping" rather than "You're such a good kid").
- *Maintain appropriate expectations:* Match your expectations to the developmental level of the student. Comments like "You ought to know that" or "I have told you a million times" usually indicate that a teacher is treating a child as an adult, or at least beyond his or her developmental level.
- *Compliment conscientiously:* Compliment students for their achievements and for their efforts toward improvement. For example, when giving a compliment about finished homework, the teacher may say, "Thanks! It takes a lot of self-discipline to complete a long homework assignment

like this one." When complimenting a child about a good grade, the parent may say, "You got an A on the final exam. This grade represents many hours of hard work!"

- *Emphasize the positive:* For example, when Karla arrived late, Mr. Kohn said, "I'm glad to see you today"—without a sarcastic tone—rather than "You are late again!" After all, it was better that she came late than not at all. Later, in private, he talked with Karla about why she was late.

Modeling respect also means that teachers treat students as important individuals, just as they would other adults. In general, adults do not like to be interrupted when they are speaking, but frequently adults interrupt children without apology. Modeling respect implies that teachers should not interrupt a child, and if they accidentally do interrupt a student, they should acknowledge and apologize for their mistake. In essence, teachers need to be willing to take responsibility for their mistakes, apologize to their students when they make a mistake, and demonstrate respect and caring for others' feelings. When teachers are uncertain about whether a certain behavior is disrespectful, they should ask themselves, "Would I treat this student the same way in front of his or her parents?" or "Would I feel proud of my behavior if it were featured in the local newspaper?" Two examples of bullying behaviors by teachers toward students are described in Box 4.4.

BOX 4.4. EXAMPLES OF BULLYING BY TEACHERS TOWARD STUDENTS

Mr. Adkins, a fourth grade teacher at Simpson Elementary School, had been teaching at Simpson for 3 years and was finding this year's group of students to have more behavior problems than the students he had taught in the past. His students frequently engaged in disrespectful behaviors toward both him and their peers (e.g., using loud voices, calling each other names, not following directions, being verbally defiant toward instructions and requests). This year, using his authority as the teacher had been the only technique that Mr. Adkins found effective for managing his students. He often yelled in class, admonished students when they defied his requests, used sarcasm to reprimand students, and belittled students when they acted inappropriately. One day, when the school guidance counselor came into Mr. Adkins' class to teach a lesson on bullying, Mr. Adkins stood in front of the class and verbally identified all the students whom he believed to be bullies.

* * *

Ms. Parsons, who had been teaching at Lehigh Academy for 15 years, was very excited about teaching and was committed to educating children. Although most of Ms. Parsons's colleagues liked her, many of them thought that she sometimes acted inappropriately with her students. Students who defied her rules or directions easily flustered Ms. Parsons. On occasions, her colleagues witnessed Ms. Parsons treating students in a bullying manner (e.g., using threats, embarrassing them, treating a select group of students unfairly). For example, one day Devon was lagging behind in the hallway talking with other students on the way to class from the lunchroom. She asked him to keep up with the rest of the class, and Devon replied, "OKAY, I'm coming!" He leisurely began walking to join the back of the line. Ms. Parsons, frustrated by Devon's lack of compliance with her request, promptly grabbed Devon's hand, dragged him to the front of the line, and scolded him in front of the class, saying, "If you can't walk like the rest of the class, then you can hold my hand like a kindergartener!" Her statement sent the class into laughter and Devon into tears.

Mastering Positive Classroom Management Methods

Mastering positive classroom management strategies can go a long way to reduce conflict, create a positive climate, and increase teaching effectiveness (Lewis, Sugai, & Colvin, 1998; Mendler & Curwin, 1999). Disruptive and disrespectful behavior (e.g., teasing and name-calling) should be handled in ways that engender a positive atmosphere or climate. For example, Myrna was teasing Samuel about his math graphs. The teacher could offer a rebuttal by highlighting the positive qualities of Samuel's work so that he knows he has done a good job on the assignment and the bully knows that the teacher disagrees with her actions. Another strategy might involve commenting on the bully's behavior: "Myrna, your comment was disrespectful. We'll talk after class." Unfortunately, ignoring or tolerating disrespectful behaviors in class conveys an unspoken message that the teacher supports or even encourages bullying and disrespect, a message that thwarts efforts aimed at establishing respect and caring in the classroom. Teacher support groups (described in the Support for Teachers section later in this chapter) can be a venue to help teachers learn new strategies to handle conflicts in the class.

Celebrating Diversity

Today, more than ever before, the American melting pot is expanding: The student population is composed of different races, ethnicities, abilities, national origins, languages, sexual orientations, religions, and geographic origins. Schools that herald and maintain respect, caring, and a positive climate embrace multiculturalism and appreciate its richness of perspectives and ideas. In other words, these schools genuinely celebrate diversity; they do not just tolerate it. They nurture environments of respect, and students learn to work as a team and to accept each others' differences rather than reject them. Celebrating diversity in school helps engender a positive school atmosphere, and learning to understand and appreciate others' points of view prepares students to live in a pluralistic society outside of school. Schools that are successful at celebrating diversity often integrate cultural characteristics of different groups (e.g., speech patterns, dialects, music, or values) into class projects and lesson plans, thereby promoting understanding and appreciation for other groups.

Solving Conflicts Without Violence

The final aspect of showing respect and caring focuses on learning how to solve conflicts without violence. Chapter 5 highlights skills students can cultivate to solve conflicts and manage anger without aggression. Solving conflicts without violence extends beyond helping students to develop positive problem solving skills: It encompasses helping teachers and administrators resolve their own conflicts peacefully. Conflicts, resentment, and negativity can just as easily exist among teachers or between teachers and administrators, and they can have a very detrimental effect on the school climate. When teachers and administrators have not solved their own conflicts, the success of violence prevention curricula targeted at students is at risk, and the curricula become more difficult to implement.

Positive Expectations

Research examining teachers' expectations of student achievement began almost half a century ago with a well-known study by Rosenthal (summarized in Rosenthal, 1994). In his study, students from 18 different sixth-grade classrooms completed an intelligence test. Teachers, however, were led to believe that the test predicted upcoming growth in intellectual competence. One fifth of the students were randomly labeled as "bloomers." The students' teachers were then informed about these students' expected rise in intellectual ability. At the end of the academic year, students completed the intelligence test for a second time. The randomly labeled "bloomers" had significant gains in intellectual achievement compared with the other students (Rosenthal, 1994). Since this research was completed in the mid-1950s, numerous studies have been conducted in an effort to understand how teachers' expectations influence students' behaviors. Three hypotheses have been forwarded: self-fulfilling prophecy, perceptual bias, and accuracy of judgment (Alder, 2000; Kolb & Jussim, 1994; Reyna, 2000; Trouilloud, Sarrazin, Martinek, & Guillet, 2002).

The *self-fulfilling prophecy hypothesis* suggests that teachers hold expectations about student achievement (that may originally be incorrect). The hypothesis posits that teachers behave according to these expectations and that teachers' behaviors influence students' academic achievement and overall performance in a way that confirms their expectations. Following this self-fulfilling premise, the hypothesis proposes that teachers who do not expect success from certain students

- spend less time with those students,
- hold nonchalant attitudes about their academic abilities,
- use more condescending language when addressing them,
- provide less feedback about their work,
- teach more simplistic materials to them, and
- prompt for answers to questions in class less frequently than those whom they perceive to be bright.

As follows, the hypothesis concludes that these biased teaching behaviors result in fewer learning opportunities and less motivation for those students perceived as less intelligent and, therefore, that these students will be less likely to succeed. In this way, teachers' perceptions are confirmed, and the original prophecy is fulfilled. An example of a self-fulfilling prophecy that led to a good outcome is given in Box 4.5.

BOX 4.5. *THE SELF-FULFILLING ERROR: HOW A LITTLE KNOWLEDGE CAN LEAD ONE DOWN INTERESTING PATHS*

The Ashley County School system was growing rapidly. Because its population was one of the fastest growing in the United States, several new schools had recently been constructed within the county. Although white-collar job opportunities bringing upper middle class families to the county were rising, the county was also witnessing tremendous growth among lower-income families, who held service jobs at country clubs and shopping plazas erected to cater to the upper middle class. With such rapid growth, the school system was understaffed and experienced frequent mixups and confusion in processing the paperwork of new arrivals.

On one particularly busy day, several new students entered the Ashley Middle School. One of the new students, a boy named Mika, was assigned to Mr. Beasley's class. At first sight, Mr. Beasley was not pleased with Mika. Most of the students in his advanced math class were pretty sharp dressers, but Mika wore plain, clean clothes. He seemed somewhat intimidated by the class, rather than showing the spunk that most of the students displayed. Mr. Beasley decided that he would have to have a talk with the counselor who handled the files and placement, because he was certain that an error had been made.

Mr. Prime, the counselor, was surprised when Mr. Beasley came in and questioned him about Mika. Mr. Prime explained that there was no error and that, in fact, Mika was transferring from a fairly elite Northeastern prep school. His family had been transferred to the new computer circuitry business that had recently opened. Mr. Beasley thought to himself that quite often computer engineering people were introverted and didn't pay much attention to attire. Maybe Mika was shy because of his "orientation to numbers."

Still, Mika was not as adept as Mr. Beasley had hoped. Mr. Beasley reasoned that it was understandable that Mika would take some time to catch up with the others after switching from another school with different books and curriculum. To help Mika make the adjustment and to get better acquainted with Mika, Mr. Beasley began tutoring Mika in the study hall and paid close attention to him in class to make sure he was mastering the material. Mika was soon performing on par with the other students and even began to shine in class discussions, confirming Mr. Beasley's anticipation that an engineering family would indeed produce someone who would do well in his class.

About 6 weeks after their meeting about Mika, Mr. Prime, the counselor, realized he had made an error. The student to whom he had been referring when meeting with Mr. Beasley was not Mika, but Michael. Michael, who should have been placed in Mr. Beasley's class but instead was sent to Ms. Baxter's class, was performing well under Ms. Baxter's tutelage. In studying the transfer records, Mr. Prime realized that Mika's files indicated that he had been an acceptable student but certainly not advanced in performance, particularly in math. Mr. Prime went to Mr. Beasley and asked about Mika's performance. Mr. Beasley said, "I was concerned at first because he didn't seem to be up to par, but I knew that he had good wiring—good genes—and that's what counts. You either have them or you don't, and the good news is he does. Mika is pulling his own and making a run for it with the others; he's becoming the leader of the pack, you might say . . . I was sure when you told me about his family that he would succeed."

Mr. Prime thanked Mr. Beasley and returned to his office. Mr. Prime was aware of the power of expectations and saw no reason to correct the very good story that Mr. Beasley had created in developing his own self-fulfilled prophecy.

Closely related to the self-fulfilling prophecy hypothesis, the *perceptual bias hypothesis* states that the confirmation of teachers' expectations comes not from students' behaviors, but from their own biased recall and evaluation of students' behaviors. For example, if Ms. Warner has low expectations of Antonio, she is more likely to be predisposed to grade Antonio's test low or prescribe a harsher punishment for an aggressive act in the classroom. This hypothesis speculates that perceptual biases are strongly influenced by teachers' stereotypes, which generally favor White, gifted, and higher economic status students. These stereotypes may also hold true, however, when teachers base their educational expectations on a student's standardized test scores. Standardized tests tend to cater to White and higher economic status knowledge bases, putting many minority and low-income students at an inherent disadvantage and confirming intellectual stereotypes (Reyna, 2000). Unfortunately, racial prejudices may extend beyond test scores, as African American children are less likely to receive in-class attention than White students, even if they are gifted individuals (Alder, 2000).

These two hypotheses—self-fulfilling prophecy and perceptual bias—identify teachers as the creators of a school's or classroom's social reality. Conversely, the third hypothesis—*teacher accuracy*—posits that teachers are actually very good judges of students' behaviors and that a skilled teacher can often predict the academic and behavioral outcomes of a student without influencing that outcome. Thus, the student's behavior is not "caused" by the teacher, but the teacher's response, when asked for his or her perceptions about a student's abilities, simply reflects an external reality. Thus, when Ms. Gonzalez states that Kipruto will probably excel in math, her prediction will not influence Kipruto's behavior. Her prediction is just a reflection of reality based on her experience.

None of these explanations is completely correct or completely incorrect. In fact, most relationships are influenced by the cognitions of the participants, which include a mix of expectations, stereotypes, and actual behaviors. Changing teachers' expectations about students' abilities may not transform an unmotivated student into the class scholar and may not confer the intellectual abilities he or she needs to succeed, but teachers' positive expectations can help create a positive classroom climate that facilitates learning and achievement. A case study of extraordinary teachers supports the idea of using positive expectations to promote a warm and welcoming class atmosphere. Hein (2004) showed that teachers hailed as extraordinary teachers consistently held high expectations of academic achievement and positive behaviors of all their students. Consequently, students who were disruptive in other classes consistently worked on task and did not display conduct problems in these teachers' classrooms.

The role of positive expectations in creating a positive school climate applies to more than just teachers and their students. It also applies to the expectations that administrators hold of teachers and staff. As in the teacher–

student relationship, the administrator–teacher relationship should encourage high expectations for academic excellence and classroom management and facilitate the communication of these expectations. In both the teacher–student relationship and the administrator–teacher relationship, it is important to distinguish between two disparate meanings of *expectations*; in many cases these meanings may be contradictory. Expectations, in the normative sense of the word, may mean that the school principal expects that Ms. Fry will finish teaching basic chemistry by the end of the semester. Expectations, in the probabilistic sense of the word, may mean that the school principal also expects that Ms. Fry will not accomplish this task. The way in which the principal communicates the latter expectation will certainly influence Ms. Fry's behavior. If he communicates with Ms. Fry in a negative manner, he may decrease the likelihood that Ms. Fry will actually finish teaching her course material. Therefore, framing probabilistic expectations in a positive way can contribute to efforts aimed at building encouraging and heartening school climates. Extensive research examining the influence of expectations on productivity in the workplace consistently highlights the importance of positive expectations to a positive workplace climate (Eden, 1990).

Support for Teachers

Teachers play a key role in creating a positive school climate, but the numerous challenges they face on a daily basis sometimes increase their stress and frustration. These challenges might include dealing with new legal requirements, handling a particularly rowdy cohort of students, tackling a new academic subject, managing an unusual number of special needs students in a class, or adjusting to a new administration's system of handling discipline problems. Workshops or in-service training sessions have served as traditional venues for supporting teachers and helping them to augment their skill sets to better address these challenges. Successful workshops leave teachers feeling energized and motivated to implement new skills. Unfortunately, teachers faced with a barrage of everyday problems frequently revert to old habits, and new skills are easily forgotten.

Although workshops may be important tools to help teachers and administrators augment their knowledge bases on specific topics, workshops may not be the best method for encouraging and maintaining long-term behavior change. In reality, continuous training, coaching, and support are likely to be more important for sustaining behavior change than a one-time event. Thus, support group meetings of teachers (who teach the same grade level or similar subject matters) can greatly enhance teachers' dedication to applying new skills in the classroom (Ialongo et al., 1999; Olweus, 1993b; Rohrbach, Graham, & Hansen, 1993; Shapiro, Dupaul, Bradley, & Bailey, 1996). A common health example reflects this same problem. Most people in the United States know how to lose weight (eat healthy food, eat less, and exercise more), but many do not abide by these simple rules, as evidenced by the high prevalence of obesity among children and adults. According to the 1999–2000 National Health and Nutrition Examination Survey, 15% of children and adolescents and 64% of adults in the United States were overweight or obese (Centers for Disease Control and Prevention, 2003). Because changing health habits is difficult, people join support groups to lose weight or get a "buddy" to maintain an exercise program. Similarly, support groups help teachers practice, maintain, and enhance new skills. Teachers who attend support groups learn from and help their colleagues in multiple ways. They teach each other how to implement new skills learned at a training workshop, coach each other on how to formulate new and creative solutions to various problems, advise each other on how to handle daily stress, and discuss schoolwide issues that affect all teachers (Orpinas et al., 2004). The support group approach is also advantageous because participants view their colleagues' classroom experiences as valuable source of practical knowledge (Smylie, 1989).

When establishing teacher support groups, we found that the most efficient and effective support groups were held every 2 to 3 weeks, started early in the school year, and ended by mid-March. Our sessions lasted 1 hour, and the sessions were divided into two parts. The first half allotted time to teachers for presenting successful bullying prevention strategies and tactics, spotlighting coworker role models and enabling brainstorming for bullying solutions. The second half of the group session was used to reinforce key elements of the bullying prevention program. In this portion of the session, participants worked to define the next social competence skill they wanted to introduce to their students (we outline a few choice social competence skills in chap. 5), role-play teaching difficult lessons, or discuss suggestions and advice gleaned from books on violence prevention or classroom management. In general, the goal of the second half of the session is to increase group members' knowledge and efficacy in preventing bullying.

Physical Environment

Although relegated to the last of the eight major components of school climate, the characteristics of a school's physical environment are not minor issues. To gain a wider perspective on the issues related to a school's physical environment, school leaders can ask themselves, "Is this a place where I like to spend many hours of my day?" "Is this an environment I would like to send my child to?" "Is this an environment that promotes intellectual curiosity and sparks a desire for learning?" Thus, when striving to create a positive school climate, school administrators should examine the following aspects of the physical environment:

- *cleanliness:* Are classrooms, hallways, bathrooms, teachers' lounges, and others areas of the school clean and properly supplied (e.g., toilet paper in the bathroom, pencils in the classroom)?

- *recognition of school community members*: Are students' scientific and artistic projects, as well as their sports accomplishments, displayed? Are students from different cultures and nationalities recognized? Are teachers and staff lauded?
- *aesthetic appearance:* Are walls painted with attractive colors? Are works of art displayed in hallways? Is graffiti promptly removed?
- *organization*: Are classrooms and common areas organized so that needed supplies are easily found? Is clutter kept to a minimum and eliminated when possible? Are other spaces beyond the classroom organized to facilitate learning (e.g., library, outdoor spaces)?
- *safety*: Is the school building safe? Does the school have a mechanism for students to report any problems? Are teachers prepared to handle an emergency (e.g., fire, weapons)? Is the playground free of rocks and other elements that could be used to hurt someone?

Safe schools are well prepared for any eventual crisis. Crises can be related to violence (e.g., weapons on campus, a suspicious stranger), a natural disaster (e.g., tornado, earthquake), or other problems that require immediate action (e.g., medical emergency, fire). To handle a crisis safely and expediently, schools need a well-developed crisis plan. The crisis plan should require training of all teachers and staff, adhere to relevant district or state procedures, involve key community agencies (e.g., fire department, police), and establish a core team that meets and revises procedures regularly. Further, the plan should also address how the response will continue after the tragedy (Dwyer, Osher, & Warger, 1998). The strategies proposed in this book will promote a safer school, thus reducing the likelihood of acts of violence. However, they do not replace having a well-thought-out crisis plan.

In daily school activities, administrators can achieve the goal of providing a safe environment without sacrificing the positive school climate. For instance, to keep track of who enters and who leaves the school, all schools ask visitors to sign in at the main office. To remind guests, a sign at the entrance of the school usually states, "For the children's security, all visitors must sign in at the office." This sign does not convey a welcoming message. The same goal of reminding visitors to sign in can be achieved with a sign saying, "Welcome to Middletown Elementary School. Parents and guests, please sign in at the office. Thanks for visiting our school." For security purposes, many schools also have police officers. These officers could be trained in problem-solving strategies. Although they may need to exert force in extreme cases, in day-to-day activities maintaining a positive relationship with students and being a model of conflict resolution will be most useful.

School budgets often constrain or limit the scale of physical improvements that can be made to the school building. However, with support from the community, teachers, and students, school administrators can accomplish some of their desired changes even with a low budget. The key is to create a physical environment that will enhance the positive climate of the school and make it a place where teachers and students enjoy working and studying.

5

SCHOOL SOCIAL COMPETENCE DEVELOPMENT AND BULLYING PREVENTION MODEL: THE STUDENT

I really like animals, I just don't like them on my plate.
—Third grader in response to being teased about being vegetarian

The School Social Competence Development and Bullying Prevention Model has two large components: the school climate and the students. Chapter 4 examined the school component (see Figure 4.1) and emphasized that implementing programs for students and teachers is unlikely to be successful without concurrently creating a positive school environment. This chapter focuses on the student component of the model and discusses students' social competence skills. The chapter first describes the six elements that together form the student component of the model: awareness, emotions, cognitions, character, social skills, and mental health and learning abilities.

INCREASING STUDENTS' SOCIAL COMPETENCE

The development of a positive school environment, as described in chapter 4, is critical for reducing bullying and promoting academic excellence. Equally important in accomplishing these objectives, however, is promoting children's social competence. Children who are socially competent are more likely to have more friends, develop positive relationships with others, and be academically successful (Welsh, Parke, Widaman, & O'Neil, 2001). As described in chapter 2, social competence frequently involves possession of the skills used to make positive decisions, solve conflicts without violence, plan for the future, resist negative peer pressure, make friends, and enjoy being around people from different cultures. In the behavioral and social sciences, however, whether an individual displays social competence is subject to interpretation. That is, different researchers present slightly different definitions of the social competence concept. To clarify our viewpoint, and to provide a basis for the discussion to come, we define *social competence* as a person's age-appropriate knowledge and skills for functioning peacefully and creatively in his or her community or social environment.

In our definition, social competence depends on the child's own skills, as well as on the characteristics of the environment. Thus, some children may be socially competent in one environment but not in another (e.g., competent with neighborhood playmates but not with peers at school). Social competence skills appropriate for one environment but inappropriate for another are exemplified in the tough, aggressive skills children cultivate to survive in their inner-city neighborhoods but that prevent them from developing the collaborative skills necessary to function well in a school environment (Masten & Coatsworth, 1998). Other children live in families and communities that do not foster social competence as it is usually defined at school or in mainstream society, and these children are not exposed to the social skills they need to excel in school. For example, Julie's parents often treated each other—and Julie—disrespectfully and frequently solved conflicts with hostility and anger. To achieve her goals at home, Julie used belligerence or domination. Unfortunately, belligerence and domination were not skills that enabled Julie to succeed at school. To survive and excel at school, Julie needed to learn about the school's norms and what was expected of her. The school, however, needed to encourage Julie's learning by providing opportunities for her, and other children like her, to learn and practice the social skills they need to succeed at school. The student component of the School Social Competence Development and Bullying Prevention Model describes the social skills that children need to succeed in school and develop relationships with peers without bullying.

COMPONENTS OF STUDENTS' SOCIAL COMPETENCE

The model is organized in six areas (see Figure 5.1):

- awareness,
- emotions,

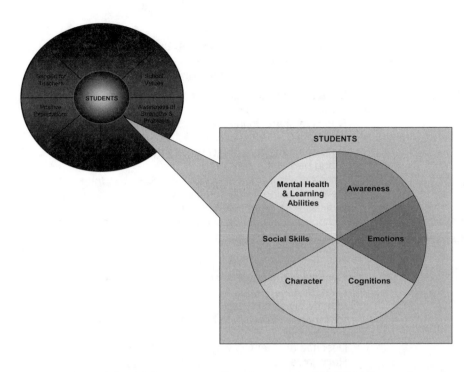

Figure 5.1. School Social Competence Development and Bullying Prevention Model: The Student Component.

- cognitions,
- character,
- social skills, and
- mental health and learning abilities.

All of the areas are equally important for bullying prevention, but teachers may choose to emphasize some specific areas, depending on the characteristics of the children with whom they are working and the types of bullying problems they are trying to influence. Exhibit 5.1 provides examples of students' learning objectives by area. These six student areas are closely related; for example, it would be difficult to teach conflict resolutions steps (from the cognitive area) to students who do not have the skills to calm down (from the emotional area).

Awareness

The first student-focused component of any bullying prevention program involves enhancing students' abilities to recognize different types of bullying patterns (i.e., aggressive, passive, and relational) and to increase students' understanding of bullying as an unacceptable behavior. It is surpris-

EXHIBIT 5.1
Student Learning Objectives, by Area

Area	Students will be able to
Awareness	Describe characteristics of physical, passive, and relational bullies
	Describe characteristics of passive, provocative, and relational victims
	Describe behaviors of bystanders that are part of the problem and part of the solution
	Recognize bullying behaviors when they see them
	Develop a schoolwide common vocabulary regarding bullying
	Discuss as a group what bullying is
Emotional development	Recognize different emotions in themselves and others
	Understand verbal and nonverbal communication of emotions
	Anger–calmness:
	Describe anger as a normal response to some situations
	Recognize the physical and emotional signs of tension and anger
	Identify triggers of anger
	Identify positive ways to handle anger (e.g., calming down, reframing)
	Describe at least two ways to calm down
	Recognize that calming down is important
	Recognize that aggressive physical and verbal responses are not acceptable in school
	Explain the consequences of aggressive behaviors
	Pessimism–optimism:
	Experience social and academic success
	Recognize automatic negative thoughts and evaluate their accuracy
	Develop context-specific attributions
	Connectedness–disconnectedness:
	Recognize common interests with peers
	Give and receive compliments
	Identify positive character traits (e.g., kindness, responsibility, honesty, respect) in others
Cognitive development	Recognize how their beliefs lead to their emotions and actions
	Modify beliefs that lead to unwanted consequences
	Identify and apply the steps for conflict resolution
	Brainstorm solutions to problems
	Identify positive and negative consequences of their choices
	Evaluate how their plan of action is working
	Explain the consequences of asking and not asking for help
	Identify adults they could ask for help
	Recognize dangerous situations and avoid them or ask for help
	Identify situations they should avoid or ignore
	Identify situations when they should solve the conflict
Character development	Tell the truth
	Be responsible for their own actions
	Work hard
	Show respect to others
	Collaborate with others

ing how many students do not know that teasing and excluding others are considered forms of bullying and are unacceptable behaviors. Moreover, students often are not aware of how these unacceptable behaviors adversely affect other children and the school climate.

Of equal concern, however, is that many adults, even those who are well educated, believe that bullying is a normal part of growing up. In our discussions of this topic with college students studying education and health, many have reported that bullying is part of school life and not a significant health problem, even though they would not accept this behavior as part of college life. This belief in bullying as normative promotes a tolerance of bullying. Bullying is never an acceptable behavior, just as learning to live with muggers and thugs in adult life is not acceptable, even for those living in unsafe neighborhoods.

Recognition of bullying as an inappropriate behavior varies greatly by the type of bullying being discussed. Most children and adults acknowledge that physical aggression is unacceptable in schools. Nevertheless, some children believe that they have to respond to verbal taunts with aggression or that they have to hit the perpetrator to save face. Often, teachers report that it is parents who encourage their children to "stick up for themselves."

Perceptions about teasing differ from perceptions about physical aggression. Although most children acknowledge that physical aggression is considered unacceptable bullying behavior, many do not identify teasing as improper behavior. In our discussions with elementary school students, some children described teasing others as fun. Obviously, these children did not perceive teasing their peers as a problem. More frequently, however, children simply were not aware that starting or passing along a malicious rumor, repeating derogatory statements to others, or excluding someone from a game are all considered bullying behaviors.

In our experience, providing children with a common vocabulary to describe different facets of bullying (i.e., types of bullies, victims, and bystanders) can be a liberating experience. Frequently, victims and bystanders express relief on learning that what happened to them has a name and that they can talk about it. This experience of relief is similar to what some women who have been harassed in the workplace report when their experience has been defined as sexual harassment. A similar relief might be felt by someone who has been suffering from rare physical symptoms and finally encounters a physician who discovers the right diagnosis. In these cases, labeling the problem (e.g., bullying, sexual harassment, or diagnosis) eases the victim's guilt: "I'm not the problem . . . I'm not crazy. This is a real problem." Labeling the experience does not solve the problem, but it can energize victims and bystanders to take action against bullying problems.

Improving student, faculty, and administrative awareness of bullying is the first step in the problem resolution process. In fact, expanding individuals' understanding of the nature and the extent of the problem, as described in chapters 1 and 4, is a prerequisite for change and will help to facilitate progress. Activities designed to increase awareness of bullying can be integrated into many classes (e.g., English literature, social studies, mathematics). Any academic situation in which students need to take turns, ask or answer questions out loud, go on a field trip, work collaboratively, give a presentation, or comment on other students' work offers opportunities for

---

BOX 5.1. EXAMPLES OF ACTIVITIES TO INCREASE AWARENESS OF BULLYING

- Define the different types of bullying (as described in chap. 1) in a handout or overhead, and ask students to work in groups to provide examples of behaviors that fit each category.
- Ask younger children to draw a bully. They frequently draw mean-looking boys who hit others and nice-looking girls who exclude and tease others. Many recognize only extreme forms of violence, such as physical fights or threatening with a weapon. Discuss the portraits and provide definitions for different types of bullies, victims, and bystanders. Help children expand their concepts of bullying by asking them to discuss why some children would want to bully others. Probing the "whys" of bullying will help children understand bullies' motivations and help those who act aggressively develop an awareness of why they behave as they do.
- During English or social studies classes—or during any writing time—ask students to write about how, where, and when bullying occurs. Ask them to elaborate on how they feel about being bullied or bullying others and what they wanted to happen when they were faced with a bullying situation. Use their comments to discuss the problem.
- During math class, involve students in developing, implementing, and analyzing a student survey on bullying victimization and aggression. Depending on the students' grade level, the class may be able to calculate frequencies or percentages of responses and even prepare graphs of the results.
- In preparation for any academic group activity, advise students about expected behaviors. For example, when students present their work to the class, provide clear norms about how to provide positive feedback and what type of comments would be unwelcome.

bullying, as well as for showing caring or respect. Therefore, bullying awareness could—and should—be integrated into class preparation for any of these learning activities (Box 5.1 lists examples of activities). In addition, several bullying prevention programs provide sample lesson plans aimed at increasing the awareness of bullying. Three programs that supply sample lesson plans are Bully Busters (Horne, Bartolomucci, & Newman-Carlson, 2003; Newman, Horne, & Bartolomucci, 2000), Bully-Proofing Your School (Garrity, Jens, Porter, Sager, & Short-Camilli, 2004), and Bullyproof (Stein, Gaberman, & Sjostrom, 1996).

Emotions

Children come to school with a variety of emotions that may facilitate or hinder their academic progress and their relationships with others. In his best-selling book *Emotional Intelligence*, Goleman (1995) highlighted the importance of emotions in one's interpersonal relationships and, ultimately, in obtaining one's goals in life. Emotional intelligence is a type of social intelligence—as opposed to cognitive intelligence, or IQ—that comprises the following social and personal skills related to handling emotions and relating to others:

- recognizing and understanding one's own feelings;
- identifying other people's emotions and needs;
- controlling impulses;
- delaying gratification;
- channeling emotions toward a goal;
- managing excitement, stress, anger, and other emotions;
- developing an optimistic view of life;
- knowing when and how to express emotions;
- motivating oneself;
- maintaining zeal and persistence in achieving a goal; and
- handling relationships with others smoothly (strongly related to understanding one's own and others' emotions).

An important component of students' emotional intelligence is learning to recognize and manage their own emotions and to identify other people's emotions. The discussion that follows highlights three dichotomies of emotions: anger–calmness, pessimism–optimism, and disconnectedness–connectedness (Exhibit 5.2 provides examples). Obviously, this discussion is not comprehensive, but these three emotional continua involve common emotions that, on the basis of our work with students, we have found to be most likely to influence bullying and its prevention.

Anger and Calmness

Some children are very angry by the time they arrive at school, frequently with good reason (e.g., negligent parents, violent home life, disrup-

EXHIBIT 5.2
Common Emotions That Influence Relationships
and Academic Achievement

Emotions that destroy relationships and reduce academic achievement	Emotions that foster positive relationships and academic achievement
Anger (irritation, fury, rage, resentment, annoyance, tension)	Calmness (peace, composure, serenity)
Pessimism (negative expectations, negativism, glumness, distrust)	Optimism (positive expectations, hope, cheerfulness)
Disconnectedness from peers, teachers, and school (sense of detachment, disengagement)	Connectedness to peers, teachers, and school (sense of belonging and caring)

tive neighborhood). But even if students have valid reasons for their emotions, anger can negatively affect how they perform academically and relate to their peers. It is very difficult to concentrate on work when one is really angry. It is also very difficult to maintain a positive conversation with someone with whom one is really angry. The paragraphs that follow describe a number of actions that teachers and counselors can take to increase children's awareness of their anger and to help them manage it.

Students can learn that anger is normal. To begin with, children need to understand that anger is common. Most, if not all, people feel angry at some time. Teachers and administrators need to explain that anger is a normal response to situations in which people feel that they have been treated unfairly, aggressively, or disrespectfully (e.g., infringement on one's personal space).

Students can learn to recognize anger. Recognizing anger is the first step in managing it. Physical manifestations of anger include an increase in heartbeat, a red face, body tension, and faster breathing. A number of activities have been designed to help children become more aware of their physical reactions. The Bully Busters program, for example, has an activity called "Feel the Heat" (Newman et al., 2000, pp. 129–130). In this activity, children receive a sheet of paper with a simple outline of a human figure. They then identify the parts of their bodies that react when they are angry. For example, some students experience anger in their stomachs, others feel it in their heads, and others feel it as tension in their arms. A school counselor we knew used this exercise with a student who had difficulty controlling his anger. On the drawing, the student indicated that he experienced anger in his head; his head would fill with angry thoughts. Because the counselor was able to pinpoint the student's physical reaction to anger, she introduced ways in which he could exercise emotional and behavioral control over his anger: thinking calming thoughts, engaging in problem-solving thinking, and then practicing slow, deep breathing.

Older elementary-age students may be able to tell a teacher or a counselor that they feel angry, but younger students often have difficulty vocalizing their feelings. Adults concerned with helping young children develop their abilities to distinguish different emotions (e.g., anger vs. fear) frequently use an exercise in which children examine, label, and discuss a chart with facial icons expressing a variety of emotions. These charts are available from a number of vendors and can also be found in anger management publications designed for children. Learning to recognize different emotions helps students develop their emotional management skills. Although anger is one of the most easily recognized emotions, it also can sometimes mask other underlying emotions such as fear, grief, jealousy, or embarrassment. Thus, learning to adequately identify different feelings will increase students' awareness of emotions that promote collaboration versus feelings that lead them to engage in bullying or aggression.

Students can increase their awareness of situations that trigger their anger. Most teachers realize that changing how students think about what initiated their feelings of anger is frequently enough to change their emotion. For example, Tom, an overweight sixth grader, was habitually teased about his weight, and his response was to become angry with his tormentor (his thought: "She is mean and is hurting me"). A school counselor talked with Tom about his reaction to being teased and explained that getting angry only eroded his power in the exchange (his new thought: "She is trying to get me angry, and she is not going to win"). The counselor practiced new response strategies with Tom, and the next time a girl teased him, he calmly said, "I know I'm fat. Let's talk about something else." As predicted, the teasing eventually stopped.

Many activities have been developed to help students recognize their own anger triggers and to manage their anger more appropriately. Newman and her colleagues (2000, pp. 124–128) provided two sample activities that teachers might consider: "Anger Is Normal" and "Cage Your Lion." The objectives of these activities are to help students identify situations that lead them to become angry, recognize how they normally respond to those situations, and discern steps they can take to handle the situation without physically acting out. These activities help students understand that anger is a normal and acceptable emotion but that an aggressive response to anger is unacceptable. Finally, anger trigger recognition activities can teach children that they can manage their angry feelings and control their behavioral displays of anger.

Students can learn to reframe their thoughts. Learning how to reframe one's thoughts can lead to a change of emotions, as detailed later in this chapter in the section on the A-to-E Process of Thought and Action. For instance, Warren frequently spread nasty rumors about his classmates. Consequently, many of his peers thought that he was very mean. However, his peers could learn to control their anger toward Warren and rechannel their emotional responses to his inappropriate behaviors by recognizing the circumstances in Warren's life that drove him to resort to loathsome behavior to gain attention. Reframing her thoughts would not stop Warren from spreading nasty rumors, but a peer hurt by Warren's tactless behavior would be less angry and better able to think about what to do next if she reframed Warren's motivation from "being mean" (and consequent emotion of anger) to "needing attention because he has a terrible life" (and consequent emotion of compassion).

Transforming anger into compassion can be very powerful. Teachers should be careful not to comment about the family life of the child acting as a bully, but they may ask the victims to reflect on why the bully displays mean behaviors; sometimes children know more about their classmates than teachers do. Likewise, activities in which students role-play both sides in a bully–victim interaction help students to learn how others may feel in bullying situations. The role-play activity can be particularly compelling if the teacher helps children understand the probable thoughts and feelings of both the bully (e.g., feeling inadequate, unpopular, or unloved) and the victim (e.g., feeling nervous, hurt, or scared).

Students can learn relaxation techniques. Relaxation techniques, such as counting to 10 before responding, tensing and relaxing each muscle, taking an imaginary trip to a favorite beach, or taking deep and slow breaths can help students manage their anger and handle stressful situations. Relaxation techniques are useful for anger management, bullying reduction, and other stressful situations students face on a daily basis (e.g., test taking). The importance of mastering relaxation techniques, however, extends beyond the classroom and childhood; they may serve to help adults obtain career and personal goals as well (e.g., through successful performance in a job interview).

Anger and calmness can be envisioned as opposite ends of one continuum. Students need to be reassured that calmness is not the equivalent of an emotional void. Rather, it can be a very positive and adaptive response to maddening situations and a solid replacement for their anger. Learning how to replace anger with calmness when faced with problems and conflicts will help students develop one of the positive social skills needed to be effective in life.

The Turtle Technique (Fleischman, Horne, & Arthur, 1983; Schneider & Robin, 1976), described in Box 5.2, has been used to teach students— particularly bullies—how to calm down when facing a conflict. It promotes alternative problem-solving strategies among elementary school children. The Turtle Technique is a very powerful activity for teaching all students relaxation techniques. Although originally designed for children with behavior problems, many teachers have expanded the Turtle Technique to include the whole classroom, sometimes using the turtle, or former bully, as a coleader in developing the skills.

BOX 5.2. *THE TURTLE TECHNIQUE*

The goal of the Turtle Technique is to help students control anger and practice positive problem-solving strategies. Using this technique, teachers establish "turtle clubs" and invite students who bully or who have problems with anger management to stay with them during a break time (e.g., eat lunch together in the room) as a member of the turtle club. Some teachers practice this technique with the whole class.

The first step in teaching students how to "turtle" is to tell the tale of Timmy the Turtle. The story goes as follows: "Timmy got into a lot of trouble until he met old, wise Mr. Tortoise, who taught him how to pull into his shell whenever he had problems. Once in the shell, Timmy learned to relax all his muscles, be calm, think about the problem that got him in trouble, think about the steps he could take to avoid getting in trouble, select the best one, and finally come out of the shell and do it."

Taking their lead from Timmy, teachers then work with students to develop specific turtle skills. Teachers guide the students in practicing relaxation and calming skills, defining problems, selecting alternative steps to take, evaluating consequences, and taking responsibility for their actions and the outcomes of their decisions.

Students are accountable for how they express their anger. Although teachers cannot make students change their emotions, they can teach students that they are accountable for how they express their emotions. Hitting and shoving classmates, calling peers derogatory names, and responding to teachers with sarcastic retorts are not acceptable expressions of anger. Students need to realize that their response to anger is a choice and that they have to assume the consequences for their behavior. When attempting to help children learn new ways of managing anger, teachers need to provide clear, consistent, and fair consequences for inappropriate behaviors, consequences that will help to solve the problem and not just punish the act or the perpetrator. When teaching accountability, teachers should stress that feeling angry is natural, but that the way people respond to their feelings is a choice—responses to anger are not driven by external events, but by one's perceptions of those events. People have the freedom to choose their best response, and then they must assume the consequences for their chosen behaviors. The concept of choice is very important and can never be overemphasized with students. In the Harry Potter series, Dumbledore, the wise headmaster of Hogwarts, explains to Harry, "It is our choices, Harry, that show what we truly are, far more than our abilities" (Rowlings, 1999, p. 333).

Students can learn appropriate behaviors to use when they are angry. Frequently, children lack appropriate repertoires of alternative, nonaggressive behaviors to use when they are angry. An impulsive victim's first reaction to a situation that has maddened him or her may be to retaliate by teasing or hitting the bully. Other victims may control their anger internally or hide their emotions altogether. Both responses can be detrimental to their health. An alternative reaction that can be taught is to be assertive rather than angry (e.g., to say, "It bothers me when you pull my hair; please don't do it again"). Although this type of response may not prevent every bully's strike, some bullies will cease their objectionable behaviors. Asking for help from an adult is another positive strategy that students can use instead of acting on their anger. Asking for adult help is most advantageous when students learn to differentiate between situations they can handle alone and those in which they need assistance. The "Strength-O-Meter," an activity developed by Newman, Horne, and Bartolomucci (2000, pp. 149–150), helps bullying victims ascertain their skill levels for managing different problems and identify when it might be necessary or appropriate to seek help from peers or adults.

Pessimism and Optimism

A second group of emotions, as important as anger and calmness, is pessimism and optimism. Optimism is an important component of emotional intelligence, as Goleman (1995) observed:

> Optimism, like hope, means having a strong expectation that, in general, things will turn out all right in life, despite setbacks and frustrations. From the standpoint of emotional intelligence, optimism is an attitude that buffers people against falling into apathy, hopelessness, or depression in the face of tough going. (p. 88)

According to Goleman, optimism predicts positive relationships and academic success.

Some children view events pessimistically for a variety of reasons; some may be seriously depressed, and others may be experiencing a sad reaction to a temporary event. By viewing the cup as half empty, pessimistic children concentrate on negative events from the past and predict an unpromising future, creating a bleak mood in the present (Seligman, Reivich, Jaycox, & Gillham, 1995). Children experiencing severe depression should receive counseling from a school counselor, psychologist, or other mental health specialist. Other children (with and without histories of depression), however, may tend habitually to view events from negative perspectives, impeding development of their social competencies.

Teachers play an important role in helping safeguard children against pessimistic thoughts and negative expectations. Teachers can take specific actions to provide students with opportunities for success and to help students change their attributions about success and failure (e.g., from "I've never been any good at math; no wonder I did poorly on the math test" to "I didn't study for this test; I could have done much better if I had studied and asked the teacher about what I didn't understand"). Encouraging appropriate attributions and providing opportunities for success throughout the school year may effectively help pessimistic students cultivate a more positive worldview. In our research with schools, we use the expression "Setting Up for Success" to highlight that teachers and administrators should seek opportunities to develop programs and learning experiences that lead to success rather than to failure.

It is very important that educators provide opportunities for success because the best way to improve one's self-confidence and self-esteem is to perform well, which usually leads to positive feelings about oneself and reduced pessimism (Seligman et al., 1995). Strategies teachers may use to increase opportunities for success in their classrooms include teaching study skills, dividing complex tasks into manageable steps, and emphasizing that success is the result of effort. Of course, the more skilled teachers are at these three strategies, the more successful their students will be at overcoming pessimism. Most important, students must perceive that the successes they experience are real successes. Children usually recognize when teachers pat students' backs simply to improve their sense of self-esteem (i.e., when students' work is subpar but lauded despite its shortcomings). However, when children do achieve success from legitimate efforts, a teacher's praise and recognition that the success resulted from the student's efforts, even if the task was small, will increase the child's propensity to be optimistic and to expect success in the next task.

Teachers should use praise and encouragement abundantly, particularly encouragement, as described in Box 5.3. Faber and Mazlish (1995), in their book How to Talk So Kids Can Learn, detailed strategies to evaluate children without demeaning them. To provide positive feedback, instead of simply praising (e.g., "This is a great painting"), the teacher—or any adult—should describe what he or she sees (e.g., "The shades of blue that you chose for the sky, the puffy clouds, and the tree slightly bent with the wind makes your watercolor look very realistic"). The description will lead the child to praise herself (e.g., "Wow, I can really paint well"). An alternative to portraying what is observed is to describe the feelings (e.g., "Your painting made me want to relax under that shady tree and enjoy the cool breeze"). When providing criticism, it is best to describe the positive and then to point out what needs to be done (e.g., "All this picture needs now is to add more variety of colors to the grass—bright in the front and dull in the back—to enhance the sense of perspective").

BOX 5.3. PRAISE AND ENCOURAGEMENT

Praise is an expression of approval or admiration used to provide positive feedback on students' work or behaviors. Examples include, "Shannon, you did great!" or "Chris, you did such a wonderful job. I'm really proud of you."

Encouragement is an expression used to motivate, support, stimulate, inspire, or promote confidence in others. For example, "Marissa, you put a lot of effort into this project; you must have found it really interesting" or "Sean, you seem very pleased with what you did; are you happy with it?"

Praise and encouragement can have a powerful influence on students and should be used abundantly, but recognizing that they are two different expressions is important as teachers try to foster self-confidence and self-esteem. Praise indicates an external evaluation but may promote student performance designed only to please the teacher or parents. Encouragement, however, has the potential to foster internalization of an activity's results, leading to personal or group ownership of the results.

In addition to providing opportunities for successfully promoting optimism over pessimism, it is also important to help children make appropriate attributions for their successes and failures. That is, teachers should help students understand that their success emerges from practice and effort (an internal, controllable attribution), rather than from luck (an external, uncontrollable attribution) or an "innate" ability (an internal, uncontrollable attribution). For example, Rita received a pogo stick for her birthday. Rita tried several times to jump with the new pogo stick but experienced dreadful results. When Rita lamented, "I'm no good at this," her mother simply responded, "You have not practiced enough. Continue trying, and you will see results." (Trying harder is an internal, controllable attribution—i.e., effort.) So Rita kept trying and practicing on her pogo stick. By the end of the day, she was able to stay on top of the pogo stick for 2 to 3 jumps; by the end of the next day, she could jump up to 10 consecutive jumps; and by the third day, she was an expert! Later, Rita's mother referred to Rita's experience mastering the pogo stick whenever Rita started to get frustrated with math or chemistry. She reminded Rita how practice had transformed her into an expert. Rita could control how much practice and effort she put into a task, whereas the general concept of skill (i.e., "I'm not good at this") was not controllable.

Two additional aspects of attribution that are important for understanding pessimism include stability (stable–unstable, permanent–temporary) and globality (global–specific). According to Seligman and his colleagues (1995), a pessimistic child attributes success either to unstable, temporary causes (e.g., "I passed the test because the teacher was in a good mood" or "I avoided being in trouble for messing with Erika because the teacher let me by this time" or "I didn't get bullied by Glen today because he was distracted talking to other kids") or to stable, permanent causes (e.g., "I failed the test because this is a crummy school" or "I got sent to the office because everybody at this school dislikes people like me"). Conversely, an optimistic child produces context-specific explanations, such as "My mom gets irritated when my room is messy" or "Ms. Jenkins doesn't like me when I'm not prepared for class" (referring only to Ms. Jenkins and not all the teachers and to a specific situation that Ms. Jenkins does not like). Unfortunately, a child cannot do anything to change external situations such as the teacher's mood or the perceived quality of the school. A child who consistently holds pessimistic perspectives may feel trapped in a system in which external, stable attributions lead to lowered self-esteem and the disappointment of failure, which students often perceive as confirmation that their attributions were correct.

To help children develop appropriate context-specific attributions, adults should attempt to model these attributions. That is, instead of Ms. Reynolds saying, "Lynda, you are always late with your homework," she could say, "Lynda, you forgot your homework yesterday and today; to get credit for today's assignment you need to finish it before lunchtime." Also, to help children develop appropriate context-specific attributions, adults can reframe the children's pessimistic attributions in more optimistic terms. When children think that they are a failure in school or in a particular subject (e.g., "I'm terrible at social studies"), teachers can help them identify the specific skills they need to improve (e.g., concentration while reading) and develop strategies to succeed. In the following exchange, the teacher reframes a pessimistic attribution in more optimistic terms with a student who is misbehaving in class:

Robert: You always pick on me. Why do you always blame me?

Teacher: Robert, I do not always pick on you. Let's talk about what you were just doing that caused me to come over here to talk with you, and then let's discuss what we can do to help make sure that it does not happen again.

In the following exchange, the teacher reframes a pessimistic attribution by a student who has been bullied:

Tanya: I'm always the one they pick on. There is no way I can keep coming to school because they always want to mess with me.

Teacher: You're right. Those boys have been giving you trouble, but it doesn't happen all the time. Both Ms. Stanislow from the counseling office and I are committed to helping you learn how to handle them better. We will also work with the boys so that their behavior stops, and we will try to teach them more appropriate ways of interacting with you.

Attributions about success and failure have also been called a person's *inner talk* or *internal dialogue*. This inner voice can influence children's self-confidence and self-esteem, as well as their overt behaviors and academic performance. The inner voice reflects personal belief statements such as "I'm bad at math" or "Kids don't like me, and I can't make any friends." One's beliefs about one's own abilities or characteristics are difficult to change, precisely because this inner voice constantly seeks evidence to support those beliefs, regardless of whether one's conviction is positive or negative (Purkey, 2000). As a result, altering one's pessimistic inner voice (or attributions) to be positive is an important task that requires practice and continued reinforcement. Although it is difficult to work with children who are pessimistic, it is worth the effort to help them move from seeing the world darkly to being more optimistic about their roles and abilities in shaping their experiences.

Disconnectedness and Connectedness

The third group of emotions we highlight in this section is disconnectedness versus connectedness with peers, friends, teachers, the school, and the family. Connectedness is related to another aspect of emotional intelligence: handling relationships and interacting smoothly with others. Relating well to others, however, is closely related to understanding emotions and practicing self-control. Students who feel connected to their school, teachers, and peers hold higher opinions of themselves, develop stronger peer relationships, and perform better academically (Eisenberg, Neumark-Sztainer, & Perry, 2003; Resnick et al., 1997).

In their efforts to successfully establish connectedness, teachers need to recognize that they first have to foster an environment of mutual respect. Establishing mutual respect is important, because students will be less likely to bully their peers if they know them, recognize their common interests, and are treated by them with respect and kindness. Thus, classroom opportunities for sharing information about one another and complimenting each other can help increase the connection among peers and reduce bullying. In addition, Nelsen and her colleagues, in their book *Positive Discipline in the Classroom* (Nelsen, Lott, & Glenn, 2000), posited that giving and receiving compliments are an important component of class meetings because they help create an environment of respect and caring. Box 5.4 provides examples of class activities for practicing how to provide compliments.

Students generally feel very uncomfortable giving compliments when they have not done so in the past, and they tend to focus on external things (e.g., "I like your shoes"). During these activities, teachers should encourage their students to move away from complimenting what their peers are wearing or how their classmates look and to focus on showing appreciation for specific behaviors (e.g., "Thank you for helping me find my coat yesterday"). If a student makes a general statement, such as "You are helpful," the teacher

BOX 5.4. EXAMPLES OF ACTIVITIES TO FACILITATE PEER COMPLIMENTS

- Prepare one 8 × 11 sheet of paper for each student in your class. Write the student's name at the top of the paper. Pass the papers around so that class members can write compliments on each person's piece of paper. Before giving the compliments to the recipient, review them and make sure that all of the comments are positive.
- Tape a piece of paper on the back of each student. As students walk around the class, their classmates write anonymous compliments on their backs.
- Ask one student to sit in the middle of a circle. Every student takes turns saying something positive about that person. Encourage students to look each other in the eye while delivering the compliment.
- Divide students into pairs, give them a list of preset questions, and ask them to interview each other. Depending on the students' grade level, the interview can start with very simple questions, such as "How many brothers and sisters do you have?" and progress to more personal questions that will help students get to know one another better, such as "What is your favorite sport?" or "Describe something good you have done for someone else that most people don't know about." Later, pull the class back into one large group, and ask students to share what they learned about each other and to describe something they have in common.

should ask him or her to give more details about when and how the peer was helpful. In addition, teachers should help students rephrase compliments that are really sneaky putdowns or empty compliments. For example, the sneaky putdown "This is the first time you have helped me!" could be rephrased as "Thanks for helping me with math." Likewise, the empty compliment "You are nice" could be rephrased as a compliment that provides real feedback, such as "It was nice of you to invite me to join your team yesterday." Exercises on compliments and appreciation may also be an opportunity to reinforce values or virtues promoted through the character education program— if the school has one—or to promote the school values ("I appreciated your honesty when you talked yesterday in class").

Appreciation and compliment activities can produce profound positive changes in students' social competence. Many children receive very little positive feedback in their lives, and these activities, besides being the highlight of their week, help foster social skills that they cannot learn elsewhere. An activity we have used in our research with schools that encourages connectivity and positive contributions is to ask students each morning to write down one good thing he or she will do during the day. At the end of the day, classmates are asked to guess each other's good deeds. This activity has many advantages: It forces each student to decide early in the morning to make a positive contribution to the class, it leads all students to "catch the other students being good" by looking for positive examples from one another, and it strengthens connections among classmates by teaching them to value each other's positive behaviors. Another teacher strategy geared to reduce put-downs is the "two put-ups for each put-down" strategy. The teacher asks the bully to give two compliments for every put-down to the student who was the target of the verbal aggression. This approach simultaneously increases students' skill in giving compliments and reduces the frequency of put-downs (Orpinas, Horne, & Staniszewski, 2003).

To summarize, recognizing and handling emotions is important not only in bullying prevention but also in helping students develop competent social skills. Thus, promoting positive emotional development in children should be a schoolwide objective. Emotional intelligence can facilitate achieving personal and academic success, but it does not replace the skills and knowledge required for academic success. However, Goleman (1995) contended that 80% of academic and professional success is defined by emotional intelligence (e.g., persistence, goal-oriented behavior, ability to work cooperatively, good understanding of one's own and other people's emotions, friendships and connection to others). It does not necessarily follow that individuals who possess high levels of emotional intelligence are morally good, honest, or truthful. It is regrettable that some students use their knowledge of others' feelings to bully their peers. Thus, character development, another component of the Social Competence Development and Bullying Prevention Model, is also important.

Cognitions

Cognitive development is a broad area of psychological study that examines how thought processes change as children mature into adults. A child's cognitive development reflects his or her ability to think, reason, and problem solve. Understanding the cognitive development of children enables school faculty and staff to develop appropriate behavioral expectations of students and to design age-appropriate interventions and evaluations. In this section, we analyze two cognitive areas that are particularly relevant to expanding social competence and preventing bullying: (a) the cognitive component of attributions, or the A-to-E Process of Thought and Action, and (b) problem-solving skills.

Children's problem behaviors are frequently related to having the wrong cognitions, as discussed in attribution theories in chapter 3. Albert Ellis (1962), Aaron Beck (1972), Maxie Maultsby (1984), and other cognitive psychologists have shown that when an event occurs, the beliefs or thoughts a person has about the event lead to certain feelings, which strongly influence how they behave in response to that situation. We use the mnemonic A-to-E—**A**ntecedent, **B**eliefs, **C**onsistent affect, **D**oing, and **E**xternal outcome—to describe this process (Box 5.5).

BOX 5.5. THE A-TO-E PROCESS OF THOUGHT AND ACTION

A *Antecedent,* or the situation or event that occurred;

B *Beliefs,* thoughts, or attributions about the event or people associated with the event;

C *Consistent affect,* or how one feels about the situation on the basis of his or her beliefs;

D *Doing,* or the consequent response to the antecedent event, typically influenced by one's beliefs and consistent affect; and

E *External outcome,* or the consequences of one's response.

Antecedent refers to external situations (i.e., what actually happened). For example, Jack called Marcos a "wetback" (offensive slang used to describe Mexicans who illegally enter the United States; the term refers to crossing the Rio Grande as a common entry point).

Beliefs or thoughts about a situation mediate the relationship between the antecedent (the external event) and resulting emotions and behaviors. For many children, learning that their beliefs, rather than external events, are the cause of their emotions is novel. Marcos's response to Jack would depend on his beliefs about Jack in addition to what happened. For example, if Marcos thinks that Jack is an ignorant kid, Marcos may challenge him to define *wetback* or simply walk away. But if Marcos thinks that Jack is being disrespectful, Marcos is more likely to get angry and start a fight.

Beliefs, sometimes grounded in temperamental characteristics (e.g., adaptability to change, inhibition, negative emotionality), are most frequently learned cognitions. When learned early in life, beliefs become automatic responses to certain topics: People do not have to really think about the topic because their response comes so quickly and naturally. For example, many people feel scared when they see a snake, no matter how small or harmless it is. Similarly, other people's behaviors may evoke certain emotions so quickly that they seem to be automatic responses rather than cognitive responses to belief. In Mr. Bell's class, for example, Lin usually looked down when Mr. Bell talked to her. Depending on his beliefs, Mr. Bell might think that she is showing respect, as students from Asian cultures might do, or he might interpret the behavior as being rude and disrespectful. His past experiences with Lin, other Asian students, and this specific behavior will influence his interpretation of her behavior.

Consistent affect refers to the emotions the person feels as a by-product of his or her beliefs about a situation. We refer to these emotions as "consistent" affect because the emotion is consistent with the beliefs the person holds. Inconsistent affect, however, might signify unstable mental health status. Marcos's feelings about Jack's behavior depend on Marcos's beliefs, so if he believes that Jack is being disrespectful, Marcos is likely to feel angry. If Marcos believes that Jack is simply uninformed about Latino culture, however, he may feel pity for Jack. The critical feature of consistent affect exemplified by this anecdote is that the emotions do not transpire from an event; rather, they occur as a result of an individual's interpretation of the event, and interpretations are grounded in thoughts, beliefs, and attitudes about the situation and the other individuals involved in the situation.

Doing refers to an individual's behavioral response to the initial event that ensues from his or her beliefs and consistent affect. If an individual thinks angry thoughts, it is likely that he or she will become angry and respond to an initial event with violence or aggression. If an individual thinks loving thoughts, it is likely that he or she will be compassionate and respond to an initial event with caring actions. Thus, beliefs and consistent affect strongly influence consequent behaviors.

If Marcos feels angry because he believes that Jack is intentionally being cruel, Marcos will likely behave in a manner that is consistent with his angry feelings: fighting with Jack, demanding an apology from Jack, or planning revenge on Jack. However, a socially competent individual can react in a way consistent with his or her angry feelings yet focus the anger into positive action. For example, Marcos could channel his anger into initiating a sincere discussion with the teacher or principal about creative ways to reduce students' racial stereotyping.

External outcome refers to the upshot of a consequent behavior. Once an individual has reacted to an initial event, that person is accountable for his or her behavior. Thus, if Marcos starts a fight with Jack, he has participated in an inappropriate behavior and will bear the external outcome (e.g., school suspension) of his actions.

To summarize the A-to-E model, the initial event does not lead directly to the external outcome. The fact that Jack called Marcos a pejorative name does not automatically mean that Marcos would have to fight with Jack and be suspended for his retaliatory actions. Rather, the emotions spurred by Marcos's beliefs led to his consequent behavior.

In the A-to-E sequence, altering individuals' beliefs can lead to changes in consequent behaviors (i.e., the "D," doing, in the A-to-E process). For example, years ago in a violence prevention workshop, we heard a story from the facilitator regarding his experience in work with prisoners convicted of serious crimes. While the facilitator was conducting a violence prevention workshop in a tough prison, an inmate who had been convicted of homicide shared a story that illustrates how significant beliefs are in the A-to-E process. On the third day of training, the prisoner reported that someone had called his mother a derogatory name the day before while he was out jogging. This prisoner admitted that before the workshop, he would have become so enraged by the other fellow's remark that he probably would have killed him. Proudly, however, the prisoner told the group that he had learned that there are many ways to save face and that name-calling is not worth a fight. Thus, instead of fighting back with aggression, the prisoner had simply turned around and said, "Wow, this is the third time someone called my mamma today." Everyone laughed, and he continued jogging.

Inevitably, and as evidenced by the A-to-E model, consequent behaviors are followed by external outcomes (e.g., peer approval, school suspension, physical injury). If a person does not like the external outcome of a consequent behavior, he or she should revisit the chain of events that led to the unpleasant outcome (i.e., antecedents, beliefs, feelings, and behaviors) and ask the following questions:

- What consequences do I want? What do I wish had happened?
- How would I have to behave to achieve this consequence?
- How would I have to feel to behave this way?
- How would I have to think to feel this way? Do I need to think differently about the situation?

Teachers have an important role in helping students understand this revisiting process and develop new, more effective thought patterns. Teachers can challenge students' thoughts about the situations they encounter and help them determine what emotions and behavioral responses will be most effective for obtaining the consequences they desire.

Problem-Solving Skills

In addition to the cognitive component of attributions, problem-solving skills are an important facet of cognitions that are particularly relevant to expanding social competence and preventing bullying. For some people, solving problems comes easily and naturally. For others, however, solving problems is a step-by-step, learned behavior. Problem solving is a cognitive process that can be learned and improved on by educators when they teach students how to manage conflicts. In addition to explaining the step-by-step process of solving conflicts, teachers can reinforce that conflicts are a normal part of life, that solving them can lead to personal growth, and that unresolved conflicts tend to fester and may escalate into aggression, resulting in negative outcomes.

To facilitate conflict resolution education, teachers and administrators should first meet to decide on a curriculum that seems most appropriate to the school's particular teaching strengths and the idiosyncrasies of its student body. Next, to promote educational consistency across grade levels and classrooms, teachers and administrators should use a conflict resolution approach and curriculum that reflects that approach schoolwide. Finally, the school's approach to conflict resolution should be deconstructed into simple language that students understand. STOPP (outlined in Box 5.6) is an example of how a conflict resolution strategy can be transformed into a simple language for students. Meyer and her colleagues proposed a different model named SCIDDLE (Stop, Calm down, Identify the problem and your feelings about it, Decide among your choices, Do it, Look back, and Evaluate; Meyer, Allison, Reese, Gay, & Multisite Violence Prevention Project, 2004). These two models, as well as many others, follow a common conflict resolution model that is outlined in the paragraphs that follow. This straightforward model can be simplified and posted as "Steps to Resolve Conflicts" in each classroom. Likewise, teachers and administrators should encourage students to use the problem-solving steps and should help students master this process.

BOX 5.6. EXAMPLE OF A CONFLICT RESOLUTION MODEL FOR STUDENTS

S   *Stop*: Stop, settle down, and be calm.
T   *Think*: Think about the problem and your goals.
O   *Options*: Think about the options or solutions to the problem.
P   *Plan*: Examine the consequences of different solutions, choose the best solution, and do it.
P   *Plan working?* Check whether the plan is working; if not, decide what would work better.

Note. From *Bully Busters: A Teacher's Manual for Helping Bullies, Victims, and Bystanders (Grades K–5)* (p. 337), by A. M. Horne, C. L. Bartolomucci, and D. Newman-Carlson, 2003, Champaign, IL: Research Press. Copyright 2003 by Research Press. Reprinted with permission.

Step 1: Define the Problem and the Goal. Clearly defining the problem and the goal with regard to that problem are important elements in the problem-solving process and influence several of the subsequent steps. For example, if Natasha is spreading nasty rumors behind Sue's back, Sue's solution to the problem will depend on her ultimate goal (e.g., Sue would like Natasha's behavior to stop, Sue would like Natasha to apologize, or Sue would like to become Natasha's friend). Thus, Step 1 requires that students learn to think about the problem, rather than simply react on the basis of their emotions or first impulse.

When discussing identification of the problem, educators and parents should help children identify situations that are dangerous (i.e., those that should be avoided or that require adult help). Dangerous situations include the following:

- A bully threatens to beat up a student or steal his or her money.
- A stranger offers a student a ride.
- A student has to traverse dangerous areas in the neighborhood.
- A student has to walk alone at unsafe times of day.

In addition, during discussions about Step 1, teachers should encourage students to report dangerous situations that their teachers may be unaware of. In discussions about dangerous situations, teachers should also inform children about which adults at school they can approach for help when faced with a particularly dangerous situation. Finally, discussions about the problem may include analyzing why the problem is occurring.

Step 2: Generate Solutions. Once students have identified the problem and their goals with regard to that problem, they are usually able to generate a number of different ideas about how to solve the problem. In this step, teachers can help students brainstorm solutions, a skill that may initially prove challenging but will improve with practice. Brainstorming solutions to different problems may be a particularly important step for students who are more aggressive, younger, or less skilled.

After generating possible positive solutions to different problems, teachers can also help students develop lists of the resources required to implement each solution. For example, if students identify fights over the pencil sharpener as a classroom problem and then subsequently identify purchasing an additional pencil sharpener as the most appropriate solution, generating a list of resources may help students pinpoint tools they might need to achieve their goal. Such a list may highlight the need to raise money to purchase an additional pencil sharpener or the need to write a letter to the principal to request an additional pencil sharpener. Similarly, if Kat is the target of verbal abuse by some of her classmates and she identifies that the best solution is to talk with the bullies, Kat may need additional resources, such as enhancing her communication skills or asking the counselor to act as a mediator.

Ignoring problems may be a good solution for minor issues (e.g., an occasional joke). Similarly, avoiding the person causing a problem may work well for issues with an individual a student does not really care much about. Learning how to pinpoint a problem and generate an appropriate solution, however, is important if the student wants to maintain a friendship.

Step 3: Examine Consequences. Once students have identified the problem and brainstormed solutions, they can examine the potential outcomes of the suggested solutions. In our research with children, we sometimes introduce Step 3 as "predicting history," or moving from spontaneously reacting to a conflict to thinking first about the impact different reactions will have. Predicting history involves generating a list of potential behavioral consequences; it is an easy process, yet it represents a more sophisticated method of addressing a problem than an emotional, spontaneous reaction.

In evaluating the potential consequences of different solutions, teachers can guide students through a process of examining each solution for its potential to solve the problem and its contribution to the student's ultimate goal (outlined in Step 1). In addition, teachers can prompt students to question whether their potential solutions will result in safe and fair outcomes for everyone involved, as well as whether the solutions will promote a positive school and classroom climate.

Step 4: Choose a Solution and Implement It. Once students have identified the best solution, they must implement it. All of the efforts exerted in the first three steps will be wasted, and the problem will remain unresolved, if students fail to implement the elected solution.

Step 5: Evaluate the Results. The last step in the problem-solving process involves evaluating the results of the implemented solution. The process does not stop with a behavioral response. An evaluation of a solution's effects on the problem and on the individuals involved with the problem allows students to reflect on their effectiveness as problem solvers. If the solution does not appear to be working, students can assess why it failed to meet their initial goals and what they can modify to resolve the problem in the future.

This five-step cognitive process for problem solving stresses an internal locus of responsibility and helps reveal how the steps students pursue can lead to specific outcomes. In addition, the process emphasizes that students have substantial control over their behaviors, because to accomplish these steps, students need to be calm and to think about the problem rather than simply react to circumstances.

Finally, the ability to apply the problem-solving process to some extent depends on the emotional development of the student. In fact, many problem-solving models add one initial "emotional" step to the cognitive steps previously described: stop, calm down, and be respectful. This initial emotional step is included in the STOPP model (Stop, settle down, and be calm) and in the SCIDDLE model (Stop and Calm down). Like the emotional component of social competence, this cognitive process may also depend on one's character. That is, students may follow all of the steps in the problem-solving process and choose a solution that "works" but that is unfair, dangerous, or against school policies. Thus, social competence programs that address emotions and cognitions should also address character.

Character

Many children—and adults—know that bullying is wrong and are familiar with strategies to solve conflicts without aggression, but they nevertheless make a decision to bully others. Consequently, bullying prevention programs must go beyond the development of behavioral, cognitive, and emotional skills. Character education, long within the domain of public education, should be an important component of any bullying prevention effort. In the 18th century English writer Samuel Johnson underscored the importance of integrating character and skills: "Integrity without knowledge is weak and useless, and knowledge without integrity is dangerous and dreadful" (Johnson, 1759/1988, p. 100).

Although character development and bullying prevention have much in common, researchers in these fields have rarely crossed paths. Most frequently, these disciplines are represented by different groups of researchers who publish in different journals and know little about each other's work. (Table 5.1 provides a brief comparison of the disciplines.) Simplistically speaking, character education strives to promote the "good," whereas violence prevention attempts to reduce the "bad." Bullying prevention and character education share the common goal of reducing violence and creating a positive school climate, although frequently through different strategies. Both disciplines strive for schoolwide comprehensive implementation, but unfortunately, both disciplines generally suffer from weak program implementation. Violence prevention programs are frequently viewed as a group of lessons implemented by the counselor, and character education is often seen as "the word of the month" that teachers randomly discuss with their students in class.

The Greek philosopher Heraclitus emphasized the importance of character, saying, "Character is destiny." Character education is a deliberate effort to help students act on ethical values or universally recognized virtues. Character education can be a thorny issue in schools, especially when it is perceived as indoctrination of students into specific values. Bohlin, Farmer, and Ryan (2001) distinguished between personal values (what the individual ascribes as being of worth or importance) and universal virtues (a moral commitment to good). People may endlessly discuss personal values (e.g., the value of life, such as the abortion of fetus vs. saving a mother's life), but it is universally recognized that being honest and hardworking is better than cheating and being lazy.

Researchers in the field of violence prevention have begun to recognize that integrating character education and bullying prevention can be a win–win situation. Currently, there is a tremendous body of knowledge on risk factors and a dearth of information on protective factors for bullying prevention. This imbalance explains, at least in part, why researchers' "profile" of a bully may be less than perfect. Moreover, the body of evidence on risk and

TABLE 5.1
Comparison of the Violence Prevention and
Character Education Disciplines

Characteristic	Violence prevention discipline	Character education discipline
Objective	Prevent and reduce violence, aggression, and bullying	Promote universally recognized ethical values or virtues
Main concepts	Violence, aggression, and bullying as not acceptable in the school community	Kindness, respect for others, hard work, and honesty as virtues that should be expected and celebrated
Types of programs	Universal programs designed to influence all students and the school environment Programs targeted to aggressive students and victims, such as counseling	Universal programs designed to influence all students and the school environment
Examples of journals	*Violence and Victims, Journal of Interpersonal Violence,* other psychological or health-related journals	*Journal of Research in Character Education, Journal of College and Character,* other educational journals

protective factors cannot explain why students who are not violent do not necessarily possess competent social skills and why students who have social skills do not always use them for positive purposes. Students' character—their internal sense of what is right and just—may indeed be the fulcrum in this delicate balancing act. From a teacher's vantage point, the bonus with respect to character education is that it can be easily integrated into many activities during the day. Frequently, schools have identified certain key character education constructs that they would like to emphasize during each week or month, and these constructs often can be melded with violence prevention activities. Box 5.7 provides some examples of teacher activities for character education. Several books on character education are available, such as *Character and Community Development: A School Planning and Teacher Training Handbook* (Vessels, 1998), *An Integrated Approach to Character Education* (Rusnak, 1998), *Building Character in Schools: Resource Guide* (Bohlin et al., 2001), and *Educating for Character: How Our Schools Can Teach Respect and Responsibility* (Lickona, 1991).

Social Skills

As pressure has grown to measure teacher performance in terms of students' achievement on standardized tests, some teachers have become increasingly concerned about using instructional time for teaching social and behavioral skills. However, as we have emphasized throughout this book,

BOX 5.7. EXAMPLES OF ACTIVITIES FOR CHARACTER EDUCATION

- Hold a class meeting to discuss what it means to have character. Brainstorm a list of characteristics or virtues that students agree on as demonstrating character, such as respect, kindness, and responsibility. Many of these virtues are crucial for bullying prevention.
- Define at the school level the character education themes or virtues that will be covered that year (e.g., patience, honesty, cooperation) and for how long they will be studied (e.g., one or two themes per month). Highlight that theme on the classroom bulletin board. Encourage students to bring in depictions of that characteristic, such as personal stories, pictures from magazines, characters from novels, or newspaper articles that demonstrate the character word of the week. Each day, set time aside to talk about new additions to the board or, if nothing new has been added, to hold a class discussion about the meaning of the word. Integrate the theme into academic activities when appropriate. For example, if the theme is patience, it could be discussed as part of a lengthy science experiment.
- Display a running list of the past themes so you can refer back to them. As you go through the year, identify opportunities to relate the themes to current or historic events and to the content of the curriculum. For example, social studies class provides many opportunities to hold group discussions about examples of character demonstrated by others. In language arts or reading, literary characters offer a vast array of opportunities to discuss the different themes. Be prepared to answer students' questions about character as they encounter events, stories, and people.
- If a schoolwide approach is established for implementing character education, students can videotape a skit demonstrating the current school theme. The tape could then be broadcast to the school or lent to individual classes for viewing.
- Do not allow unkindness in the class. Respect and caring behaviors can be tied to many virtues.

developing a behavioral repertoire that fosters constructive relationships is key to creating a positive school climate and will have a major impact on children's future. Although teaching academic content is essential, developing effective interpersonal skills is also central to children's development and success later in life. In both our research and our personal lives, we have encountered many individuals who have reported experiencing conflicts in their families or jobs because they lacked the social skills to "get along" with others. We have not met a single individual, however, who reported experiencing interpersonal conflict over not remembering the history of his or her state. Yet many schools teach history and ignore interpersonal development.

Some children may get involved in aggression, or be victimized, because they lack social skills such as those presented in Exhibit 5.3. In prior sections, we discussed several skills that can reduce aggression and victimization: conflict resolution, emotional management, and character education. We also discussed positive relational skills, such as giving compliments, thanking others, or showing other signs of respect. General communication skills are also important for bullying prevention. They include verbal and nonverbal behaviors related to speaking, listening, and showing respect. Positive communication skills will enable students to support their academic lives and achieve success. Because lack of academic achievement is a risk factor for bullying, teaching academic and study skills can have a positive impact on improved learning and reduced aggression. As students move into adolescence, other skills, in addition to the ones listed in Exhibit 5.3, become necessary, particularly those related to dating and personal relationships.

Given the long-term effects that positive verbal communication skills can have on students' happiness and productivity in their adult lives, no teacher should begrudge the practice of including verbal skills as part of his or her regular academic instruction. Teachers also need to be aware that lack of verbal ability is a risk factor for aggression (Buka & Earls, 1993). Helping children who are the target of aggression to develop nonaggressive verbal comebacks may prevent some bullying. When 8-year-old Carla was teased at summer camp because she was a vegetarian, she was taken aback. Her parents decided not to complain because her camp experience was nearly over, but they rehearsed with her possible responses. The next day, after the first negative comment on being a vegetarian had been directed at her, she said, "I really like animals; I just don't like them on my plate." Everyone laughed and stopped bothering her. Many children we have worked with have not even thought about the possibility of using assertive verbal responses rather than acting out aggressively in reaction to bullying. Chapter 10 discusses more strategies to help victims.

Fortunately for educators and counselors who wish to teach these skills at school, many books provide examples of activities for children of different ages, including the following: *Skillstreaming in Early Childhood: New Strategies and Perspectives for Teaching Prosocial Skills* (McGinnis & Goldstein, 2003); *Skillstreaming the Adolescent: A Structured Learning Approach to Teaching*

EXHIBIT 5.3
Examples of Specific Skills

Type of skill	Specific skills
Conflict resolution skills	Apologize
	Ask for help when faced with a problem
	Resist peer pressure to engage in high-risk and aggressive behaviors
	Avoid dangerous situations
	Ignore taunting and other behaviors meant to provoke anger
	Solve conflicts without aggression
	Set positive goals
	Accept the consequences of one's own behavior
	Negotiate
	Handle wanting something from others positively
Emotional management skills	Calm down
	Manage anger
	Reframe situations to portray a more optimistic view of a problem
	Maintain connectedness to peers and school
	Use self-control
Character education skills	Be honest
	Be responsible
	Work hard
	Respect others' opinions and things
	Be a good team member
Skills in showing concern and respect	Say please and thank you
	Ask for permission
	Offer help to peers
	Offer to help in the classroom
	Contribute to class activities and experiences
	Express concern for others
	Give compliments
Verbal communication skills	Introduce oneself
	Interrupt others politely
	Keep a conversation going
	Express feelings without blaming others or damaging relationships
	Express ideas without attacking others
	Time speech (say the main points first, without going into unasked-for details)
	Focus on the behavior, not the personality
	Engage in a conversation
Listening skills	Be attentive to others' conversation
	Repeat and summarize what others have expressed
	Pay attention to verbal and nonverbal communication
	While listening, try to understand rather than responding or providing advice
	Maintain eye contact while listening
	Follow directions
Academic skills	Develop study skills
	Listen to and follow teachers' directions
	Read for pleasure
	Manage one's time
	Organize one's work
	Complete assignments doing one's best job

Prosocial Skills (Goldstein, Sprafkin, Gershaw, & Klein, 1980); *Making and Keeping Friends: Ready-to-Use Lessons, Stories, and Activities for Building Relationships Grades 4–8* (Schmidt, 1997); *Ready-to-Use Social Skills Lessons and Activities for Grades 7–12* (Weltmann & Center for Applied Research in Education, 1996); and *Confronting Sexual Harassment: Learning Activities for Teens* (Sabella & Myrick, 1995).

Mental Health and Learning Abilities

Some bullying problems require specialized medical, psychological, or psychiatric attention or specialized educational services. Not all problems are within the students' or teachers' volitional control. For example, Kamphaus and colleagues found that 4% of a random national sample of elementary school students could be classified as severely psychopathological and that 12% could be classified as having a learning disorder (Kamphaus, Huberty, DiStefano, & Petoskey, 1997). According to these numbers, if the children with serious mental health issues were randomly distributed across classes, every class of 25 children would contain one child with severe psychopathology and three children with some type of learning disorder. Most likely, these students require medication or specialized educational treatment, or both. In addition, the researchers found that 8% of the sample—which would translate to two students per class—exhibited disruptive behaviors. Students who act in a disruptive manner may or may not require medication, but they definitely require special attention.

Students with mental health and learning disabilities issues represent a small portion of the school but require a large amount of resources. Most important, teachers need to be aware of these students' needs and seek support when necessary. Teacher support may be found in a small group setting (informal or formal), as described in the Support for Teachers section in chapter 4. In addition, it may be necessary for teachers to obtain specific training in work with special needs children.

Although special needs children may occasionally require specialized treatment, many also benefit from the strategies described in this book. In one of our teacher discussions, a special education instructor told us that she was amazed at the dramatic improvements one of her students had made after several anger management, conflict resolution, and social competence sessions. This student, who has previously had terrible anger management problems, had made the instructor an advocate of the program—"He made me a believer."

Most of the skills discussed in this chapter are simple, but many children have not seen adults or peers using them. In addition, although some children may have been exposed to these skills, they may not have been walked through the process of transforming a more complex skill into smaller, manageable steps. For example, a shy student who would like to develop a new friendship might find it helpful if a teacher or counselor were to briefly outline a course of action: Think about the person you would like to talk to, choose a topic, decide on a good time, start with a short and friendly question, and so forth. Skills development is a fundamental component of violence prevention.

6

EVALUATION OF BULLYING AND AGGRESSION PROBLEMS AND INTERVENTION PROGRAMS

The gods had condemned Sisyphus to ceaselessly rolling a rock to the top of a mountain, whence the stone would fall back of its own weight. They had thought with some reason that there is no more dreadful punishment than futile and hopeless labor.

—Albert Camus, *The Myth of Sisyphus and Other Essays*

This chapter highlights the importance of evaluating bullying prevention programs and provides guidelines for conducting these evaluations. The first section examines why the evaluation of the problem and the evaluation of the programs are important. The second section outlines the steps to follow when evaluating the problem and the impact of the programs. Finally, the last section details data collection procedures involved in conducting an evaluation, including the types of information, sources of information, methods used to gather the information, and available scales.

WHAT CAN EVALUATION ACCOMPLISH?

As Sisyphus learned, activities that take place year after year but produce no accomplishments constitute a dreadful view of the future. Evaluation can enhance what education professionals do—and help them stop rolling the rock uselessly—by highlighting what works and what needs improvement. Thus, evaluation is necessary and important to all endeavors.

In the prevention of bullying, evaluation is necessary in two areas. First, schools need to assess the seriousness and characteristics of the bullying and aggression, as well as the assets and protective factors of the school community. This assessment will guide the selection of the best programs to address the problem. Second, schools need to evaluate the efficacy of the programs they implement to prevent and reduce bullying. This evaluation will help school professionals refine the programs and make informed decisions about future prevention programs.

Patton (1996) defined *program evaluation* as "the systematic collection of information about the activities, characteristics, and outcomes of programs to make judgments about the program, improve program effectiveness, and/or inform decisions about future programming" (p. 23). Evaluation helps school professionals understand where they started, where they arrived, and how to further advance toward their goals. Although assessment is part of everyday school life, administrators frequently fear program evaluation. Box 6.1 lists commonly held myths about program evaluation, and Box 6.2 discusses why program evaluation is important.

BOX 6.1. *MYTHS ABOUT PROGRAM EVALUATION*

Program evaluation will indicate whether the program is a success or a failure. The possibility of failure scares most people. However, effective program evaluation is a process of examining the value of the program that provides feedback to participants and identifies the program's strengths and areas that need improvement. Thus, evaluation enables continued program effectiveness and refinement to occur.

Program evaluation is boring and produces useless results. This may be true for some evaluations, but a good program evaluation is practical and relevant and provides meaningful results to the providers. Having teachers and other school personnel involved in developing, conducting, and using the evaluation will ensure its meaningfulness.

Program evaluation is too expensive and a waste of resources. It is true that program evaluation may require additional resources. But it is probably more expensive to waste resources on programs with unknown effects or on programs that have demonstrated efficacy in other situations but not in the current situation or school setting. In addition, results from the evaluation can be used for continued program improvement and for sharing information with parents, the school board, and community agencies. Results may also be used in applying for grants for continuing or additional services.

Program evaluation is too complex and requires significant new skills. Most schools have done some program evaluation. For instance, many schools have assessed students' strengths and weaknesses in an attempt to identify areas for further teacher training. Thus, evaluation is rarely completely new to a school. Program evaluation can range from fairly simple to very complex. Even students can be involved in parts of the evaluation process and can conduct some of the analyses, for example, by calculating frequencies and creating graphs in math class. For more complex data analysis, a joint venture with university researchers can be a win–win situation for everyone.

BOX 6.2. WHY IS EVALUATION IMPORTANT?

Evaluation enables school professionals

- to understand the characteristics and magnitude of the problem (needs assessment) by identifying
  - prevalence of bullying and victimization,
  - types of bullying and where it occurs,
  - risk and protective factors, and
  - prevalence of positive behaviors;
- to improve the program (formative evaluation) by identifying
  - strengths and weaknesses of the program,
  - need for local adaptation of the program,
  - feasibility of the program implementation plan,
  - students' comprehension and liking of the program, and
  - teachers' need for training for program implementation;
- to monitor program implementation (process evaluation) by identifying
  - quality and quantity of program implementation and
  - fidelity of program implementation to original plan; and
- to examine program effectiveness (outcome and impact evaluation) by identifying
  - overall success in achieving the desired ultimate or outcome goal,
  - overall success in achieving intermediate or impact goals, and
  - costs and benefits of the program.

Four types of evaluation are important for examining the impact of programs: formative, process, outcome, and impact. *Formative evaluation* examines the quality of new programs and procedures as well as the feasibility of implementing them. Formative evaluation can start as soon as the ideas for prevention programs are conceived and continues as programs are added or modified. Formative evaluation can also help untangle issues in implementation that are difficult to foresee. Frequently, teachers, administrators, parents, and students form a committee to examine new programs. After defining the possible programs that could be implemented, educators assess the strengths and weaknesses of each program. Teachers can test some lessons of a curriculum to examine students' comprehension and interest in the program and propose how to adapt the curriculum to local needs. Teachers may propose different programs or special revisions for each grade level. Administrators need to assess the implementation of new policies and refine the process as needed. Finally, the committee decides on what kind of training is needed to implement the programs and who should participate in these training programs.

After developing intervention objectives and designing implementation processes, program execution should be monitored. This tactical monitoring, often termed *process evaluation*, can be an important step in helping administrators determine what went wrong if a program fails to meet its objectives. Many programs fall short of their marks not because they are ineffective at achieving their intended goals but because they were not implemented as intended. For example, policies that were developed may not have been enforced; some teachers may have implemented only half of a 20-lesson curriculum. In other instances, teachers may neglect to model what they teach. For example, a teacher who shouts at students and loses control will not be a credible source when trying to teach anger management skills to students.

Administrators ultimately want to know whether the program has achieved its intended objectives of reducing bullying and victimization and promoting social competence skills. Determining the extent to which a program has met its final objectives, typically labeled *outcome evaluation*, helps administrators ascertain whether a program can be deemed a success. *Impact evaluation* refers to changes in skills, knowledge, attitudes, or other theoretical constructs that the program is designed to change. Theoretically, changing these constructs will reduce bullying and victimization (the final outcome). The selection of constructs to be evaluated depends on the theory chosen to guide the intervention. Thus, outcome and impact evaluation are needed to examine how successful the program is and how to improve program effectiveness.

For example, in School A, teachers identified sexual harassment—considered a form of bullying—as a problem. Results from a student survey indicated that over 50% of boys and girls had been involved in at least one harassment incident since the beginning of the school year. In addition, students wrote personal testimonies with compelling descriptions of what they had been through. Teachers also identified other problems: Students were unaware of school policies regarding sexual harassment, students did not know whom to contact when they had been victimized, some students had had their experiences trivialized by the teachers from whom they sought help, and some harassers did not suffer any consequences for their behavior. To address these issues, a team of teachers gathered to develop, implement, and evaluate the intervention. The outcome objective was to reduce sexual harassment incidents by 30% by the end of the academic year. To achieve this outcome, they defined three program objectives:

- to increase by at least 50% the number of students who know the school's rules and consequences related to sexual harassment and who know whom to contact if they are harassed,
- to increase teachers' knowledge and self-efficacy to handle incidents of sexual harassment so that at least 80% of the teachers and administrators know how to handle the problem, and
- to increase students' satisfaction with the process of handling sexual harassment incidents to a minimum of 70% satisfied.

To achieve these program objectives, all teachers and administrators participated in a 6-hour workshop on sexual harassment. In addition, all students and their parents received a one-page flyer describing the school policy on sexual harassment and providing examples of harassing behaviors and of respectful relationships among students. Students had ample opportunity to ask questions during class discussions with their teachers, and follow-up school assemblies were planned for every 9 weeks, during which the principal explained the policy, the consequences, and the process of reporting. Most important, a sexual harassment prevention team was created to review and act on each reported incident.

Did this program reduce the harassment incidents by 30%? The only way to know is to evaluate the program. It is normal and expected that reporting probably will increase in the first weeks after the program starts. As more students learn the definition and behaviors related to sexual harassment, they will be more likely to recognize it and report it. Thus, it is critical that the evaluation differentiate between actual victimization and reporting.

Formative, process, impact, and outcome evaluations can help identify ways to improve a program. In the sexual harassment example, an evaluation—complete with both quantitative data (e.g., surveys of teachers and students) and qualitative information (e.g., focus groups, essays, interviews)—can provide information about maintaining or modifying a program by helping to answer the following questions: Does the school need to provide resources to train new teachers? Does the school need to meet with students only at the beginning of the year, or intermittently throughout the year? Does the school need a sexual harassment prevention team, or can the assistant principal handle all of the cases?

For additional resources on program evaluation, including formative, process, impact, and outcome evaluation, educators can review the document *Demonstrating Your Program's Worth: A Primer on Evaluation for Programs to Prevent Unintentional Injury* (Thompson & McClintock, 2000). This publication is free and was created by the National Center for Injury Prevention and Control at the Centers for Disease Control and Prevention (www.cdc.gov/ncipc).

WHAT DOES EVALUATION LOOK LIKE?

Many people associate evaluation with traditional research studies in which researchers administer a pretest at the beginning of the intervention and a posttest at the end the intervention and then determine from these data whether the intervention succeeded or failed. Patton (1996), Hughes (2003), and others, however, have presented program evaluation as less linear and as a more ongoing, spiraling process. This process, which includes the eight steps described in the following paragraphs, emphasizes evaluation activities that should be considered during the assessment of the problem of bullying and throughout the development, implementation, and evaluation of programs for reducing bullying and fostering positive relationships. In addition, this process stresses the idea that evaluation does not end at Step 8; rather, the last step involves refining the process and continuing to improve the intervention and evaluation methods. Ideally, evaluation should be an upward spiral in which the program implementers assess the problem, select and implement a program, and evaluate the outcomes; use the evaluation results then to improve the program and its implementation; re-evaluate outcomes; and improve the program again and again, continuously ensuring that the program grows in value and relevance to the school.

Step 1: Establish a Team. The bullying prevention or social competence development team should include a number of stakeholders, such as teachers, administrators, students, parents, community members, program funders, and if available, professional consultants from local universities or other agencies. To ensure that the program realizes its full potential impact, key decision makers who have budgetary or programmatic influence should be part of the team from the start. Patton (1996), in his well-known book *Utilization-Focused Evaluation*, defined the participation of key stakeholders as a critical element in the success of this eight-step process. In addition to administrators and community members, the development of an intervention should involve future participants at the beginning of the process. After all, an evaluation should be, above all, useful to everyone who is going to be affected by it. Forming a well-rounded bullying prevention team or a social competence development team composed of a variety of stakeholders is also an important step because it pools collective local knowledge about a school's aggression problem, generates community interest and support for the intervention that is ultimately chosen or developed, increases the capacity of community members to solve their problems, and secures community support for the idea of expanding resources to address the problem (Hughes, 2003).

Step 2: Define the Problem of Bullying. The prevention team established in Step 1 could define relevant questions, such as the following:

- What is the prevalence of bullying and victimization?
- What types of bullying are most frequent?
- Where does bullying occur?
- What are the risk factors that need to be reduced and the protective factors that should be enhanced?
- What are the characteristics of the children who are victims and of those who bully others?
- How intense are the emotional and physical consequences of bullying?
- What is the current prevalence of positive behaviors that should be enhanced?

This baseline information is used to develop objectives in Step 3. Regardless of which questions the team identifies, their wording should be concise and unambiguous enough to elicit clear responses. A good diagnosis is imperative to selecting the best and most appropriate interventions for a problem. Schools must "mine" needed information about where, when, and how frequently children bully their peers, as well as where, when, and how frequently children and teachers establish positive, caring relationships to build a foundation for success. Box 6.2 lists four sets of questions related to assessing the need for a bullying prevention program, evaluating a program's effectiveness, and gauging the quality of a program's implementation.

Educators have many different perspectives on bullying and aggression. Some teachers and administrators admit their school has a bullying problem but recognize only overt, physical pushing and fighting as bullying. Many do not view occasional incidents of psychological aggression as bullying, dismissing rumors and malicious gossiping as "kids' stuff." Other educators, particularly in recent years, have adopted a more comprehensive view of bullying. They recognize that both hitting and passing rumors that hurt other students can be classified as a form of bullying and that neither are acceptable in schools. These differences in perspective highlight that it is imperative for each school or school district to conduct a needs assessment before beginning to develop or adopt a bullying prevention program.

Not only definitions and awareness of bullying vary from one school to another; the nature and intensity of the problem also differ. Because not all schools face the same bullying and aggression issues, each school must clearly identify its problem. For instance, one school may have a serious problem with gangs, another with racial tension, a third with frequent physical fights, and a fourth with painful relational aggression among cliques of students. The reasons why children are involved in aggression may also differ by school or groups of children. Aggression may be related to teachers' lack of classroom management skills, to a school climate in which impunity reigns, or to children's dysfunctional family environments. Given this potentially wide spectrum of problems, a school's first step toward developing or selecting a bullying prevention program is to clearly understand the problem and to identify the risk and protective factors.

Step 3: Identify Clear and Measurable Objectives. Three different categories of objectives are needed. First, *outcome objectives* refer to the extent to which a program has achieved its ultimate goal (e.g., reduction of bullying and victimization). These objectives should include a specific time frame, goal, and audience—for example, "to reduce the prevalence of victimization by 30% by the end of the academic year." Second, *impact objectives* refer to the degree to which the program is achieving its intermediate goals, such as increased knowledge about the problem, changed attitudes toward the problem, enhanced connectedness to the school, or improved conflict resolution skills. The impact objectives will address the relevant constructs of the theories chosen to understand the problem and to guide the development of the intervention, as examined in chapter 3. For example, an impact objective might read, "By the end of the school year, 50% of the students will demonstrate their understanding of the school policies about sexual harassment" or "By the end of the school year, 80% of the students will demonstrate attitudes that renounce sexual harassment."

Finally, *process objectives* have two components: coverage and delivery. *Coverage* refers to whether a program is reaching its targeted population. Examples of a target population are all students or teachers in a school, students or teachers in a specific grade level, all students at high risk for violence, parents, and bus drivers. Different target audiences can be identified within the same intervention program. For example, a school might set integrated objectives specifying that 100% of the students will receive a pamphlet on sexual harassment and at least 90% of the teachers will discuss the pamphlet in class. *Delivery* refers to whether the program was implemented according to the design specifications outlined in the execution plan. Of course, delivery assumes that the prevention team specified the key components of the program and how these components should be delivered. A primary facet of an implementation plan involves specifying who should be trained, how much training people should receive, and which components should be emphasized during implementation (i.e., delivery). Any of the following examples are valid delivery objectives: (a) 100% of social studies teachers will receive at least 6 hours of training in bullying prevention, and at least 50% of other teachers will receive at least 2 hours of training; (b) at least 60% of students will participate in a three-session curriculum on sexual harassment; and (c) all sessions will be implemented following the instructions prescribed in the manual.

Step 4: Identify the Intervention Best Suited to the Needs of the School. In the fourth step, the team's primary efforts should focus on locating or developing a program that addresses the concerns identified in the previous stages of this process. The team should define whether it will implement a universal or a targeted intervention (or both). *Universal interventions* are developed for everyone in the school community, independent of their level of risk for violence or their record of prior aggressive behaviors. A universal program, for example, would include a bullying prevention curriculum delivered to all students in the school or to all students in a grade level (not just those who are aggressive). Likewise, a classroom management workshop for all teachers would be deemed a universal approach. *Targeted interventions* can be directed at two types of individuals: (a) those who are identified as being at risk for a particular problem and (b) those who have already been identified as having a problem. An intervention that targets the former group of individuals is sometimes termed a *selective intervention*, whereas an intervention targeted at the latter group of individuals is often called an *indicated intervention*. In schools, for example, students who have reported being the target of bullies or students in in-school suspension may be identified for a particular intervention. Teachers whose racial or socioeconomic background differs from their students' may receive special training on cultural diversity, or new teachers may be offered a workshop on positive classroom management. Parts II and III of this book expand on the development of universal and targeted interventions, respectively.

Step 5: Define the Methods to Evaluate Whether a Program is Achieving Its Goals and to Examine Whether It Was Implemented as Desired. In the Gathering Data for Evaluation section later in this chapter, we discuss different aspects of this step in detail, including what information is needed for the evaluation, who are the sources of information, how to gather the information, and what scales are available. Obviously, some methods may be more effective than others in certain situations. We also discuss a variety of qualitative and quantitative methods that evaluators can use to strengthen the rigor of an evaluation, keeping in mind Albert Einstein's sage advice, "Not everything that can be counted counts, and not everything that counts can be counted."

Step 6: Do It! The prevention team must implement the intervention and conduct the evaluation as planned.

Step 7: Analyze the Data Collected During the Evaluation and Report on the Results. Using the expertise of university consultants or other professional consultants at this point in the process can be a win–win situation for everyone: University consultants acquire access to real-life, practice-based settings, and schools obtain access to a higher level of statistical analyses than those normally conducted in-house. Frequently, data analysis is the weakest part of many school evaluation plans. If a prevention team will need the assistance of university consultants to analyze the data, including them at the start of the program planning process probably will yield a more positive response. Working with the team from the start, university consultants will have a stronger investment in the project, and they can assist throughout the process by highlighting recent research studies, helping identify relevant constructs, proposing scales that have been successfully used in other schools, and analyzing the data.

Step 8: Evaluate and Refine the Process. On the basis of the results from the prior steps, the team identifies what works and what needs to be adjusted. In this final step, the team should reevaluate the program's goals and develop new objectives or modify existing objectives as needed. Last, the prevention team should weigh the pros and cons of the intervention and evaluation methods, eliminating or augmenting the program or the methods when appropriate. Essentially, the team then goes back to Step 1 and reevaluates the entire process.

GATHERING DATA FOR EVALUATION

In the eight-step evaluation process, Step 5 recommends that an evaluation methodology be specified before implementing an intervention. This section expands on Step 5 and addresses the following questions: What information is needed for the evaluation? What sources of information should one use to evaluate a program? How will this assessment information be gathered? What scales are available? The answers to these questions depend on the purpose of the evaluation and the type of program implemented. This section advises practitioners on some of the dos and don'ts of evaluation planning.

What Information Is Needed for the Evaluation?

During the needs assessment phase, at a minimum, evaluators should collect information on the extent and prevalence of the bullying and victimization problem. More specifically, the evaluation should attempt to answer the following questions:

- How frequently do the different types of bullying and victimization behaviors occur (i.e., physical, verbal, relational, and—among older students—sexual harassment)? Ideally, evaluators should ask specific questions for each type of bullying.
- How serious is the bullying problem in the school (or grade level or classroom)?
- What are the physical and emotional consequences of bullying for the victims?
- How effectively do teachers and administrators control bullying?

- How do victims and bystanders handle bullying?
- Where, and under what circumstances, does bullying most frequently occur?
- What are the characteristics (e.g., demographic, academic, cognitive) of bullies, victims, and bystanders?

The collection methods used to glean these data will need to be tailored to each problem and each intervention. For example, depending on the specific time frame in which evaluators are interested, questions about the prevalence of bullying should require respondents to indicate the frequency of the behavior during a specified time span (e.g., within the last 7 days, within the last 30 days, from the beginning of the semester, or since the beginning of the school year). For younger children and for very frequent behaviors, the time period should be short—no longer than 1 week.

In addition, the way in which questions are worded can be very important in ensuring that respondents provide the specific information evaluators were targeting for collection. The wording of questions can be particularly critical in studies conducted with younger children. For example, if a survey asks whether students have been bullied in the last week, they will often answer no. But if students are asked if they were teased, pushed, or left out of an event, they may respond yes, because they may not recognize these behaviors as bullying. Consequently, if questions use the general term *bullying,* evaluators should be sure to supply a definition of bullying before asking these questions.

In addition to bullying and victimization, evaluators should collect data on the theoretical constructs that the intervention is intended to modify. These constructs might consist of knowledge about what behaviors can be considered bullying, knowledge about how to stop bullying if one sees it happening, attitudes about whether bullying is accepted under the umbrella norm of "just part of being a kid," attitudes that support alternatives to violence, the degree of empathy that students express for bullying victims, feelings of connectedness that students associate with school, students' and staff's skills in conflict resolution, or the relationship that students have with teachers. Some of these data can be collected from both students and teachers and compared. Other questions might collect data exclusively from teachers, administrators, or students. For instance, teacher evaluations could be designed to include questions about their connections with students, their personal classroom management styles, their relationships with colleagues and administrators, and their perceptions of administrative support.

Who Are the Sources of Information?

Although it may be obvious that an evaluation of a bullying prevention program should ascertain the perspectives of the students involved in or exposed to bullying, it is also important to gather information from other members of the community to provide different points of view on the problem. Members of the community may include individuals from within the school system (e.g., teachers, school administrators, or support staff) and from outside the system (e.g., police, judicial officials, or religious and spiritual leaders). Program evaluations that use multiple methods of data collection and gather data from multiple sources yield the most robust program assessments (Leff, Power, Manz, Costigan, & Nabors, 2001); no single approach to program evaluation can fully reveal the extent of a bullying problem or the power of a prevention program's impact on the problem. However, the larger the evaluation, the bigger the cost. Thus, a prevention team should prioritize which sources of information will provide the most insightful and compelling data, if for no other reason than to minimize costs.

Students

In most evaluations, students are the primary—and sometimes the only—source of data, because they are the most likely to be affected by bullies or to act as bullies themselves. Because students are minors, a school should decide before an evaluation is conducted how it will maintain data confidentiality, whether it will seek parental consent for any aspect of the evaluation, and how it will handle information that indicates any kind of risk for the child (e.g., reports of suicidal thoughts or harassment by a teacher). Because bullying frequently occurs when adults are not present, obtaining students' reports in an evaluation provides unique perspectives on the problem. In general, the prevalence of bullying is much higher in students' self-reports than in teachers' reports.

To collect data from students, evaluators can use a variety of methods, which are discussed in more detail later in this section. Briefly, these methods include self-reports; teacher and parent evaluations; or archival data such as behavior or conduct reports (school office records), academic achievement (report cards or school records), standardized test scores, or reports from nursing logs. Nursing logs may be particularly relevant for investigating fights or the use of nursing services by victims of bullying.

Teachers

Teachers are an important audience from whom to collect evaluation data. They typically have a strong connection to the school, and their input and perceptions are important for evaluating prevention programs' impact on bullying. In addition to their day-to-day observations of their students' behaviors, teachers may also be victims of student aggression themselves and so are uniquely positioned to provide insight into the depth of a bullying problem. Teachers frequently implement some, if not all, elements of a prevention program. As a result, they may be able to provide information to help evaluators determine how carefully an implementation plan has been followed (i.e., program fidelity) and how committed they and their colleagues were to the program's curriculum (e.g., was a whole curriculum covered or only a portion of it?).

Administrators

Without administrative support, neither the program nor its evaluation will ever come to fruition. Administrators usually are responsible for defining the range of resources (money, time, personnel) available for the program and its evaluation and prioritizing the intervention in the school's needs hierarchy. Thus, administrative support is essential to the success of a bullying prevention program and should be obtained early in the program development process.

Other School Staff

In general, school staff include other administrative personnel (e.g., counselors, school psychologists, school social workers, and secretarial staff) and operations personnel (e.g., cafeteria workers, bus drivers, and custodians). Often overlooked, school staff can play a critical role in establishing school climate and should be considered stakeholders in bullying prevention programs. Similarly, these individuals should be considered as a potential source of data in program evaluations. Program evaluations can tap this audience to examine their perceptions of the bullying problem, the program curriculum, and the program's impact. Neglecting to capture staff perceptions of the problem and the intervention program may inadvertently exclude valuable information about the total environment being examined.

Parents

Although parents generally do not have direct information about the extent of problems within the school, they do understand the concerns of their children. They may also provide a unique perspective, albeit generated from hearsay and their children's reports, on the prevalence of bullying at school. As such, parents can also provide valuable insight into outsiders' perceptions of the school's bullying problems.

Community

Finally, community members, although frequently excluded from intervention development and evaluation, may be a very important group from whom to collect evaluation data. Not only can they help researchers identify the extent to which a community is experiencing bullying or aggression problems; they may also be crucial players in collaborative efforts intended to facilitate the extension of an intervention beyond the school to the entire community. Community members that the evaluation team may want to query include law enforcement officers, judicial leaders, community agency staff (e.g., YMCA or YWCA, Boys and Girls Clubs, mentoring programs), local business owners, and religious or spiritual leaders. Box 6.3 provides an example of how community members can be included in the program planning process from the initial needs assessment through impact and outcome evaluation.

BOX 6.3. EXAMPLE OF A COMMUNITY PROGRAM EVALUATION: THE PARTNERS FOR SUCCESS PROGRAM

The Partners for Success Program was established in the Springfield, Massachusetts, schools in collaboration with the Smith College School for Social Work to address the socioeconomic problems that put a large number of children at risk for emotional, behavioral, and academic problems. The program emphasized a team approach in which school members, college faculty, and community agency personnel worked together to create an inviting climate that would facilitate learning and promote school and community safety. As part of this positive climate, they emphasized multicultural sensitivity and appreciation for personal and group differences, so that all members of the community would be included. These three groups identified goals for educational reform and social service integration. They coordinated their efforts to developed school and community programs that allowed the best use of resources.

After the 3rd year of their program, the intervention team conducted both a process evaluation and a consumer satisfaction assessment. The process evaluation was used to detail the number of services offered and the number of client contacts that had occurred during the prior 3 years. The consumer satisfaction assessment was conducted using surveys and focus groups. In the survey, students, families, and school personnel rated their level of satisfaction with the services offered as very positive, and they provided multiple examples of program effectiveness. In addition, respondents' feedback matched the program's stated objectives. In the focus groups, stakeholders provided strong support for the program. The evaluation provided valuable information that was used by the intervention team to refine the program. The Partners for Success Program is a practical demonstration of the ongoing spiral of program development, evaluation, refinement, and continued progress needed to address the problems of at-risk youths and to reduce aggression and violence in schools (Sessions, Fanolis, Corwin, & Miller, 2003).

How Will the Information Be Gathered?

No data collection method is ever perfect; each has its advantages and disadvantages. Exhibit 6.1 summarizes some of the benefits and shortcomings of popular data collection methods. Preemptive planning can be a strong weapon against anticipated problems. In addition, using more than one data collection method almost always strengthens the results of an evaluation. In the sections that follow, we highlight surveys, behavioral observations, peer sociometric measures, and archival data.

Surveys

Surveys completed by students are most commonly used for two main purposes: to assess how widespread a school's bullying problem is and to examine whether an intervention was effective at reducing the problem. When designing student surveys, evaluators must select carefully the number of questions, the content of the questions, and the type of response categories that will be appropriate for the age of the respondents. Surveys for young children often use pictorial response categories. Frequently, researchers use facial icons when working with primary and elementary school students (e.g., smiley faces, neutral faces, or frowning faces). When students' reading abilities are low, researchers may read the survey questions aloud while presenting the questions on overhead projectors. Surveys can also be programmed into computers. The computer can recite questions to students using computer-assisted survey interview (CASI) technology. Unfortunately, CASI technology is expensive and often not readily available to schools. If CASI is available, researchers should consider leveraging the strengths of this technology: CASI provides a strong sense of privacy for students, which may encourage them to provide more sincere responses to survey questions, and CASI can help ensure that students with low reading levels accurately comprehend written questions.

Although surveys provide a greater sense of confidentiality for respondents than do interviews or focus groups, other problems may affect the trustworthiness of the survey results: Students may not remember bullying incidents well, they may exaggerate the incidents, or they may not remember whether the incident occurred within the time frame in question. Responses from students who bully other students may not fully reflect the frequency or intensity of their aggressive behaviors or may exaggerate the consequences of their behaviors. Students who are victims of other students' aggressive behaviors may covet adult help, and thus they may exaggerate the frequency or seriousness of their experiences. Other victims may minimize the amount of bullying that they have endured, not wanting to admit that they are unable to protect themselves or fearing the reaction from bullies if it is discovered that the bullying has been reported.

EXHIBIT 6.1
Advantages and Disadvantages of Different Data Collection Methods

Advantages	Challenges
Surveys	
Provide results that are easily quantified and analyzed	Are difficult to construct when available scales do not fit the needs or areas of interest of the school; new scales or items may have to be developed locally
May provide a more accurate prevalence rate, because many bullying behaviors are frequently hidden from adults and not always reported	Provide little assurance of the quality of the responses; thus, it is important to convey the importance of the survey and to ensure confidentiality
Are the best method to evaluate verbal and relational aggression	Are strongly influenced by the reading level of students; teachers may need to read the surveys out loud or use computer-assisted technology
Can capture the unique perspective of victims and bullies	Have very low response rates when they are not completed in the school
Are less expensive than interviews or observations in terms of cost per respondent	Cannot be linked to other measures, such as school records, if they are administered anonymously (no names or codes attached); comparisons of pretest and posttest results are done at a group level, and impact on specific students cannot be examined
Provide more anonymity than other methods; thus, respondents are more likely to tell the truth	May increase students' fear of telling the truth if they are administered with name or a code attached
Can use evaluated scales for measuring different types of bullying and victimization	Preclude a more in-depth, qualitative understanding of aggression
Behavioral observations	
Do not require extra class time to be completed	May change the behavior to be observed because of the presence of the observer
Can provide information about bullying in different settings (e.g., playground, cafeteria, classroom, hallways)	Are difficult to use when evaluating relational and verbal bullying, which are tricky to observe; microphones and videotapes are needed to measure these types of bullying
Provide a firsthand account of bullying and of the relation among bullies, victims, bystanders, and other contextual factors	Require trained interviewers, particularly to distinguish rough-and-tumble play from aggression and to code more complex behaviors and sequences of behaviors
Can provide information about the sequence of events that led to a fight	Are time consuming
May provide information about students who have difficulty expressing verbally or are afraid to speak	Are not useful for very low frequency behaviors
Can use available behavioral observation systems	

Peer sociometric measures	
Have shown good psychometric properties	Are banned in some school districts out of concern that some children will be stigmatized or further categorized by fellow students and teachers
Provide information from multiple children (a whole classroom) in one evaluation	
Are sensitive to verbal and relational aggression	Are time consuming and require specific knowledge and skills to analyze the data
May provide information about students who are at risk because of being rejected by many students and about students who are influential among peers	May increase students' fear of reporting bullying if the management of the information is not clearly explained

Surveys can also be used to collect information from teachers and administrators. Such surveys might ask teachers and administrators about being bullied and victimized by students. A survey might also question teachers and administrators about the frequency and severity of bullying incidents at their school. Finally, a survey developed to capture responses from teachers and administrators could ask them to report on other personal and school characteristics they consider to be related to the bullying problem or to its solution.

Because of the small number of teachers employed at any one school, anonymity may be a source of concern in completing a survey. Some teachers may not respond honestly to survey questions from fear of administrators' or colleagues' reactions should their responses be revealed. For example, teachers may "soften" their responses if they know colleagues who previously reported considerable bullying in their classrooms and subsequently received a negative annual evaluation because administrators concluded that they were ineffective classroom managers. More specifically, in our research with teachers, we often used self-report forms that queried teachers' perceptions of the school's environment. Such sensitive questions may be worrisome for teachers who fear administrative reprisals. Along these same lines, teachers may be reluctant to share personal or emotional reactions to bullying-related issues in a survey (e.g., their personal level of depression, fatigue, or discouragement in the teaching process) if they believe that the information will be reused for reasons other than improving the school or research (e.g., performance evaluations).

To reduce anxiety among child and adult respondents, the evaluation team should give clear information about how the data will be handled. The team should openly describe the individuals who will have access to the survey data, the individuals who will analyze the data, and the aggregate measures that will be used to report the results. The importance and purpose of the information should be conveyed to all participants.

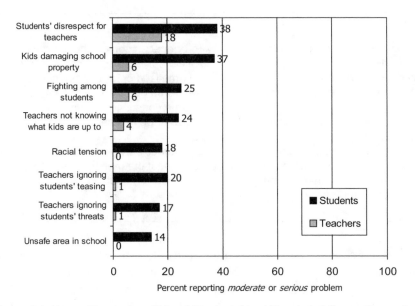

Figure 6.1. Upper Elementary School Students' and Teachers' Perceptions of Moderate to Serious Problems of School Safety in School District A.

Teachers and students often have very different opinions regarding whether bullying and aggression are problems the school should address. They also have different perceptions about how responsive the school is to these problems. For example, in recent surveys we have conducted about school safety, teachers and students gave very different responses to the same survey questions (Figure 6.1 and Figure 6.2). In School District A, teachers reported almost no safety problems, whereas students reported significantly more. Student reports of moderate to serious problems ranged from 14% (unsafe areas at school) to 38% (student disrespect for teachers). In School District B, we found the reverse: For most questions, teachers reported significantly more safety problems than students. Overall, teachers and students perceived more safety problems at School District B than A. In School District B, student reports of moderate to serious problems ranged from 19% (unsafe areas at school) to 53% (student disrespect for teachers).

Teachers' and students' responses to questions about the prevalence of bullying and victimization usually vary. Response disparities between these two groups raise questions as to whether the students' or teachers' reports best reflect reality. The correct answer is often difficult to ascertain; bullying can be a covert, private event that is not observed by teachers. This factor, compiled with the fact that students can also be influenced by rumors that have no basis in reality (e.g., someone brought a gun to school), may account for students' reporting a larger problem with bullying and aggression than teachers generally report. However, in schools in which problems with ag-

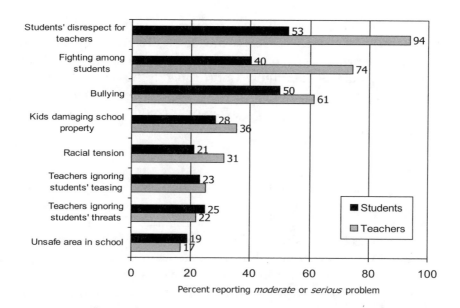

Figure 6.2. Upper Elementary School Students' and Teachers' Perceptions of Moderate to Serious Problems of School Safety in School District B.

gression are grave (such as School District B), students may become numb to aggression and stop recognizing it as a serious problem.

Students and teachers may also have different perceptions of how effective a teacher or the school administrative staff is at handling bullying problems. Students often report that teachers do not take bullying problems seriously or that teachers' responses to bullying worsen the problem rather than improve it. Teachers, however, report that they frequently take action but that they do so privately or discreetly rather than publicly. Thus, students who have been victimized may be unaware of the teachers' actions. Private reprimands can be problematic, though, because if victims do not believe they will be taken seriously and be protected, they will be less likely to report bullying incidents. Disparate perceptions of bullying between teachers and students is a topic that should be addressed during the development of the program.

Behavioral Observations

Behavioral observations have been an important data collection procedure in aggression research for more than three decades. This technique was a major component of the early work of Patterson, Reid, and their colleagues at the Oregon Social Learning Center (Patterson, Reid, Jones, & Conger, 1975; Reid, 1978). More recently, Pellegrini (1996; Pellegrini & Bartini, 2000) also used behavioral observation methods. Behavioral observations are objective and naturalistic. They occur in the students' natural social settings, allowing researchers to watch students interact in their normal environment. Some observation systems, such as having an observer keep a simple tally sheet of bullying incidents observed within a specified time period, are very simple and require little training. More frequently, however, observation systems are more complex and require observers to have extensive training in how to reliably record specific behaviors or interchild interactions over varying time spans and in differing locations.

Peer Sociometric Measures

Peer sociometric measures, which evaluate behaviors and relationships within social groups, have been used in research for over two decades (Coie & Dodge, 1983, 1988; Leff, Power, & Goldstein, 2004; Terry, 2000). These measures may take the form of peer ratings or peer nominations. In the peer rating process, students rate all other students in their class or group on a specific characteristic or construct. For example, students may rate their peers using a 5-point Likert-type scale indicating how likely they are to pick on other students, be left out of a group, or cooperate with others.

In the peer nomination process, students nominate a limited number of classmates whom they like or dislike. A variation on this technique might ask children to nominate peers who exhibit specific negative characteristics (such as bullying or getting angry easily) or positive traits (such as being willing to help or playing fair). Peer nominations can provide valuable information about peer acceptance: Children may be popular (receive many positive votes), rejected (receive many negative votes), controversial (receive positive and negative votes), or neglected (not receive any votes). Further comparison of nominated children with other sources of data can inform evaluators about whether a child's popularity is related to being prosocial (behaving in ways that help or benefit other students) or to being an influential bully. Such comparisons might also reveal other helpful information about the characteristics of rejected, controversial, and neglected children.

Not all school administrators are comfortable with the use of sociometric measures because they worry that the results might prompt students to stigmatize specific classmates. In research, institutional review boards, which hold responsibility for approving research procedures used with people, are not very keen on their use either. However, research provides no support for this argument. Most students know who the bullies and the victims are, and the nomination process is unlikely to change their cognitions. An alternative to peer nomination is teacher nomination. However, when teacher and peer nominations were compared, teachers identified only 47% of the peer-reported elementary bullies, 22% of peer-reported middle school bullies, 46% of the peer-reported elementary victims, and 16% of peer-reported middle school victims (Leff, Kupersmidt, Patterson, & Power, 1999).

Archival Data

Students' school records contain valuable information on each child. Specifically, discipline referrals and nurse's logs, which are discussed in the paragraphs that follow, become particularly important in bullying prevention program evaluations. In addition, school records contain information about academic performance in class and on standardized tests. Depending on the program's objectives, improvements in academic performance might be expected as a result of a reduction in bullying and, therefore, would be important to monitor and track.

Many schools have computerized databases that track referrals to the office for disciplinary action. These databases can be tapped in an evaluation to examine the impact of bullying intervention programs. For example, Newman and Horne (2004) found that teachers who participated in a bully prevention training program made significantly fewer discipline referrals to the office after the program than they had before, as measured by the computer tracking system used by the district. Similarly, the system's data showed that teachers who participated in the program made fewer discipline referrals than teachers who did not participate in the program.

If school discipline reports are computerized, data collection is straightforward. Evaluators can easily compile information by various fields within the database, such as teacher, student, offense, or location. The process of pulling data from an existing computer system is inexpensive and does not interfere with class time. In addition, the computer's record of discipline referrals may contain information about behavior problems in other locations outside of the classroom, such as in the cafeteria or on buses. However, if the school discipline reports are not computerized, the process of collecting the data and entering it into a computer will be time consuming and labor intensive.

Using disciplinary data as a single outcome measure of a bully reduction program, however, has many drawbacks. First, behavior problems tend to increase during the school year. Referral rates are likely to be higher later in the year, thus concealing intervention effects. Second, consistency among teachers' disciplinary referrals is generally low. What is acceptable or tolerable behavior for one teacher may be unacceptable and intolerable for another, thereby resulting in significant variation in referrals by class period and from teacher to teacher. Some of these problems can be reduced, however, with appropriate planning. Tracking disciplinary referrals over several years allows evaluators to consider the seasonal nature of referrals when analyzing intervention results. Also, referral consistency across teachers can be increased by developing clear referral guidelines and providing training on when and how to enact these guidelines. In addition, some schools keep a record of every referral to the office, whereas others record only severe cases in which parents were notified. Many school districts are establishing a standard disciplinary referral process for all schools within the district, an action that will facilitate evaluators' cross-school comparisons.

A final major concern for relying solely on disciplinary referrals to evaluate an intervention is that not all children who bully others are referred to the office. Discipline referrals largely depend on teachers' classroom management skills, their tolerance for disruptive behavior, school policies, and the number of problem students in the class. Furthermore, some teachers may be hesitant to refer misbehaving children to the office simply because they worry that their principal will deem them ineffective as classroom managers. A recent study confirmed that a discrepancy exists between the number of office referrals and teachers' ratings of students. A relatively high number of children who were identified as clinically problematic according to the Child Behavior Checklist were not referred to the office for disciplinary purposes (Nelson, Benner, Reid, Epstein, & Currin, 2002). Consequently, relying solely on discipline referrals will likely underestimate the number of children with behavioral problems at school.

Because students who are injured at school are generally referred to the school nurse, nurses' logs can be a valuable tool to assess whether the bullying prevention program reduced injuries due to violence. To use nurses' logs, schools need to be aware that two conditions must exist: The intervention program must be designed to reduce physical bullying along with verbal or relational bullying, and the nurses' log must specify the cause of the injury to discriminate between intentional and unintentional injuries. Nurses' logs have a number of advantages. They are readily available and, thus, easy and inexpensive to collect. They can provide baseline information for several years before implementation of the intervention. They do not require class time or parental permission to collect and access the data. And they can provide comprehensive, schoolwide information.

Data from nurses' logs do have limitations, however; variations may exist between schools and school nurses with regard to how they collect and record data, yielding inconsistent data for analysis; data from nurses' logs may be unavailable, incomplete, or even lost, introducing missing data problems to the evaluation (Brener, Krug, Dahlberg, & Powell, 1997); and injury prevalence may be low, affecting the power of the analyses. This latter point may be the most critical detriment to using nurses' logs as an evaluation measure. In 2003, only 4% of high school students reported being injured in a physical fight (Grunbaum et al., 2004). Moreover, these injuries may have occurred outside of school because the survey did not prompt respondents to limit their answers to a school setting. Consequently, before deciding to use nurses' logs to monitor an intervention's impact, the school should evaluate the quality of the data that have been collected and the prevalence of injuries. Nevertheless, examining nurses' logs can be an important evaluation tool if the school has a problem with children being injured by bullying. The logs should be used, however, in tandem with other tools that measure verbal and relational bullying.

It is important to remember that surveys, behavioral observations, peer sociometric measures, and archival data are not the only data collection alternatives available. Other options include interviews, focus groups, and student essays. Each of these options has inherent benefits and limitations that should be considered before use. Interviews of key persons can provide valuable information about the problem and ideas for solutions. However, it can sometimes be difficult to generalize interview findings from a few individuals because these individuals may or may not be representative of the whole population of interest. Focus groups with students allow for group reflection but may limit feedback if a bully is present in the group (other students may be too intimidated by the bully to share their thoughts and feelings). In addition, analyzing focus group data requires specialized skills and is time consuming.

Student essays can provide rich insights into students' feelings about bullying, perceived bullying problems, and possible bullying solutions. Student essays are easy to collect; they can be requested as part of English class and thus do not require additional class time to complete. Although they cannot be quantified to assess progress toward programmatic goals, essays can provide an in-depth description of the bullying problem, thus assisting evaluators in understanding the meaning that certain behaviors hold in a school setting. Finally, student essays can yield constructive information, supplemental to survey findings, that may help clarify ambiguous survey answers. For example, the students in one elementary school rated the school as very unsafe in a survey. The principal, who was confused by this unexpected result, asked teachers to request essays from students about why they thought the school was unsafe. Most students wrote about a construction site next to school, not about bullying.

What Scales Are Available?

When searching for scales that students can complete and assessments of students that teachers complete, evaluators can consult the document *Measuring Violence-Related Attitudes, Behaviors, and Influences Among Youths: A Compendium of Assessment Tools* (Dahlberg, Toal, Swahn, & Behrens, 2005). This publication is free and was created by the National Center for Injury Prevention and Control at the Centers for Disease Control and Prevention (www.cdc.gov/ncipc).

Figure 6.3 provides the Reduced Aggression and Victimization Scales, which are free and available for schools to use on request from the author. The scales were developed by Pamela Orpinas as an elementary school version of the Aggression Scale (Orpinas & Frankowski, 2001). The Reduced Aggression Scale and the Reduced Victimization Scale are composed of six items each. Two of the items measure relational aggression or victimization, and the other four measure overt aggression (teasing, name-calling, threats,

Think about what happened DURING THE LAST 7 DAYS, when you answer these questions.

During the last 7 days:	0 times	1 time	2 times	3 times	4 times	5 times	6 or more times
1. How many times did a kid from your school tease you?	0	1	2	3	4	5	6+
2. How many times did a kid from your school push, shove, or hit you?	0	1	2	3	4	5	6+
3. How many times did a kid from your school call you a bad name?	0	1	2	3	4	5	6+
4. How many times did kids from your school say that they were going to hit you?	0	1	2	3	4	5	6+
5. How many times did other kids leave you out on purpose?	0	1	2	3	4	5	6+
6. How many times did a student make up something about you to make other kids not like you anymore?	0	1	2	3	4	5	6+
7. How many times did you tease a kid from your school?	0	1	2	3	4	5	6+
8. How many times did you push, shove, or hit a kid from you school?	0	1	2	3	4	5	6+
9. How many times did you call a kid from your school a bad name?	0	1	2	3	4	5	6+
10. How many times did you say that you would hit a kid from your school?	0	1	2	3	4	5	6+
11. How many times did you leave out another kid on purpose?	0	1	2	3	4	5	6+
12. How many times did you make up something about other students to make other kids not like them anymore?	0	1	2	3	4	5	6+

Victimization Scale: Overt victimization = questions 1–4, relational victimization = questions 5–6.
Aggression Scale: Overt aggression = questions 7–10; relational aggression = questions 11–12.

Figure 6.3. Upper Elementary Aggression and Victimization Scales.

pushing, or hitting). These scales were developed for upper elementary school children. In a study of fourth and fifth graders ($n = 411$), the internal consistency of the scores, measured with Cronbach's alpha, was .86 (range by gender and race = .84–.89) for aggression and .84 (range by gender and race =

.80–.87) for victimization. The original Aggression Scale, composed of 11 items, was developed for middle school (Orpinas & Frankowski, 2001).

Espelage and her colleagues developed the University of Illinois Aggression Scales for Grades 3 to 12, which measure bullying (9 items), fighting (5 items), and victimization (4 items) during the month prior to the survey (Espelage, Bosworth, & Simon, 2001; Espelage & Holt, 2001; Espelage, Mebane, & Adams, 2004). Swearer and her colleagues developed the Bully Survey, which comprises a student, a teacher, and a parent survey (Swearer, Song, Cary, Eagle, & Mickelson, 2001). The student component is a four-part, 31-question survey that queries students regarding their experiences with bullying, perceptions of bullying, and attitudes toward bullying. The survey is available on request from the author. Crick developed scales for different grade levels to measure relational aggression (Crick, Casas, & Ku, 1999; Crick & Grotpeter, 1995). A number of scales are available to evaluate intrapersonal characteristics that may influence aggression, such as attitudes (e.g., Funk, Elliott, Bechtoldt, Pasold, & Tsavoussis, 2003), beliefs (e.g., Huesmann & Guerra, 1997), and altruism (Solomon, Battistich, Watson, Schaps, & Lewis, 2000).

Few scales are available to measure teachers' knowledge and skills. One of them is the Teacher Inventory of Skills and Knowledge (TISK), which measures teachers' awareness of bullying and the frequency with which teachers use bullying prevention and intervention strategies. The questions asked in the TISK were developed to parallel the Bully Busters intervention, but the items could be adapted to evaluate other similar interventions. An elementary and a middle school version of the TISK are available (Horne, Bartolomucci, & Newman-Carlson, 2003; Newman, Horne, & Bartolomucci, 2000). Finally, the Maslach Burnout Inventory measures three components of educator burnout in the workplace: emotional exhaustion, depersonalization, and personal accomplishment (Maslach & Jackson, 1993). This inventory, however, is not free.

Before instituting an evaluation, it is especially important that the evaluation procedures be reviewed to ensure that they are culturally sensitive (i.e., that they are relevant for the cultural groups being evaluated or using the evaluations). This review includes addressing a number of cultural characteristics that schools often overlook, such as gender bias, sexual identity and sexual orientation issues, race and ethnicity concerns, socioeconomic stereotypes (e.g., children from rural vs. urban backgrounds, children who ride the bus to school vs. children who walk, or children who receive reduced-price lunch vs. children who pay full price). In addition, when multiple methods are used to collect evaluation data, comparing student, teacher, and parent results can provide interesting insights into different groups' perceptions of the problem and the intervention. Using multiple methods of data collection and gathering data from multiple sources will help schools feel more confident in their interpretation of intervention results.

7

SELECTION AND IMPLEMENTATION OF UNIVERSAL BULLYING PREVENTION PROGRAMS

Thank you . . . this program has changed my life. You have taught me how to solve my problems without violence and to respect not just my friends but my family and teachers too.
                    —Letter from a sixth grader to the facilitator, at the
                    end of a 20-lesson violence prevention curriculum

This chapter provides an overview of existing universal programs to reduce and prevent bullying and aggression. Universal programs are meant to influence all students, independent of the level of risk for aggression or their actual aggressive behaviors. The first section discusses strategies to identify programs from accessible databases. The second section discusses principles of implementation of successful programs. The final section examines criteria to select programs and lists a sample of existing programs for reducing bullying and aggression. Each of the programs presented has demonstrated some evidence of being effective.

IDENTIFYING HIGH-QUALITY PROGRAMS

During the past two decades, interest in school violence prevention has increased, a trend that has been accompanied by the development of numerous commercial and not-for-profit programs. Some of these programs have undergone rigorous assessment, but the large majority of these programs have never been evaluated. The evaluations that have been performed have not always yielded positive findings: Some programs have not been effective, some have been effective only with regard to particular measures or certain types of students, and some have even shown detrimental effects. Differences in the degree of success may be due largely to the quality of program implementation. Fortunately, empirical evidence in support of well-designed and well-implemented programs continues to grow, attesting to their influence in reducing substance abuse, increasing academic learning, improving mental health, and decreasing antisocial behavior (Greenberg et al., 2003). Thus, choosing the right intervention on the basis of the problem, the objectives, and prior evaluations is essential for successfully reducing aggression and bullying.

Several strategies have been used to identify promising programs. Chambless and Hollon (1998) maintained that certain criteria must be met for a program to qualify as "empirically validated." These criteria include

- experimental group design, including random assignment to conditions of treatment or no treatment;
- well-documented treatment procedures (manuals developed);
- strict adherence to program monitoring procedures;
- uniform training of program implementers;
- well-validated and reliable outcome measures targeting multiple areas of measurement;
- follow-up of treatment effects at least 6 months post hoc; and
- replication of the process by different, objective researchers.

These criteria are very rigorous and very difficult to achieve in bullying prevention. The cost of implementing the first criterion alone, in which schools would be randomly assigned to intervention or control conditions, is enormous (Multisite Violence Prevention Project, 2004a). Random assignment to different conditions, however, is an important step in empirical evaluations and is considered the gold standard for mitigating the effects of extraneous factors on the results of the research. In a clinical trial, for example, when 10,000 women are assigned to receive either a particular medication or a placebo, one can be fairly confident that differences between the two groups in disease or mortality are due to the medication. In bullying prevention, however, assigning a limited number of schools to intervention or control conditions does not guarantee control over the effect of extraneous variables (e.g., turnover of school administration, differences in student demographics, intensity of teacher implementation) on the outcomes of interest. Further, in research studies, random assignment does not allow for the tailoring of the intervention to the specific needs of the school.

Two strategies have been used to overcome limitations in program evaluation: conducting meta-analyses of published evaluation studies and contracting experts to review curricula, informal research, and published evaluation research to subsequently rank bullying prevention programs on the basis of specific classification criteria. Wilson, Gottfredson, and Najaka (2001), in a meta-analysis of 165 published school-based prevention intervention evaluations, concluded that the programs appeared to be effective in reducing alcohol and drug use, dropout rates, absenteeism, and other conduct problems. Across the evaluated prevention intervention, the strongest effects were associated with programs promoting self-control and social competence that used cognitive and behavioral strategies rooted in social learning principles. Strong positive effects were also found for interventions designed to change the overall school environment: establishing clear norms for behaviors, improving classroom management, revising overall school discipline management, and reorganizing grades or classes. Wilson et al.'s meta-analysis and other studies of this kind (e.g., Mytton, DiGuiseppi, Gough, Taylor, & Logan, 2002) suggest that prevention programs work but that their effectiveness varies greatly by type of intervention, quality of implementation, and the school's initial climate. Thus, the generalizability of programs is still in question (Gottfredson, Gottfredson, & Skroban, 1998; Greenberg et al., 2003; Skroban, Gottfredson, & Gottfredson, 1999).

The second strategy, a review of programs by a panel of experts, has been used by several government and nonprofit agencies. These organizations have contracted expert researchers in the field of violence prevention to conduct more thorough evaluations of programs that appear theoretically sound and that have shown some evidence of initial success. Depending on the organization, experts have been asked to prioritize reviewed programs into two or three groups. Although labels vary by agency, most organizations have used the following categories: promising, effective, model, or exemplary. It is regrettable that the criteria used when assigning programs to these categories has varied by agency. Thus, a program may be considered exemplary by one agency but only promising by another. The following paragraphs list some of the contracting organizations and provide a short description of the categories they use to prioritize programs. We strongly recommend visiting their Web sites for more detailed information about various evaluated bullying prevention programs.

The Substance Abuse and Mental Health Services Administration (SAMHSA; 2005), an agency of the U.S. Department of Health and Human Services, has identified successful substance abuse and violence prevention programs in three categories: promising (some positive outcome), effective (consistently positive outcomes), and model (available for dissemination, with technical assistance available from developers). Their review includes 55 promising programs, 38 effective programs, and no model interventions. The programs focus on a variety of risk behaviors, such as drug use or bullying and aggression; other programs focus on developing assets relevant to numerous risk behaviors, including bullying. Programs can be reviewed at http://modelprograms.samhsa.gov/.

The U.S. Department of Education (2002) has published a book describing 3 exemplary (sufficient evidence of effectiveness) and 29 promising (some evidence) violence prevention programs. The report, entitled *Exemplary and Promising: Safe, Disciplined, and Drug-Free Schools Programs—2001*, is available free of charge at http://www.ed.gov/admins/lead/safety/exemplary01/exemplary01.pdf. It contains an excellent table that compares programs on emphasis (targeted behaviors or goals), grade levels, duration and intensity, and costs. A number of the programs address the reduction of tobacco, alcohol, and drug use, but the majority of the programs focus on reducing aggression and increasing social skills. Only 12 programs from this review were also selected in the review presented by SAMHSA.

The American Federation of Teachers (AFT; 2001) has published *Building on the Best, Learning From What Works: Five Promising Discipline and Violence Prevention Programs*, available at www.aft.org. Three of the five promising programs are included in the U.S. Department of Education review.

The National Association of School Psychologists has published *Exemplary Mental Health Programs: School Psychologists as Mental Health Service Providers*, available at www.naspcenter.org/ (Nastasi, Pluymert, Varjas, & Moore, 2002). Their review includes a parenting bully reduction program.

The Center for the Study and Prevention of Violence (n.d.), at the University of Colorado at Boulder, with the support of the Office of Juvenile Justice and Delinquency Prevention, published the *Blueprints for Violence Prevention*, available at http://www.colorado.edu/cspv/blueprints. The criteria for selecting which programs would be evaluated include clear deterrent effect, strong research design, sustained effects for at least 1 year, and multiple replications. Consequently, the total number of identified programs is relatively small: 11 model and 18 promising programs; not all are school based, and a number of them do not focus directly on bullying reduction. The exemplary program called Functional Family Therapy, for example, addresses working with delinquent and highly aggressive adolescents through a family therapy model, which is not likely to be implemented in a school setting.

The Development Services Group (n.d.) has one of the most comprehensive databases to search for programs. Its Model Programs Guide and Database is available at http://www.dsgonline.com/. Programs are prioritized into three categories based on research design: exemplary (experimental design, random assignment), effective (experimental or quasi-experimental design), and promising (limited research, but promising results). The programs can be searched by 17 topical categories (e.g., gang prevention, academic skills enhancement, behavior management), but not all of the categories are directly related to schools. Finally, database users can also search for programs by target population characteristics (e.g., age group, gender, race and ethnicity, and other characteristics such as school dropout rates). When reviewing individual programs, the site also provides useful information about endorsement from other agencies.

The Virginia Best Practices in School-Based Violence Prevention (http://www.pubinfo.vcu.edu/vabp/) presents an extensive list of programs evaluated for effectiveness. The site provides brief descriptions of a large number of programs that are appropriate for school settings (Virginia Commonwealth University, n.d.).

IMPLEMENTATION OF PREVENTION PROGRAMS

The success of programs in reducing student aggression and bullying varies greatly by school. Success of prevention programs typically depends on two factors: the characteristics of the school environment and the quality of implementation (Gottfredson & Gottfredson, 2002; Greenberg et al., 2003).

Characteristics of the School Environment

A bullying prevention program—no matter how good it is—can never replace the development of a positive school climate (see chap. 4). In fact, a program will work best in environments in which good will exists between teachers and administrators, the discipline plan is based on a responsibility model, positive strategies to prevent aggression are common, and teachers are skilled in classroom management (Bear, 1998). Of course, extensive planning, as well as involving teachers in decisions about what to teach and how to integrate prevention concepts into daily class routines, will increase ownership of the program and foster a more seamless implementation of the program into daily activities (Gottfredson & Gottfredson, 2002). Short-term, fragmented initiatives without teacher support and without a clear tie to the mission of the school will likely prove ineffective (Greenberg et al., 2003).

In addition to teacher acceptance, administrative leadership and support are critical for ensuring a successful implementation of a schoolwide bullying-reduction program. Administrators typically define how much time should be allocated to implementing a curriculum and how many resources are available for purchasing a curriculum and training the teachers. They can also help creatively integrate the activities from the prevention curriculum into different academic subjects and with other components of the program. Without administrative support, teachers will not receive high-quality prevention training, the curriculum will not be allocated sufficient time in the classroom, and the program implementation will not be monitored. Finally, administrative support is also necessary for facilitating a program evaluation, as well as for deciding how to improve the program over time.

Quality of Implementation

Many programs fail simply because they are not implemented properly, instructions provided by the curriculum developers are not followed, or the plan is halted before its recommended "run time" expires. Generally, short-term interventions produce short-term results; multiyear programs are needed to seed and maintain improvements in social competence and school climate (Greenberg et al., 2003).

Successful intervention programs should be implemented with the following four basic social learning principles in mind:

1. *Modeling the desired behavior:* Part of learning competent social skills involves observing others—in this case adults—acting in a socially appropriate manner. To expect students to behave in ways that adults do not model is unrealistic. The old saying "Do as I say, not as I do" does not apply in schools. Teachers and staff must set behavioral standards by modeling appropriate positive behaviors (Bandura, 1986; Bear, 1998).

2. *Defining program objectives and designing multiple tactics for reaching them:* The overarching goal of the school is to create a positive environment that promotes academic excellence and positive interpersonal relationships. To achieve this goal, teachers and staff need to define the specific student learning objectives that they might adopt (see examples in Table 5.1) and that are congruent with schoolwide objectives. Frequently, the implementation of a program is deemed successful when the recommended activities have been conducted. It is important to remember that the purpose of a program is to achieve its objectives, not to simply complete a list of activities. Achieving some program objectives may require a teacher to implement different activities in different classes because students may have varying needs. Moreover, in our research, many teachers have told us that sometimes they need to complete the same activity several times (e.g., a relaxation technique) for students to fully understand it. Sources of activities are numerous. Many teachers, through years of experience, have collected their own effective activities for developing social competence and fostering a positive classroom climate. Successful activities can be shared through informal or formal communications, such as teacher support groups (see the Support for Teachers section in chap. 4) and online discussion groups. Finally, administrators can choose a formal curriculum to achieve some of the objectives, like those discussed later in this chapter. Having a formal curriculum for teachers to follow has the advantage of increasing program implementation.

3. *Providing knowledge about the desired behavior:* Knowledge is an important component of behavior change, yet alone it is of-

ten insufficient motivation to drive people to adopt new behaviors or abandon old ones. For example, consider how many things people do knowing that they are unhealthy or unsafe. To address bullying issues, teachers and administrators still need to ensure that students possess basic information about appropriate and inappropriate behaviors (e.g., how to recognize a bully, how to calm down, how to solve disputes cordially) and why such behaviors are suitable or unsuitable in specific situations.

4. *Supplying opportunities for reinforced practice:* To learn competent social skills, children need to practice them. Just as one cannot learn to swim by watching a video, children cannot learn appropriate social skills without opportunities to practice them. To start, administrators and teachers should provide students with nonthreatening environments in which to practice (e.g., one-on-one practice time with the teacher or class role-play). In addition, students will gain confidence in their new skills only through adult reinforcement and encouragement. As students become more comfortable with their new skill set, teachers can expand practice opportunities to different environments and diverse situations.

During our research, many teachers voiced concern about the generalization of new behaviors beyond the classroom. That is, many teachers worry that children are unable to transfer the skills learned in the classroom to other environments. Expanding practice opportunities beyond the classroom (e.g., playground, cafeteria, school bus, gym) will help address this concern. Sometimes applying skills learned in one setting and transferring those skills to another setting can be difficult even for adults; children have an even harder time generalizing specific skill sets. Although some students may perform superbly in an in-class role-play, they may stumble when trying to apply what they have learned once they exit the classroom. McGinnis and Goldstein (2003) offered the following suggestions to promote behavior transfer to new environments:

1. *Teach students the new skill over and over*. Provide students with the opportunity to practice the new behavior in different environments, assign related homework, provide feedback on learning progress, and abundantly reinforce the new behavior. What students learn in the classroom will not transfer to other areas of the school unless teachers, administrators, and staff make a special effort to help them practice the new behavior in those areas. Instruct students to use the skill. Provide the students with prompts to help them recognize when

it is appropriate to apply the new skill. Envision with students new situations in which they might need to use the new skill.

2. *Wean students from instruction.* As time progresses, teachers should provide helpful reminders to students that prompt them to use the skill, but only when students have not recognized that the situation is appropriate for using the skill.

3. *Provide students with novel situations.* Students need to practice new skills in new situations. For example, playing a cooperation game in the schoolyard rather than in the classroom can help students get prepared for an upcoming field trip. Likewise, having students work as a group on a large mural for the school during art class can help them practice conflict resolution skills and become acquainted with their classmates.

4. *Maintain a schoolwide plan.* Teachers and administrators need to expect and reinforce appropriate student behaviors throughout the school. Using a common conflict resolution model and demonstrating desired behaviors usually enhance students' learning.

A schoolwide program that provides support for change and that allows teachers the opportunity to implement an effective curriculum is likely to result in a reduction of bullying and an increase in positive social relationships in schools.

SELECTED PROGRAMS TO PREVENT AND REDUCE BULLYING AND AGGRESSION

Several programs have proved to be somewhat effective at reducing school bullying and aggression. The information we provide here is meant to serve as a convenient reference for educators but should not be construed as our endorsement of any particular program; in addition, the listing is neither extensive nor comprehensive. Rather, the programs reviewed are the ones with which we are familiar and that have some demonstrated level of efficacy. More detailed information on each program can be found on the Web sites provided. To address all of the topics discussed in chapters 4 and 5, educators may need to select more than one program or curriculum or may even need to develop an amalgam of programs to support their own strategies. In deciding whether to purchase or acquire a program, the following criteria will help educators in their selection processes:

1. *Goals of the school:* Depending on the breadth of a school administration's goals, the school needs to select one or more curricula. Administrators may decide to implement a program

that combines environmental and skill development strategies, such as changes in the school's discipline plan, training of faculty to teach a conflict resolution model, and implementing a curriculum to increase students' social skills.

2. *Evidence of success:* Administrators and educators should examine what kind of success a curriculum has achieved in other localities, as well as the school context in which the program was successful.

3. *Training:* Educators should examine whether the program was more successful when implemented by teachers or by outside researchers, keeping in mind that a program implemented by a skilled violence prevention specialist may not produce the same results when applied by untrained school personnel. However, violence prevention specialists are sometimes viewed as outsiders and, consequently, may lack the amount of acceptance teachers enjoy in their classrooms. Consideration should also be given to how much and what kind of training teachers and staff will need to successfully implement a program, as well as whether resources will be available to meet this training need.

4. *Instructional strategies:* If educators decide to implement a curriculum, they should determine whether the curriculum being considered has clear objectives and step-by-step procedures for implementation. The extent to which a curriculum is well organized and easy to implement can be gauged by how well the instructional activities match the program objectives, the number of exercises available to foster practice, the variety of activities to accommodate students with different learning styles, and the degree to which the curriculum engages students.

5. *Cultural relevance:* Before selecting a program, educators should assess whether the curriculum is relevant to the school's students. Also, educators should make sure that the program does not inadvertently promote a biased or stereotyped view of a particular group of students. Educators will need to assess whether the program requires modifications to make it culturally relevant.

6. *Cost:* Finally, administrators need to determine whether a program fits their budget. Is the curriculum, including books, additional teaching materials, student handouts, and training, affordable? How many additional staff members and additional staff training hours will be needed to implement the program?

Examples of Programs to Prevent and Reduce Bullying

From our experience with developing, selecting, and implementing different bullying prevention programs, including curricula, we believe that choosing a good curriculum is important but that rigorously implementing that curriculum is even more important. The programs discussed in the paragraphs that follow meet the criteria we have reviewed.

The Peaceful Schools Project and the Back Off Bully Program

The Peaceful Schools Project and the Back Off Bully Program are directed to Grades K through 5 (http://www.backoffbully.com/). The Peaceful Schools Project is a systemic intervention that allows schools to personalize the philosophy of the intervention while keeping an organized set of measurable principles and materials available in manuals. The Peaceful Schools project is a large-scale school change program to reduce aggression and create a positive school climate, whereas the Back Off Bully is a curriculum for reducing school bullying. Students and all adults in the school community are challenged to become helpful bystanders. The program includes a step-by-step teacher manual to teach the K–5 curriculum, a video for students and one for parents, artwork (e.g., posters, magnets, patches), measures to evaluate the extent of the problem, and a discipline manual. The program emphasizes creating an environment that encourages cooperation and avoids power struggles, highlighting effective problem solving and choice making (Twemlow et al., 2001).

Bully Busters

Bully Busters was developed for Grades K through 5 (Horne, Bartolomucci, & Newman-Carlson, 2003) and 6 through 8 (Newman, Horne, & Bartolomucci, 2000; http://www.bully-busters.com; www.researchpress.com). Two manuals, one for each group, provide a complete training for teachers and numerous activities for children. The program is designed to increase awareness about bullying and increase teachers' skills to prevent and reduce the problem. Research results show an increase in teachers' knowledge about bullying and effectiveness in handling bullying problems. Improved skills in preventing bullying were reflected in a reduction in disciplinary referrals to the office. (*Note:* An author of these manuals is also an author of the current text.)

Bullying Prevention Program

The Bullying Prevention Program, designed for students in Grades K through 12, works on a school, classroom, and individual level to deter bullying (http://www.colorado.edu/cspv/blueprints/model/programs/BPP.html). Developing class rules, having class meetings, and reinforcing positive behaviors are the key aspects of the Bully Prevention Program. Teachers, students, and parents work to improve peer relations and classroom climate. The Bullying Prevention Program has been successful in reducing new victimization incidents and has ameliorated bully and victim problems (Olweus, 1993b; Limber, 2004).

Bully Proofing

Developed for use with Grades K through 5 and 6 through 8, Bully Proofing provides several manuals and other teaching materials for reducing and preventing bullying (http://www.sopriswest.com). Information is available showing a reduction in bullying. A parent component is part of the program (Bonds & Stoker, 2000; Garrity, Jens, Porter, Sager, & Short-Camilli, 2004).

Target Bullying: Ecologically Based Prevention and Intervention for Schools

The Target Bullying program, for Grades 5 through 9, is designed to help school personnel first collect data on the bully–victim problem in the school and then use the data to make decisions about the potential effectiveness of intervention and prevention efforts that could be implemented in their school and community. Bullying behaviors are reduced when teachers, school personnel, students, and families are engaged and take ownership of prevention and intervention efforts. The program is described in *Bullying in American Schools: A Social–Ecological Perspective on Prevention and Intervention* (Espelage & Swearer, 2004; Swearer & Espelage, 2004).

University of Illinois School Bullying Taskforce

The University of Illinois School Bullying Taskforce, developed for Grades 2 through 12, assists school administrators, faculty, and staff in designing bullying prevention and intervention programs that are tailored to their school (a Web site is unavailable; contact espelage@uiuc.edu for more information). Surveys are administered to assess teacher and parent attitudes, peer pressure, and school climate. Students, faculty, and parents are asked to identify what types of bullying are occurring, where they are occurring, and how these behaviors are being maintained. After in-house data are collected, the program staff work closely with an advisory committee to tailor a program to fit the school's or community's needs (Espelage, 2004).

Examples of Programs to Prevent and Reduce Aggression

CASASTART

The National Center on Addiction and Substance Abuse (CASA) has created a program entitled Striving Together to Achieve Rewarding Tomorrows (START), targeted to Grades 3 through 8 (ages 8–13; http://www.modelprograms.samhsa.gov/pdfs/FactSheets/CASA.pdf). The CASASTART program is intended to prevent youths from engaging in substance abuse and delinquent behaviors. The program assembles motivated individuals from community-based organizations, the police force, and school districts to achieve its goals.

Good Behavior Game

The Good Behavior Game is a behavior management exercise for Grades 1 and 2 that is based on a system of positive rewards (http://www.bpp.jhu.edu). The manual describes how teachers can promote positive behaviors and deter aggression by dividing students into classroom groups and rewarding them for positive behaviors. After 1 year of implementation, teachers reported a decrease in aggressive behaviors in first-grade students (Embry, 2002; Ialongo, Poduska, Werthamer, & Kellam, 2001).

I Can Problem Solve

The I Can Problem Solve program, developed for Grades pre-K through 6, aids teachers in helping children to resolve conflicts peacefully (http://www.researchpress.com). Teachers incorporate pictures, role-playing, puppets, and group discussions into their skills training lessons. The program increases children's prosocial behaviors and problem-solving skills (Shure, 2001).

Life Skills Training

Developed for Grades 6 through 9, the Life Skills Training program is designed to build social skills, prevent violence, and prevent substance abuse by helping students identify their personal management skills (e.g., set goals, solve conflicts, reduce stress), their skills to avoid substance abuse, and their general social skills (http://www.lifeskillstraining.com/program.cfm). Students who develop skills in these three domains are less likely to engage in risky behaviors throughout adolescence (Botvin, Mahalic, & Grotpeter, 1998).

Linking the Interests of Families and Teachers

The 10-week Linking the Interests of Families and Teachers program, for students in Grades 1 through 5 and their parents, has three major components: classroom-based problem-solving and social skills training, playground-based behavior modification, and group-delivered parent training (http://www.colorado.edu/cspv/blueprints/promising/overview.html). The components address specific deficiencies in children's social skills (e.g., opposition, deviance, and social ineptitude), as well as deficiencies in adults' parenting practices (e.g., disciplining and monitoring). This intervention is effective in decreasing overall rates of aggression (Eddy, Reid, & Fetrow, 2000).

Peace Builders

Designed for use with Grades K through 5, Peace Builders seeks to change the characteristics within a school setting that trigger aggressive, hostile behavior (http://www.peacebuilders.com/). The program has been used in urban and suburban schools with children of mixed ethnicities. Research has found that this program improved the social competence of its students and buffered expected increases in their aggressive behavior (Flannery et al., 2003).

Positive Behavioral Interventions and Supports

This program, which is also called Positive Behavior Supports, was originally developed for special education programs in Grades K through 12, but it has been successfully used in regular school programs (http://www.pbis.org/schoolwide.htm). The program emphasizes the development of a positive school environment by promoting a systemwide intervention that contains components for the entire school (e.g., support for staff, data-based decision making, improved discipline system), for the individual classroom, and for students (e.g., social competence and academic achievement; Sugai & Horner, 2002).

Promoting Alternative Thinking Strategies

Promoting Alternative Thinking Strategies (PATHS) is a school-based intervention for Grades K to 5 designed to foster emotional competency in children (www.preventionscience.com). Teachers and paraprofessionals are trained to implement the program. PATHS is effective in improving social cognition, social and emotional competencies, and problem solving, as well as in reducing aggression and depression (Greenberg, Kusche, & Mihalic, 1998).

Responding in Peaceful and Positive Ways

The Responding in Peaceful and Positive Ways prevention program teaches violence prevention using behavioral and cognitive strategies to students in Grades 6 through 8 (http://www.modelprograms.samhsa.gov/pdfs/FactSheets/RiPP.pdf). The program encourages students to apply critical thinking skills to solve problems and manage their behavior. The program has shown some effectiveness in reducing student physical aggression (Meyer, Farrell, Northup, Kung, & Plybon, 2000).

Second Step

The Second Step program has an elementary school (from pre-K) and a middle school version (http://www.cfchildren.org/). The elementary school version teaches empathy, impulse control, and anger management and includes a 6-week parent education component. The middle school version includes a larger cognitive component to promote understanding of the violence problem. It also targets empathy, anger management, problem solving, and skills application. The program has shown some effectiveness in reducing student physical aggression (Grossman et al., 1997).

III

ADDRESSING THE PROBLEM: PERSISTENT BULLIES

8

PERSISTENT BULLYING: COUNSELING INTERVENTIONS

Things do not change; we change.
> —Henry David Thoreau, *Walden and Other Writings*

A few children continue to bully despite positive changes in the school environment and classroom; we label these children *persistent bullies*. Working with persistent bullies in individual or family counseling is not easy, because these children require interventions customized to their individual problems. This chapter delineates the foundation for developing an intervention for persistent bullies and describes individual counseling interventions. The first section discusses the importance of a comprehensive evaluation of the bullying problems. The second section examines the skills that counselors and other mental health workers must possess to successfully work with these children and their families, and the final section reviews successful interventions that school counselors can implement with individual bullies.

COMPREHENSIVE EVALUATION OF THE PROBLEM

Even in the best school environment—one in which the climate is positive and most children practice appropriate social skills—not all children develop peaceful and positive interpersonal relationships with their peers and their teachers. Persistent bullies continue their inappropriate or even violent behaviors for many reasons. Quite likely, persistent bullies have multiple risk factors (e.g., living with a dysfunctional family, mingling with delinquent peers, living in a high-crime neighborhood) and few protective factors (e.g., having a caring adult in their lives, belonging to a religious group that eschews aggression). As described in chapter 2, the sum of risk factors for violence mitigated by the sum of protective factors ultimately equates to a child's level of risk. When emotional problems, such as anxiety or depression, occur simultaneously (comorbidly) with behavioral problems, such as oppositional defiant disorders and conduct disorders, it is particularly important to understand the interaction of all these elements to develop a successful plan of action for persistent bullies. Regardless of why persistent bullies are not influenced by a caring schoolwide culture, it is necessary to help them change their behavior.

Counseling persistent bullies is generally beyond the purview of teachers. In most schools, persistent bullies are referred to the school counselor or school psychologist by the individual in charge of handling discipline problems or by the classroom teacher. The school counselor usually conducts a comprehensive evaluation of the child's problems, establishes a working alliance with the child, and develops a plan of action. In addition to counselors' leadership in evaluating bullying problems with an individual child, the feedback of other school personnel is relevant and helpful. For example, many schools have a Student Support Team (SST) composed of teachers, support staff, and sometimes parents that reviews students who are referred because of academic or behavioral problems. The goal of the SST is to identify roadblocks to the student's success and develop a remedial plan. The team brainstorms ideas, identifies the most promising strategies, develops a plan, and supervises its implementation. It is an evolving process where goals and strategies are developed and revised as needed. SSTs, as well as classroom teachers, frequently undertake a functional behavioral analysis to determine what is maintaining the inappropriate behavior and then develop a behavior intervention plan to decrease inappropriate behaviors and increase more appropriate ones. Data collection about where, when, why, and how the problems occur is essential to this process and, therefore, may require the involvement of many people. The functional behavioral analysis is often thought of as being part of the special education process, but it can be used for any student and at any grade level. Psychologists, social workers, family therapists, and other community mental health workers may also be engaged in working with persistent bullying behavior. They may facilitate the evaluation of the problem and the implementation of individual or family therapy in the school or the community. We use the term *counselor*, regardless of the professional degree, throughout this chapter.

As the first step in establishing an intervention program for persistent bullies, the counselor evaluates the nature, extent, and seriousness of the bullying behaviors. When bullying is not deterred or diminished by schoolwide reduction interventions, there is a strong possibility of the co-occurrence of bullying with other problems, such as depression, learning disabilities, family dysfunction, or addictions. To develop an intervention, counselors need to investigate the factors maintaining the behaviors. In addition to the child's assessment, a counselor must investigate the characteristics of the family and the community, including parental attitudes toward bullying, parental awareness of the problem, individual and family strengths, characteristics of the family environment, and features of the community and culture.

Assessing the Child

Seriousness of the Bullying

The first step in developing a program to help persistent bullies is to gather information about the specific behavior and its surrounding circumstances. How frequently does the bullying happen? Is it an ongoing behavior or a recent development? Is it verbal, physical, relational, or a combination of all these behaviors? Where does it happen (e.g., classroom, playground, bus, gym)? What has the school (or referring authority) done to solve the problem? What has the family done? What have been the outcomes of these steps? Because repeated bullying incidents at school generally result in students being referred to the school counselor or psychologist, the problem is likely to have been documented by school personnel. These records—the more detailed the better—can provide valuable input for evaluating the extent and nature of the problem. A thorough assessment will expose the magnitude and seriousness of the child's problem. If the family is asked to participate in the intervention, a detailed description of the problem will increase the family's awareness of, and commitment to, the intervention program.

Co-Occurring (Comorbid) Conditions

Bullying may not be an isolated problem. The literature on conduct disorders and oppositional defiant disorders indicates that aggressive behaviors are likely to coexist with other problems. For example, in one study more than 70% of children diagnosed with oppositional defiant disorder also had a comorbid condition (Simonoff et al., 1997). Another study reported that 39% of girls and 46% of boys diagnosed with oppositional defiant disorder also had other diagnoses such as depression, dysthymia, or anxiety. Hyperactivity and aggression were commonly linked (Maughan, Rowe, Messer, Goodman, & Meltzer, 2004). In addition, aggression was frequently found to occur concurrent with other problem behaviors, such as drug and alcohol use, tobacco use, early sexual activity, multiple sexual partners, and suicide attempts (Orpinas, Basen-Engquist, Grunbaum, & Parcel, 1995). Given that bullying is most often a behavioral manifestation of other underlying issues, the facilitator needs to address the whole spectrum of problems to identify the most effective intervention. Causality among problems, however, should not be assumed. For example, if a child is a bully and is also depressed, one cannot assume that bullying caused the depression or that depression caused the bullying. They may coexist independently, and each may require treatment.

Counselors have a range of methods and instruments available to gauge the extent of aggression and to identify co-occurring problems. The two most widely used behavioral ratings for children and adolescents are the Behavior Assessment System for Children (BASC; Reynolds & Kamphaus, 1992) and the Achenbach Child Behavior Checklist (CBCL; Achenbach, 1991). These instruments, when completed by multiple sources (e.g., student, teacher, parents), can be cross-referenced to provide information on multiple dimensions of the child's problem, identifying externalizing behaviors, including aggression and hyperactivity, and internalizing behaviors, such as depression and anxiety. These instruments also measure adaptive skills, such as study and social skills. An individual score from the BASC or the CBCL may be compared with national norms that are available by age, gender, and race and ethnicity.

Another widely used instrument is the Eyberg Child Behavior Inventory, which parents complete (Eyberg, 1992). More narrowly focused than either the BASC or the CBCL, it measures a child's specific aggressive behavior. The Sutter–Eyberg Student Behavior Inventory is a parallel instrument that teachers complete (Eyberg, 1992). Of course, observation of persistent bullies can provide insight into their aggressive behavior, the antecedents of that behavior, and its consequences. Therefore, observation should not be overlooked as an assessment tool. Behavioral observation systems, described in detail in McMahon and Wells's (1998) *Treatment of Childhood Disorders*, range from very basic to fairly sophisticated and may be used in classrooms, other areas of the school, and at home.

Factors That Maintain the Behaviors

For developing an intervention, it is fundamental to understand what maintains the behaviors. As discussed in chapter 1, aggression can be instrumental (i.e., aggressive behaviors used to obtain valued goods) or reactive (i.e., aggressive behaviors used to retaliate to a perceived or real offense). When bullying is instrumental, the bullying is maintained because it pays off: Bullies gain access to the playground equipment more often; bullies take lunch money and have more cash to spend; and bullies tease other children and get recognition and attention from their peers. For these bullies, the personal satisfaction and other social and tangible payoffs obtained from bullying may be more important than the occasional negative response from a teacher. Clearly, empathy for their victims is not the bullies' strong suit, and their inappropriate behaviors are reinforced when they learn that the rewards of bullying outweigh the risk of the occasional punishment. To stop this type of persistent bullying, adults who play a significant role in bullies' lives must make the payoffs more costly and the alternatives more attractive.

Persistent reactive bullying generally occurs because the children involved lack the required social skills to manage situations in a more effective way. Because bullies generally lack self-control, they react aggressively to even minor offenses, perceived or real, such as a mean look or a passing comment. Some of these children live in such disorganized family environments and are so angered by the way they are treated at home that regular schoolwide interventions may be insufficient to prevent their reactive bullying. Four years ago, after implementing a schoolwide bullying intervention in an elementary school, we asked teachers how effective they thought the program was. Most teachers commented that the program effectively reduced students' aggressive behaviors, with the exception of one or two students in each class (Orpinas, Horne, & Staniszewski, 2003). Accompanied by the teachers, we interviewed the families of these children. In short, their family environments were chaotic. Children coming from unorganized family environments may benefit from the family programs we discuss in chapter 9.

Meaningful intervention requires an understanding of the motivations behind children's problem behavior. Adler defined four motivations underlying children's misbehaviors: attention, power, revenge, and inadequacy (Dagley, 2000). Bullies may harass their peers to gain attention, and frequently harassing others is the only way they know how to gain this attention. Normally, this is a mild form of bullying and one that may be easily addressed by helping the child find other ways of gaining recognition (Box 8.1 describes the example of John, an attention-seeking bully). However, a deeper need than attention may drive bullying, and Adler defined this second need as power. Many children engage in negative behaviors to be influential over their peers and over adults. Most schools provide developmentally appropriate activities, such as sports and academic achievement, to help students develop a positive sense of power and influence. Bullies, however, who may experience a more intense need for power or may lack the ability to achieve power in positive ways, may act cruelly and aggressively to validate their own power (Box 8.2 describes the example of Roberto, a power-seeking bully).

BOX 8.1. JOHN: MOTIVATED BY ATTENTION

When the school year began, John seemed fine, but as the weeks went by he began to act more and more aggressively in the classroom. In particular, he began to bother two quiet, nonaggressive classmates. He would purposely bump into these children, and if they fell over or stumbled, he would tease them about being spastic and dumb. Other children in the classroom would smile and sometimes even laugh at John's antics.

His teacher, noting that his inappropriate behaviors were escalating, referred John to the school counselor. During an interview, the counselor learned that John had felt very confident at the beginning of the school year, but as the school year progressed, he had felt more and more inadequate. Other students were learning faster than he was, and several of the other students seemed to be much more popular. The counselor met with the teacher, and together they identified several ways that John might take a stronger leadership role in class, including taking responsibility for getting sports equipment out on the playground and assisting with lunchroom duties such as turning the daily count in to the cafeteria. He also was designated "team leader" of his reading group.

At the same time, the teacher and John developed a "private" signaling system to alert John that he was out of order and needed to rein in his behavior. Maintaining the leadership role that the teacher had assigned to him was contingent on his self-control. Further, the teacher met with John's parents and presented them with information as to how they could help John catch up academically with the other students in school. John's inappropriate behaviors quickly decreased, and as he gained recognition for his classroom leadership, he stopped bullying. He still had a strong need for attention and recognition, but he found ways of meeting that need through proactive channels.

BOX. 8.2. ROBERTO: MOTIVATED BY POWER

Roberto was new to the school, and within the first few days he had fought with several other students. When his teacher attempted to identify the cause of these fights, Roberto's opponents complained that he was very bossy, even though he was a newcomer. Roberto tried to tell everyone what to do, saying he was "the king" and better than any of the other students. When students would defy Roberto, he would become very angry and taunt them, continuing the conflict until they either gave in to Roberto or a fight ensued. When the counselor met with Roberto to talk about the situation, he said that in his neighborhood the "kings" were in charge and that he intended to be "king" of his classroom.

A consultation with his parents confirmed Roberto's assertion that neighborhood residents were perceived as either leaders or lackeys who answered to the leader. Roberto's parents clearly wanted their son to be in charge. The counselor explained to

Roberto's parents that although the leader–lackey model may work in their neighborhood, it was unacceptable in the classroom. The school counselor offered to help Roberto demonstrate his power in other ways, including sports and other classroom activities. Roberto continued to have an explosive temper when he was challenged, but by working with the counselor, he came to understand that sometimes power is demonstrated by self-control rather than by losing control.

Although seeking attention and power are clearly forms of instrumental aggression, revenge, which Adler identified as the third goal motivation for misbehavior, is clearly a form of reactive aggression. Students may seek revenge for any offense, real or perceived (e.g., treated unfairly, humiliated in front of peers, called a derogatory name), by peers, teachers, or administrators. Revenge has frequently been cited by the media, and a study conducted by the U.S. Secret Service identified it as the motive behind school shootings (Vossekuil, Fein, Reddy, Borum, & Modzeleski, 2002). In interviews with elementary and middle school bullies conducted during the past 10 years, they often express their anger, citing an "unfair" situation and claiming a right to respond to it with aggression (Box 8.3 describes the example of Yancy, a revenge-seeking bully).

BOX. 8.3. YANCY: MOTIVATED BY REVENGE

Yancy was somewhat larger than the other girls in her sixth-grade class, and she did not do as well academically as the other students. Learning activities, particularly reading, were difficult for her, and she was clearly one of the slower readers in the class. Although no student made direct comments, the other girls would occasionally roll their eyes or sigh when Yancy was called on to read aloud in class.

Several of the higher achieving students in class began to complain that things were happening to their school supplies: Their pencils were broken, papers were torn, and other supplies were damaged. The teacher suspected Yancy, because she was often seen near the desks where vandalism had occurred. When the teacher asked her about the damage, Yancy denied any involvement. Later, when several of the girls confronted her, Yancy said, "You just better watch out, 'cause more than pencils are going to get broken . . . Other things might get broken too, like your faces . . . You think you're so damned smart." The negative environment persisted for several days.

The teacher informed the school counselor about the confrontation between Yancy and the other girls. During a counseling session, Yancy again denied any involvement in the vandalism incidents but reiterated that the other girls deserved their misfortune. When the counselor inquired what that meant, Yancy told the counselor that the girls seemed so confident and sure of themselves and acted as if they could do no wrong, so it "served them right" to have their supplies damaged. The counselor reflected that it must be painful to see the other girls getting all the breaks—learning easily, having good supplies, making friends easily—and that sometimes Yancy must want to make them suffer for their good fortune. Yancy immediately confirmed the counselor's observations but admitted that she really did not want bad things to happen to the girls.

Over the next few weeks, the counselor developed a plan, in collaboration with the teacher, to involve Yancy in cooperative learning activities with several of the other girls in the classroom, in which she was responsible for the distribution of materials and supplies for the learning activities each morning. At the same time, the teacher gave Yancy a leadership role in the classroom. In addition, she was put in charge of activities in the common area, such as helping with the school lunch. The counselor also set up weekly meetings with Yancy and began to work with her on developing more effective social skills. Yancy gradually learned to work with the other girls in less competitive, more cooperative ways. Finally, a mentor was asked to come to Yancy's afternoon school program to help her improve her reading skills.

Adler's fourth motive underlying misbehavior is inadequacy or inferiority. Adler explained that some children act as if they believe they are inadequate or unable to develop appropriate social and problem-solving skills. Some of these children may not develop an overt aggressive problem behavior, instead simply giving up on themselves and wanting to be left alone. Others "hide" behind very disruptive—and sometimes even bizarre—behaviors that deflect attention from their perceived inadequacy. If they act aggressively, they whine that the situation is not fair because others are more popular or skilled then they are. These students' inadequacies afford them special privileges or opportunities because adults and children will eventually "write them off," maintain low expectations of them, and allow them to get away with behaviors that may be disruptive and problematic for other children. The low expectations by teachers and peers confirm the negative self-image that these children hold about themselves. In a very dysfunctional way, these children excuse themselves from the responsibility of improving

BOX 8.4. RUTH: MOTIVATED BY INADEQUACY

Ruth had never been a major troublemaker but had nonetheless been distracted in class. She had had difficulty with her work and had often sat idly without attempting to finish her assignments. Recently, however, she had begun to pester others, particularly two other girls who sat near her, and the pestering was escalating. The other two girls began to complain to the teacher, whose efforts to cajole Ruth into doing her assignment would be met with Ruth's grumbling that the work was too hard and impossible to master. Only when the teacher stood beside her and walked her through the activities did Ruth manage to accomplish anything. Ruth's harassment of the other two girls began whenever the teacher's attention was required elsewhere in the room. The school psychologist recommended several strategies to Ruth's teacher:

- Use encouraging statements with Ruth to persuade her to try harder, to move ahead, and to take ownership of her work. Statements like "Ruth, you've had some difficulty, but continue trying; stick with it for the next 10 minutes. Then I'll come over and help you some. I'll be with you when I've seen you try for 10 minutes."
- Provide opportunities for collaborative learning. Evaluate whether the other two girls can be enlisted to work with Ruth. It is evident that Ruth wanted attention from the other two students but gained it inappropriately. Legitimate interaction among the three girls could help Ruth learn more suitable ways of behaving in the presence of other children.
- Provide negative consequences (e.g., such as after-school assignments) when Ruth fails to complete her class work. The after-school activities may include finishing incomplete assignments and academic tutoring. Care must be taken, though, that the after-school activity does not become reinforcing, which can lead Ruth to cause problems to spend time alone with the teacher after school.

their behavior by claiming that they are not capable of learning effective social skills (Box 8.4 describes the example of Ruth, a bully motivated by inadequacy).

In each of the examples presented in Boxes 8.1 to 8.4—John, Roberto, Yancy, and Ruth—the inappropriate behaviors highlighted were goal oriented and determined by the emotional needs of each child. These cases are representative of children who do not respond well to the universal programs for bullying and for whom a more targeted or specific program must be implemented.

Assessing the Family and Community

Strengths

Intervention measures to eliminate bullying behaviors may capitalize on existing individual strengths (e.g., athletic skills) and family strengths (e.g., the security of an extended family). Whatever strengths bullies possess need to be explored and encouraged. Indeed, many bullies demonstrate skills, such as leadership, that need only to be redirected into positive actions.

Attitudes Toward and Awareness of Bullying

Parents' perceptions of bullying are especially germane to assessing a child's behavior problems and determining whether an individual or a family intervention is warranted. Do they believe bullying is wrong? Or do they accept bullying as normal and appropriate? These parental attitudes can strongly influence bullies' behavior. In family therapy programs, although the child is the targeted client, the child's anticipated change occurs through modifying the parents' behaviors and attitudes. Parenting styles need to be addressed early in family counseling sessions, because parental disposition will influence how sincerely the family engages in the change process. Motivated parents—those who recognize a problem when they see the child interacting inappropriately with siblings or other children—welcome intervention, because they have already resolved to improve their child's behavior.

When parents blame their child's bullying problem on someone else, such as the teacher, and reject the notion of family influence, they are less inclined to endorse family participation in any intervention program. Often parents who do not perceive the bullying behavior as problematic define it as typical children's behavior, expressing their beliefs in such terms as "boys will be boys" or "that's just how kids are." Despite displeasure with their child's behavior, they do not recognize it as being unusual or extreme. Indeed, they may become aware of the problem only after a teacher or family member has identified the behavior as being more aggressive than normal. One child with whom we worked put urine in a bottle and tricked a first grader into drinking it, saying it was a "new drink." The parents of the bully excused his behavior as typical "kids' stuff." Some parents sanction bullying by encouraging their child to fight back whenever they are threatened or insulted. Failing to understand their parents' motives, bullies may perceive such parental advice as a blessing for their behaviors. They may not realize that their parents' counsel to "fight back" may be an unacknowledged admission of their inability to find any other means to protect their child from being a victim.

Taking care not to denigrate parental motives and to explain parents' approval to fight back in protective terms, counselors working with bullying children must clearly state that fighting is *not* an option at school.

Family Environment

Whether the counselor is working with the individual child or the whole family, he or she needs to investigate and understand the family environment. If the family is not functioning well as a result of drug or alcohol abuse, depression, marital conflict, or unemployment, interventions that focus only on bullying behaviors are likely to be unsuccessful. Given such stress factors, parents may be too debilitated to effectively engage in a parenting program or support the child's new behaviors. In addition to working with the child, the counselor may need to work with the parents or refer them to an appropriate community agency for assistance.

Community and Culture

Bullies come from a wide range of cultural backgrounds and live in a variety of different communities that may influence how their aggressive behaviors are learned and maintained. The level of support for bullying and the general acceptance of violence vary greatly among communities. Although bullies come from all backgrounds, children living in communities with high rates of neighborhood crime, gangs, and drug dealing face additional risk factors when compared with children living in low-crime neighborhoods. Some children who have bullying problems in school are those who are marginalized by society. Struggling economically and emotionally, they may feel a cultural clash with the school and may hold an "us against the world" attitude learned from their parents. The counseling program needs to be sensitive to and address the multiple and varying child, family, school, and community factors. The counselor, within his or her realm of influence, needs to understand the families' plight and to take steps to alleviate their problems.

FACILITATOR SKILLS

All adults who work with bullies need a set of skills to achieve some measure of success in modifying these children's behaviors. Teachers need to be able to engage students in a respectful and yet authoritative manner. Administrators need to demonstrate care for students while establishing clear school guidelines. The particular skills that counselors and other mental health professionals need to be effective in working with persistent bullies are divided into three sets: skills for designing an intervention with a solution-focused approach, skills for connecting with the bully, and skills for working with the family of the bully.

EXHIBIT 8.1
Comparison of the Problem-Focused Approach and the Solution-Focused Approach

Problem-focused approach	Solution-focused approach
What is wrong?	How can I solve the problem?
Why is the child aggressive?	How can I help the child be less aggressive?
What skills are not present?	How can I help the child develop necessary skills?
What did the child do? When? Where? Why?	How can we find a solution to prevent a similar situation from happening again?

Skills for Designing an Intervention With a Solution-Focused Approach

The comprehensive evaluation of a bullying problem should lead to the development of an intervention focused on the solution rather than the problem (Exhibit 8.1). Frequently, bullies who are referred, tested, and diagnosed by professional counselors are subsequently left on their own, failing to receive the help they need. The solution-focused approach is designed to avoid such shortcomings by

- shifting the focus from what a child cannot do to what he or she can do;
- focusing on what will work to resolve the problem, instead of on the problem itself;
- creating change by altering beliefs about and expectations for the child;
- generating hope, a sense of control, and a focus on positive strategies for change; and
- providing models of change by focusing on what has worked in the past.

The solution-focused approach is described in detail in *Solution-Focused Counseling in Middle and High Schools* (Murphy, 1997). This book examines theoretical constructs and empirical support for using a solution-focused approach with students and suggests strategies for using the approach. Murphy presented specific examples of working with children with problems of aggression and bullying and outlined the steps one should follow when using solution-focused counseling. The solution-focused model is a helpful resource for counselors and other mental health professionals who address bullying and victimization problems. It is the recommended approach for all interventions described in this book and is particularly relevant when working with persistent bullies who do not respond well to universal interventions.

Skills for Connecting With Children Who Bully

It is essential that the counselor be able to connect with the bully, in essence establishing a therapeutic alliance. Because failure to forge a positive connection greatly reduces the likelihood of change in bullies' behavior, we highlight five skills that are particularly important:

1. *Establishing an invitational approach:* Frequently, bullies are not invited to participate in the process of counseling; they are ordered, demanded, or forced. When they are required to attend, the relationship automatically begins as confrontational or adversarial, evoking belligerence and defensiveness. The invitational model provides the opportunity to have an open dialogue, illustrated in the following exchange, about the problem:

   Counselor: Mike, I'd like you to come and talk with me.

   Mike: What did I do now? What are you going to fuss about?

   Counselor: There have been some problems in your classroom, in the hallway, and even in the bathroom. I'd like to talk with you about what's going on, to get your sense of what's behind the problems. Perhaps you and I might work together to find some way of resolving these problems. Think you can help with that?

   Mike: Well . . . I guess I can help you.

2. *Showing respect and dignity:* Generally, persistent bullies are used to being in trouble and expect to be treated ignominiously, without positive regard. It is important that they be afforded respect and dignity. When in doubt about whether the adult's behavior is respectful, ask, "Would I treat a guest in my family—an adult guest—the way I am treating this child?" The following exchange exemplifies respectful communication:

   Mike: So, what are you going to yell at me about today? I'm so tired of you people being on my case.

   Counselor: I know what you mean. I wouldn't like to have someone yelling or getting on my case. I don't intend to do any yelling, and as for being on your case, I'd rather we talk about what's been happening between you and Gene and see if we can't find some way of resolving the conflict that's going on. I respect you and your ability to find a different way of dealing with problems. Let's talk about how you have seen the conflict, and I'd like your thoughts on what we might do about it.

3. *Being honest and direct:* Bullies are adept at identifying insincerity and become very suspicious when people are not can-

did with them. The counselor needs to identify a problem and state what is necessary to resolve the problem without moving into blame and condemnation.

> *Mike:* You counselors always act nice, but I know you're just trying to jerk me around to get me to do what you want.

> *Counselor:* You are right, I do want to be nice to you, just as I want you to be nice to me. I also want us to find some ways of changing what has been happening, because it cannot continue. We will not allow one student to bully and threaten another student in our school. I want you to be happy here, but those are the rules: Safety comes first. Let's talk about what can be done to resolve the problem, rather than sit and talk about whether I'm trying to blame or trick you. My goals are clear: First, the bullying has to stop; then, we can find other ways for you to accomplish your goals, perhaps by taking on a different leadership role, whatever will work for you without harming others.

4. *Being understanding, but not approving:* The counselor needs to understand the bully's perception of the problem but, at the same time, avoid condoning or giving the impression of approving the inappropriate behavior.

> *Mike:* Well, it really isn't my fault that Gene's an idiot. He's so stupid, I can't help but tease him. He even asks for it, with that dumb laugh of his.

> *Counselor:* Mike, I understand that you find Gene frustrating and that his laugh irritates you, but I don't accept that teasing and hitting Gene is the solution. We need to find a different way for you to manage your anger and a way for you to tolerate other students, even if you don't like them.

5. *Accepting that the bully and others associated with the bully, such as parents and teachers, are doing the best they can given their circumstances:* Counselors must avoid making judgments. They must operate on the basic belief that bullies and others involved in the offensive behavior do the best they can given their circumstances and that, if possible, they would have done better. Counselors may need to accept the premise that bullies may simply lack the problem-solving, decision-making, or self-control skills to be more adaptive than they are. The following dialogue and Box 8.5 exemplify this point.

Mike: You're just sticking up for the goofball. I can't help it if he drives me crazy.

Counselor: No, that's not accurate. I understand that he drives you crazy, and I think that you are doing the best you can right now to deal with Gene, but what you've been doing isn't working. The good news is that other things can be done. My goal is to spend some time helping you identify new ways of getting along with Gene and other people, ways you haven't been able to use because you didn't know about them. Mike, I don't think you are a mean person; I think you have been doing the best you can, but that hasn't been good enough because you've hurt Gene. We'll go over some things you can do instead.

BOX 8.5. *EXPECT THAT PEOPLE DO THE BEST THEY CAN, GIVEN THEIR CIRCUMSTANCES*

As a new counselor in a mental health agency, Andrew was assigned to work with a family, but he was ill prepared to address their situation. When the family's son refused to obey the father's directive, the father became so angry that he grabbed the first thing at hand (in this case, a frying pan in the kitchen) and began to hit the boy. The boy required hospitalization, and the father was arrested for child abuse. Andrew scheduled a meeting to discuss whether it would be possible for the family to reunite and to determine whether the father was even fit to parent.

The counselor expected to feel nothing but contempt for the father, but during the interview Andrew realized that he was remorseful and was seeking forgiveness. The father had no record of violent behavior in his past, and when he elaborated on a set of mitigating circumstances—he had been physically ill with the flu, he had recently lost his job, a parent was dying of cancer, and he had had a bitter argument with his wife just before his argument with his son—his anger was more understandable. He said, "I just reacted . . . I just didn't think right."

Although no circumstances can excuse such behavior, counselors need to recognize that numerous extenuating circumstances may surround an aggressive or inappropriate behavior. Frequently, counselors must work with people who are doing the very best they can under a variety of difficult economic, social, or familial stressors. Counselors should strive to help these individuals change their circumstances if possible or develop more adaptive stress management techniques.

Several resources are available to further understand and develop these skills. Hazler (1996) described how counselors can be invitational by establishing a therapeutic relationship with bullies, while still maintaining a focus on the importance of changing the problem. Purkey and Schmidt (1996) also provided an extensive discussion of how counselors may develop an invitational approach to working with difficult children. For mental health workers inexperienced in establishing therapeutic relationships, Hill (2001) edited an excellent book on developing therapeutic skills.

SCHOOL COUNSELING FOR PERSISTENT BULLYING

The foundation of counselors' work with persistent bullies—the comprehensive assessment of the problem and the facilitation skills—has been described in the previous two sections. In addition, intervention programs targeted at persistent bullies will be more effective if the school has developed a positive school climate and operates with these three tenets in mind: All children can learn, all people in the school community should be treated with respect and dignity, and no aggressive behaviors are acceptable at school. These beliefs, as well as the positive school climate, were described in chapter 4. It is unreasonable to expect success with any individual or group therapy program if the school has a dysfunctional emotional climate, poor leadership, and little commitment to growth and learning. This section examines what works and what does not work in school counseling, provides two examples of counseling programs for bullies, and discusses the role of peer support in bullying prevention.

School Counseling: What Works? What Doesn't?

The process of evaluating the success of school counseling is not simple. School counselors' multiple responsibilities include performing administrative duties, teaching bullying prevention lessons to classes of students, and intervening with the most difficult children at the school. They address a wide spectrum of issues: They help children overcome bullying problems, avoid use of illegal drugs, cope with stress and bereavement, make career decisions, and more. Counselors also may provide training for parents, teachers, and administrators. Counseling sessions can take on a variety of configurations, including the standard practice of one-on-one interventions, large group counseling, family therapy, and self-help training.

It is regrettable that the few counseling and other therapeutic school-based interventions for children that have been evaluated have had mixed reviews. Wilson, Gottfredson, and Najaka (2001), in a review of 165 school-based prevention studies, concluded that counseling in general had a negative effect. However, the authors indicated that individual interventions using cognitive and behavioral strategies did have a positive effect. When counseling was used to promote self-control and social competence, it was consistently successful. Similar results were described in the report of the Surgeon General (U.S. Department of Health and Human Services, 2001) on youth violence, based on the meta-analyses conducted by Lipsey and Wilson (1998) and Andrews et al. (1990).

In general, research indicates that neither individual nor group counseling is effective when it is used as amorphous "talk therapy" and when it does not focus on the development of skills. Group counseling of bullies or aggressive children is not recommended either, because increasing contact with deviant peers may lead to an escalation or reinforcement of aggressive behaviors (Dishion, McCord, & Poulin, 1999). When used as part of a bullying prevention program, group counseling should be conducted with mixed groups of aggressive and nonaggressive children. On the basis of these studies and our own experience working with counselors, we propose the following components as most efficacious in school counseling:

1. *Comprehensive evaluation:* Before beginning the selection of an intervention, the counselor must conduct a thorough evaluation of the nature, background, causes, and influences of the persistent bully to identify which strategies are likely to be most effective at reducing or eliminating bullying.

2. *Skills development:* Interventions with a strong skills development orientation are more likely to be successful. Recommended skills, similar to those discussed in chapter 5, include problem solving, decision making, moral reasoning, empathy, and anger management. To help students master these new skills, counselors may use many social learning strategies, including giving verbal instructions and performance feedback, reinforcing the practice of the skills, teaching self-monitoring, shaping complex behaviors, and modeling new behaviors.

3. *Behavior management:* A number of strategies can be used to help the child manage specific aggressive behaviors. Counselors need to remove whatever maintains the behavior and help the child satisfy his or her needs in a constructive way.

4. *Multimodal approach:* Because the emphasis is on skills development and behavior management, interventions in which parents and teachers participate are more likely to yield positive results. These adults play an important role in helping the child apply the new skills and reinforcing the child's positive behaviors.

5. *Support for academic development:* Reducing academic failure not only fulfills the educational mission of the school by rais-

ing students' level of scholastic achievement; it is also an important strategy to reduce aggression. If a child who has bullying tendencies progresses academically, the child's self-esteem improves, and the likelihood of future aggressive behaviors is reduced.

Finally, the use of a solution-focused approach and the ability to develop an invitational, positive relationship with bullying children should be fundamental components of any intervention efforts if difficult children are expected to alter their behavior. Children cannot be mandated to change. In a positive relationship, they are more likely to cooperate and reap the benefits of the program.

Examples of Counseling Programs for Persistent Bullying

Despite the pervasiveness of bullying problems in schools, the number of counseling programs that have been developed to specifically address persistent bullying is relatively small. We highlight two of them—Aggression Replacement Therapy and Promoting Issues in Common. Both programs emphasize skill development, a recommended and effective strategy (Wilson et al., 2001).

Aggression Replacement Therapy

Goldstein and his colleagues have worked for several decades on reducing aggression among children and adolescents. His group has developed an extensive intervention program called Aggression Replacement Training (ART; Goldstein, Glick, & Gibbs, 1998), which can be useful for hard-to-change bullies. The program addresses several aspects of the student component of the School Social Competence Development and Bullying Prevention Model (see Figure 5.1). Goldstein and colleagues contended that anger is an overt behavior that children and adolescents use because they lack prosocial abilities. The emotional anger they experience is influenced by the cognitive misperceptions these youths hold of the world, and it prompts their inappropriate bullying behaviors. Thus, according to Goldstein's group, aggressive behavior is an interaction of behavioral, cognitive, and emotional experiences. To address these components, they have introduced three levels of intervention—social skills training (named *skillstreaming*), anger management, and moral reasoning. All have been incorporated into an overarching model for aggression control and reduction, the ART.

The ART model posits that all aggressive behavior, whether in school or elsewhere, is a function of both internal and external influences. Counselors must address these influences to effectively reduce the problem behavior. At the external level, a number of factors contribute to aggression (similar to the risk factors presented in chap. 2), including peers, parents, neighborhood, economic status, and media messages. At the internal level, the ART model identifies aggressive children as lacking interpersonal and cognitive problem-solving skills, as displaying anger control problems, as relying on aggression to resolve most of their conflicts, as operating at a low level of moral reasoning, and as exhibiting little or no evidence of personal ethics.

Primarily, the ART model is offered as a group psychoeducational counseling intervention rather than as group counseling. In other words, it is most often used as a classroom behavioral skills training program. ART's psychoeducational group model is the preferred delivery approach because it uses the group to train and reinforce new behaviors. By being in a group of students with a wide range of skills, aggressive students may learn from more skilled children, receive support for positive behaviors, role-play new behaviors, and be challenged to change their irresponsible behaviors. This group model follows very specific skills-building exercises, making it very different from unstructured counseling groups.

The ART intervention is planned to take as long as necessary, but a minimum of 10 weeks is recommended. The sessions, which generally last 45 to 60 minutes, are offered three times a week. Each of the three sessions has a different focus: skills development, anger control, and moral development. ART can also be conducted as one-on-one training with individual students who do not function well in groups. When the skills are taught to individuals without the group support, they lose the opportunity to role-play and interact with peers, but the counselor may compensate for this loss by participating in role-plays himself or herself.

The social skills component—or skillstreaming—of the ART model includes 50 prosocial skills, such as making a complaint, preparing for a difficult conversation, dealing with someone else's anger, and avoiding fights. Teaching manuals have been developed for preschoolers, elementary-age students, and adolescents (Goldstein, McGinnis, Sprafkin, Gershaw, & Klein, 1997; McGinnis & Goldstein, 2003). To introduce a skill, the facilitator first demonstrates how to execute it effectively; in other words, the counselor walks his or her audience through the skill using positive role modeling. Each skill is demonstrated step-by-step. It is very important that all group members clearly understand how the behavior is performed and why it is important. Next, to enhance skill proficiency, students practice the new skill (by role-playing). In the group, each member receives feedback, encouragement, and supportive criticism. Each group member is afforded the opportunity to continue practicing until he or she correctly demonstrates the skill (positive performance feedback). Next, to facilitate the transfer of knowledge to new environments, the facilitator must work with students to practice the skills as though they were in different settings (e.g., classroom, cafeteria, home, or shopping center). Finally, the students evaluate how successful they have been at applying their newly learned prosocial skills.

The anger control component is based on a long line of research studies that examine effective methods for managing anger, beginning with the work of Novaco (1975), building on the stress inoculation training conducted by Meichenbaum (1977), and adapting the work of Feindler and Ecton (1986). During these sessions, students learn self-control skills and calming methods. The facilitator helps students become aware of what triggers their anger and how their body responds to those cues. Students practice strategies to reduce anger, such as deep breathing, counting backward, or developing positive images that will compete with the negative stimuli. Students also learn cognitive strategies to reduce anger. These include evaluating the consequences of anger, using self-reinforcing statements designed to reduce anger, and reinterpreting the cues to be less negative.

The third component, moral development training, evolved from the work of Kohlberg (1984). He found that group discussions of moral dilemmas advanced all members of the group to the level of the highest performing person. During the past two decades, as the model evolved to be more inclusive of diversity and gender, it has proved to be an effective intervention for reducing antisocial behavior that normally would have required school disciplinary actions or police contacts (Arbuthnot & Faust, 1981).

The ART program's solid theoretical background, balanced by the years of practical trial-and-error experience of its developers, has had some evaluation (Goldstein et al., 1998). In the short-term, skillstreaming and anger control training are effective in reducing aggression; research studies have not been able to demonstrate comparable long-term effects. Evaluations of moral reasoning training have indicated modified moral values but have not verified that changes in moral values translate into improved ethical behavior. The studies do confirm, however, that the combination of all three components of ART produces a cumulative impact on bullies. It reduces their aggression while concurrently improving their behavioral skills, emotional control, and moral reasoning. Although the authors have applied the program in youth detention centers, mental health facilities, and schools, the most positive changes have occurred in school settings.

Promoting Issues in Common

Hazler's (1996) Promoting Issues in Common (PIC) program was developed specifically for counselors working one-on-one with bullies and victims. The counseling process is implemented in three stages. In the first stage, students involved in a conflict are referred to a counselor. In a safe, comforting environment, they share their perceptions of the problem with the counselor, who listens to everyone's view of the event without attempting to identify who is at fault or assign blame. This delay in passing judgment and assigning blame lays the groundwork for a trusting and supportive relationship between the counselor and the students. In the process, the counselor models how to listen, to be empathic, and to remain open to various interpretations of an event. In this first stage, the counselor also demands that the bullies stop their behavior.

During the second stage of PIC, the counselor consults with the bully and the victim individually to examine prior relationships between the two. During these preliminary sessions, the counselor determines whether joint or separate counseling is the best strategy to use. During the individual meeting, the counselor also assesses the extent of other problems each student might have and begins to address some of the individual concerns. As part of the individual work, the counselor reflects on the problem and tries to help each member understand the other's point of view.

In the third stage of PIC, if the counselor determines that the bully and the victim may be able to work together, joint counseling is scheduled. Once joint counseling sessions begin, counseling efforts are geared to promoting a mutual understanding of the incident that prompted the referral and of the perceptions of one another's behavioral motivations. Hazler (1996) did not promote any specific techniques but instead indicated that interventions should arise from the interactions between the bully and the victim. Most school counselors would be able to adapt the PIC model to meet their counseling needs.

In a review of counseling programs to reduce bullying, Greene (2003) also mentioned, in addition to PIC, the Shared Concern method (Pikas, 2002) and the No Blame Approach (Maines & Robinson, 1992). None of these three methods are comprehensive, nor do they actively engage teachers or parents. Furthermore, none have reported evaluations of their effectiveness (Greene, 2003).

Peer Support

Frequently organized and supervised by counselors, peer support strategies may include a variety of possibilities, such as peer counseling, peer mentoring, and peer leaders. Peer programs involve having a school adult— generally, a counselor or teacher—organize and offer specific groups, such as peer mediation. In the peer mediation training, the counselor coaches students in basic mediation skills, including listening for content and affect, paying attention to both sides of a story, understanding the conflict, and following problem-solving steps with peers who are in conflict. Unfortunately, most of the evaluations of peer-led bullying prevention programs have shown that they are ineffective at reducing youth violence. The Surgeon General's report on youth violence specifically discouraged the use of peer counseling, peer mediation, and peer leaders, concluding that these strategies may cause harm. Adult-led programs are generally more effective than student-led programs (U.S. Department of Health and Human Services, 2001). A major concern about peer-led bullying prevention programs is that they allow peers to have a very strong influence over classmates and entrust participants with confidential information that they may be ill prepared to handle. Usually, the responsibilities concomitant with confidential information should be reserved for adult professionals (Ross, 2003). Implementing peer-led programs can be cumbersome, another concern for counselors and administrators. Some of the peer counseling programs require extensive training—up to 45 hours— and ongoing supervision provided by an adult counselor (Carr, 1988). The training is not easy; it may include a wide array of topics such as personal growth, appreciating diversity, self-assessment, and counseling skills (Robinson, Morrow, Kigin, & Lindeman, 1991). Finally, practical implementation issues may complicate peer programs. Peer-led curricula require an extensive amount of adult monitoring, and the peers may need to miss class to perform their duties.

To counterbalance criticism of peer-led programs, Naylor and Cowie (1999) conducted an extensive evaluation of peer support systems in secondary schools and colleges in England. They concluded that peer support systems did reduce the negative effect of bullying on victims and helped to create a school climate in which students felt that others cared for them. They also reported that children and adolescents often perceived peer supporters as having more relevant experiences, being more trustworthy, and being more easily available than adults (Cowie, 1999).

To conclude, we stress that changing persistent bullying is difficult and requires a commitment to solve the problem, for aggressive behavior escalates when not addressed. A prime focus of counselors' work should be to stop and reduce bullying. To achieve this goal, counselors should enlist the cooperation of different members of the school community. The student support team is an excellent venue for including the school community in developing a plan, which different members of the school can take responsibility for implementing, and for evaluating how the plan is working. In addition, counselors need to become familiar with a variety of methods of addressing the problem, including conducting a comprehensive evaluation, using a solution-focused approach, and developing skills to connect with persistent bullies. One of the most powerful approaches to reduce persistent bullying is to include families, the topic of chapter 9.

9

PERSISTENT BULLYING: FAMILY INTERVENTIONS

In every conceivable manner, the family is link to our past, bridge to our future.

—Alex Haley

This chapter discusses family interventions for persistent bullies. For the most part, it is geared to professionals with some training in work with families, particularly those who have had experience working with families of children who persist at bullying, aggression, and violence. The chapter comprises four sections. The first section charts the development of parenting programs for reducing violence and aggression. The second section examines seven core elements of parenting programs that have successfully facilitated behavior changes in aggressive children. The third section delineates the core skills necessary for working with the families of bullies, including skills for connecting with the family and skills for structuring the sessions and intervening. Finally, the last section discusses general and specific strategies for intervening with persistent bullies and their families.

HISTORY OF FAMILY AND PARENTING PROGRAMS

When educators and researchers question why some children persist in bullying their peers, frequently the answer points to a dysfunctional family.

As discussed in chapters 2 and 3, families play a key role in how children behave. In fact, the family is the first learning environment for most children, and the emotions, beliefs, and social skills they bring to school are most often rooted in the family environment. As a result, family therapy, parenting programs, or even family support groups are frequently the preferred intervention for children with aggression problems.

Because of the recognition that families are so important in people's lives, researchers have studied, for the past half-century, how families influence the development of childhood aggression, how troubled families can be distinguished from nontroubled ones, and how family therapists can lessen the emotional pain and hurtful behaviors of family members. In sum, family therapy and parent training are some of the most thoroughly researched programs for violence prevention. Furthermore, family programs are some of the most successful in modifying children's aggressive behaviors (Christophersen & Mortweet, 2001; Dadds, 1995; Forehand, Kotchick, Shaffer, & Dorsey, 2002; Horne & Sayger, 1990; Kazdin, 1987; Kazdin & Weisz, 1998, 2003; Kotchick, Shaffer, Dorsey, & Forehand, 2004; Reid, Patterson, & Snyder, 2002).

This section summarizes the history and successes of research with the families of children who are aggressive. Examining this brief history of family research provides a glimpse at the breadth and depth of what researchers and therapists can expect from family interventions. Although research on family interventions has assessed their effectiveness in reducing only aggressive behaviors, rather than bullying behaviors, it has consistently demonstrated a positive impact on aggression. Because persistent bullying is a subset of aggressive behavior, and because bullying and aggression are frequently linked (Nansel, Overpeck, Haynie, Ruan, & Scheidt, 2003), violence prevention practitioners should be confident that family interventions can help reduce persistent bullying problems as well. The chronology of this family and parenting research can be broken into three stages (Forehand et al., 2002).

During the first stage of parenting research (1960–1975), researchers tested the efficacy of parenting programs that consisted of a family facilitator working with the parents (who served as mediators) to change the behaviors of the child (who was the target of the intervention). Results from this early research, which consisted mostly of descriptive studies and single case designs, indicated that parenting programs had positive short-term effects on reducing aggressive and destructive behaviors, all characteristics related to children who bully.

During the second stage of parenting research (1975–1985), researchers focused on whether parent training programs could be successfully generalized to other settings. Research in this period held serious implications for future violence prevention interventions. First, research indicated that parent training could be generalized to other settings (e.g., from a clinical setting to the home or school). Second, the short-term behavior changes seen in research studies conducted before 1975 demonstrated long-term changes as well. Third, the interventions studied were proved to affect change not only in the targeted child's behavior but also in the behaviors of other family members (e.g., siblings). Finally, the research revealed that parent training interventions also led to improvements in other areas of the child's life, such as school performance (Forehand et al., 2002; Horne & Sayger, 1990; Kotchick et al., 2004; Reid et al., 2002; Sayger, Horne, Walker, & Passmore, 1988).

The third stage of parenting research began in 1985 and continues to the present. The issues addressed in research and intervention today are far more complex than those addressed in the first two phases of parenting research. Current studies focus on determining which specific components of parent training induce change and what effect the intervention setting has, two issues that have important implications for reducing the time and cost of a family program. In addition, family researchers have expanded their area of study beyond familial and marital characteristics to include the multiple influences on a child's maturation, including developmental traits, socioeconomic conditions, community and neighborhood features, and ethnic and cultural factors. Current interventions have even explored novel relationships, such as a family's connection with the community and the influence of that connection on the child's behavior. As a consequence of this phase of parenting research, interventions have been more tailored to the distinct needs of aggressive children and their families (Blechman, 1998; Calhoun, Glaser, & Bartolomucci, 2001; Conduct Problems Prevention Research Group, 1992; Prinz & Miller, 1996; Smith et al., 2004).

In summary, over 40 years of research on family therapy and parenting programs for reducing aggression in children have demonstrated empirical support for judging family interventions as effective. Family interventions have had consistently positive results, regardless of the professional characteristics of the facilitators (e.g., clinical psychologists, school guidance counselors, or social workers as facilitators) and the characteristics of the setting (e.g., home, school). The Substance Abuse and Mental Health Services (SAMHSA) Web site provides examples of exemplary and promising family programs (http://www.mentalhealth.samhsa.gov/schoolviolence/initiative.asp). Some family programs worth mentioning are Karol Kumpfer's Strengthening Families Program (http://www.strengtheningfamilies.org), Lynn McDonald's Families and Schools Together (FAST; http://www.wcer.wisc.edu/fast/), Matt Sanders's Positive Parenting Program (http://www.triplep-america.com/), William Quinn's Family Solutions for first-time offenders (Quinn, 2004), and Parents as Teachers (http://www .parentsasteachers.org).

Although research on aggressive behavior dates back to the 1960s, research aimed specifically at bullying prevention has developed only during the past two decades. A particular dearth of research exists for family interventions that help parents shape their child's bullying behaviors or their child's bullying victimization. Understanding the successful principles of family research for aggression and violence is important for developing family interventions for persistent bullies, which are built on many of the same principles. In spite of the limited research on the families of bullies, a few books have been published that can help counselors aid parents in addressing issues related to their child's bullying or victimization. Several are presented in the annotated bibliography at the end of this chapter. Most frequently, books advise counselors on how to help parents—or advise parents how to help themselves—handle their child's aggression.

CORE ELEMENTS OF EFFECTIVE
FAMILY AND PARENTING PROGRAMS

On the basis of over 30 years of research at the University of Georgia, Forehand and colleagues (2002) recognized seven core elements common to parenting programs that are effective at reducing aggression. Although further research is needed to delineate the differences between family research to reduce bullying and family research to reduce aggression, we propose that the following seven elements be used as a foundation for the design of parenting programs to reduce bullying (Box 9.1). The following sections discuss how these elements have been incorporated into existing parenting programs.

Focus the Intervention on the Parents

Parents have considerably greater potential influence over an aggressive child than any other adult will have because they spend the greatest amount of one-on-one time with the child and, most likely, have the strongest emotional relationship with the child. A teacher's 6-hour-a-day contact with a child may be almost as much time as a parent may spend, but teachers have little opportunity for individual and personal exchanges in a typical classroom. Teaching parents how to intervene with their child also provides the greatest opportunity for the child to transfer social skills to new situations. As the parents learn to help their child use prosocial skills at home, they can also help the child apply those skills in a variety of new settings (e.g., at the local store, mall, or grandparents' house).

Similarly, when working with parents who have a child who bullies his or her peers, the inappropriate behaviors should first be addressed at home before an attempt is made to address the behaviors in other settings. Parents who are unable to influence the child's behavior at home will be even less likely to influence the child's behavior at school. In short, the initial focus of an effective parenting program should center on helping parents master new parenting strategies that will affect their child's behavior at home when the

BOX 9.1. CORE ELEMENTS OF EFFECTIVE PARENTING PROGRAMS

1. *Focus the intervention on the parents* because they have (a) presence and influence with the child, (b) authority within the family and often within the community, and (c) incentive to work to solve the problem.
2. *Focus on prosocial behaviors* rather than antisocial problems because effective programs build on strengths of family members rather than concentrating on dysfunctional family characteristics.
3. *Teach parents to understand, identify, and track behavior* because to change their child's behavior, parents must first increase their awareness of the problem, understand the extent of the problem, gain insights into the behavioral antecedents of the problem, and acknowledge the inappropriateness of bullying.
4. *Teach parents social learning principles* (e.g., reinforcing prosocial behavior, modeling appropriate problem-solving skills, demonstrating effective conflict resolutions) as a framework for understanding how bullying behavior develops, is maintained, and can be changed. Then teach parents the skills to change their child's behavioral patterns.
5. *Teach new parenting skills* such as implementing new family rules, developing new strategies for positive interaction, and improving family cohesion.
6. *Transfer skills* from the clinic to the school or other settings so that change may occur in a variety of situations.
7. *Address parental and family risk factors* that may require specialized attention or hinder the family program, such as parental drug abuse.

child is under their direct control (e.g., new problem-solving skills, appropriate behavioral responses to frustration). Unfortunately, convincing parents that they need to focus on bullying problems at home can be difficult when the inappropriate behaviors occurred at school or in the community, as illustrated in the following exchange:

Parent: So why do we have to do this? It is the school's problem. Why do we need to be involved?

Counselor: Good questions. I am working with Lance's teacher, and I will ask her to be involved with us after a short time, but first it is important that we ensure that you can influence Lance's behavior while he is under your supervision. Because pushing other students at school is not OK, the school wants to get this problem under control. We are asking for your help. If you can help Lance stop bullying at home and in the neighborhood, there is a better chance that we will be able to help Lance act appropriately at school. In other words, if you can help Lance at home, we can work together to influence his behavior at school too. That's the goal . . . good monitoring and teaching at home, then generalize the behaviors to the school. Let's talk about how you can do that.

Once parents have mastered strategies for influencing the child's behavior at home, parenting programs should teach parents how to help the child generalize new social skills and appropriate behaviors beyond the familial interactions. New social skills can be transferred to new environments such as playgrounds, school activities, and after-school care programs.

Focus on Prosocial Behaviors

An effective parenting program builds on the existing strengths of the child and the family. Counselors often hear absolute complaints, such as "He never behaves" or "He's always out of control." Still, most children, even bullies, exhibit some cooperative and compliant behaviors at some points in time. Because most parents focus on the negative behaviors, a difficult task for counselors is to help parents identify the positive attributes of their children. In Patterson's early research (e.g., Patterson & Forgatch, 1987), he referred to aggressive families as "aversive." He reported how family discussions about conflicts escalate until members become aggressive. Helping parents learn to recognize their child's positive behaviors and to build on their child's strengths breaks the aversive relationship. Parents instead focus on cooperation and "catching the child being good." Parents can then increase the frequency of those positive behaviors by rewarding them. In the process, parents help their children change not only their behavior but also their self-image as a troublemaker to a more positive definition of themselves. Children and families work much better with a positive and affirming approach than with one that is continually focused on negative behavior. Another way of defining this process is as follows: "Nastiness leads to nastiness, whereas kindness leads to more kindness." The goal is to promote cooperation so that the family moves from being aversive to inviting.

The facilitator for the program (e.g., clinical psychologist, school counselor) should strive to identify the circumstances that lead to and maintain positive behaviors in the persistent bully. The facilitator can then build on these situations by teaching parents how to recognize instances that spark their child's positive qualities. Most parents need to be shown how to catch the child being good and how to avoid focusing on the child's misbehavior.

Teach Parents to Understand, Identify, and Track Behavior

Teaching parents to be able to identify their child's positive and negative behaviors is generally a very difficult task. The process starts by helping parents define their child's problem behaviors, an inherently complex task, given the wide spectrum of bullying behaviors (e.g., physical fights, verbal threats, taunts, passing rumors, sexual jokes) that should be analyzed.

An effective way of helping parents become more adept at defining and tracking good and bad behaviors is to ask them to keep a log or diary of events. A checklist, such as the one presented by Horne and Sayger (1990, p. 172) and reproduced in Box 9.2, can be kept on the refrigerator or hung in some other common area at home. To develop the checklist, the facilitator needs to help parents identify specific areas of concern. Recording general events or using the general notation "not being good" or "being mean" is too imprecise. To facilitate the process of generating a functional list, the counselor can ask parents to imagine that they are watching their child on a video camera. "If we were watching the video playback, how would you describe what you were seeing on the television monitor? What would the child be doing?" In the process of defining the behaviors, the facilitator may encounter resistance from parents who do not perceive certain behaviors as bullying or as problematic but rather define them as "what kids do." Thus, the facilitator may need to help these parents understand that although many children may act in a similar manner, ultimately such behaviors are inappropriate and can hurt others.

BOX 9.2. COMMON PROBLEMS CHECKLIST

1. My child started a fight with his or her brother or sister.
2. My child did not help his or her brother or sister when needed.
3. My child played music or the TV too loudly.
4. My child was late coming home.
5. My child did not clean up (kitchen, bathroom, etc.) after doing something.
6. My child interrupted conversations.

7. My child answered me rudely.
8. My child acted inappropriately in front of company.
9. My child didn't listen to me.
10. My child left clothes lying around the house.
11. My child refused to help around the house.
12. My child lied to me.
13. My child stole something.
14. My child used dirty words.
15. My child bothered me while I was on the phone.

Note. From *Treating Conduct and Oppositional Defiant Disorders in Children*, by A. Horne and T. Sayger, 1990, Elmsford, NY: Pergamon Press. Copyright 1990 by Pergamon Press. Reprinted with permission.

Teaching parents to understand, identify, and track behavior also involves helping them understand how behaviors can be a function of a complex sequence of events. The A-to-E Process of Thought and Action, outlined in chapter 5 (Box 5.5) for use with all children, may help illuminate this sequence for parents. The A-to-E Process of Thought and Action is an effective tool for clarifying the triggers of inappropriate behaviors; it can help parents connect an event to the beliefs and emotions that ultimately lead to a specific behavior. The model can clarify how parents can help the child modify his or her behaviors. An example of the process is described in Box 9.3.

BOX 9.3. EXAMPLE OF THE A-TO-E PROCESS OF THOUGHT AND ACTION

Antecedent or external event that triggers the sequence: "He called my mom a bad name."

Beliefs related to the event: "I think he was disrespectful to me." "I think people who are disrespectful should be beaten."

Consistent emotions: The emotions are not caused by the event but arise from thoughts and beliefs (**B**) the person has about the event. "I am so mad about being disrespected in front of my friends."

Doing: Individuals' behaviors are consistent with the emotions. "I am so angry that am going to make him apologize, even if I have to hit him."

External outcome: The person's behavior is followed by an external outcome or consequence (e.g., being suspended from school). The outcome is not predetermined by the

antecedent, although people often speak as though it is—
"He was disrespectful, and that is why I am being suspended
from school."

Teach Parents Social Learning Principles

Most behaviors are learned by observing others. When parents model effective problem solving and decision making, their children learn by observing them. Practicing with parents how to serve as effective role models can be very powerful and ultimately may come full circle to change the child's behavior. In addition, bullying behavior is reinforced by its payoffs (e.g., the persistent bully gets to use playground equipment longer than other children or gains status among a group of peers). Just as bullying behavior can be perpetuated through rewards, prosocial behaviors can also be sustained through appropriate rewards.

To change aggressive behaviors, parents need to learn how to change the payoffs or rewards for bullying. Like a police officer who looks the other way and leaves a mugger to work out his conflicts with the person being robbed, parents who ignore or leave disruptive children to work out their own conflicts cannot expect change. In addition to changing the rewards for bullying (what comes after the behavior), parents also need to understand and change the antecedents to bullying (what comes before the behavior). By changing the circumstances that prompt inappropriate behaviors, the behavior may be averted before it occurs.

Teach New Parenting Skills

Parents of aggressive children need to learn new skills (e.g., scheduling or structuring family life), which may then affect the entire family. In our experience, parents whose children persistently bully others often have chaotic lifestyles where at-home routines are ill established or nonexistent. In working with these families, counselors may suggest that the parents work on their scheduling skills, prompting the parents to establish a regular routine for a set period of time (e.g., 3 months). The counselor can ask the family to meet and work out a schedule that includes, at a minimum, agreeing to be home together at the same time once every day and to have a meal together. Although parents may be concerned that such a schedule will be too constricting, the counselor can explain that the routines are necessary only for a short time and can be adjusted after the family is functioning more smoothly.

The facilitator can use a number of other activities to help introduce parents to new parenting skills. For example, counselors can teach parents how to apply the Premack Principle, or "Grandma's Law," which states that less desirable activities should be done before more desirable activities:

- "Eat your peas; then you can have dessert."
- "Cut the grass; then you can play basketball."
- "Do your homework; then you can watch TV."

Too often parents apply the Premack Principle backwards:

- "OK, you can have some cookies now, but in a little while you have to eat your dinner."
- "You can have Robbie over now, but later you have to do your homework."
- "OK, you can play basketball today, but then this weekend you have to mow the lawn."

Counselors can also teach parents how to foster a positive home atmosphere by using an activity that prompts families to identify the strengths they see in other family members. Paralleling the classroom activity presented in chapter 5, family members begin their day by silently identifying a positive act they will perform for another family member by the end of the day. At night, family members gather together to guess what positive thing each did for the others that day. As a result, families focus on positive behaviors and identify ways of helping each other. The positive changes that parents experience as a result of their new skills carry over into other positive interactions by showing respect for family members through positive communication. As they begin to genuinely like themselves, their spouse, and their children, parents find the time spent with other family members to be more interesting and fun.

Finally, all parents have some conflicts with their children, but most can solve them effectively. Those who have not learned how to effectively solve conflicts through proper communication resort to hitting or shouting at the child. Counselors can teach and help parents master effective communication skills, such as those displayed in Box 9.4. Parents may benefit from booklets, handouts, or videos that demonstrate the new skills. Counseling sessions can be videotaped and played back so that ineffective communication strategies can be identified and alternative, more respectful and solution-focused expressions can be practiced. Most important, the facilitator must model and reinforce effective communication skills with the family. By practicing effective skills and receiving positive reinforcement from the facilitator, the family will learn new ways of communicating, and ideally, the family climate will improve as well.

Transfer Skills

Most persistent bullies have a difficult time applying new skills in new settings. Their parents will need instruction in how to teach the child to

BOX 9.4. EXAMPLES OF GOOD AND BAD COMMUNICATION

- Use "what, where, when, why, and how" expressions
  - *Good:* "I want you to clear the dinner dishes from the table. We need to clean up the kitchen because we have to do some other things, including your homework. Please do it now."
  - *Bad:* "Get in here and clean up the kitchen. You never do what you are supposed to do." The use of negative language and an absolute—the word "never"—does not provide constructive feedback.
- Give a reward *after* the expected behavior
  - *Good:* "Work on your homework now. When you have finished and I have looked it over, you may watch television for an hour."
  - *Bad:* "Watch TV for an hour, and then do your homework."
- Treat family members as well as you would treat a stranger
  - *Good:* "Please take off your shoes before coming in the house. You have mud on them."
  - *Bad:* "Were you born in a barn, you idiot? Get your shoes off!"
- Own the problem
  - *Good:* "I am very angry that you hit Buster. We do not do that in our family. Now, let us talk about what is going on here and what we are going to do about it." The tone is kept calm.
  - *Bad:* "Did you hit him?" Never ask a question when you already know the answer. "You really make me angry." The parent is not taking responsibility for his or her own anger.

apply newly acquired skills in different environments and circumstances (e.g., store, school, aunt's house). This transfer needs to be planned and rehearsed to be successful. The facilitator can help parents manage possible stumbling blocks in their child's transfer process (e.g., another child at school who frequently lures the persistent bully into acting inappropriately), as well as teach them how to capitalize on possible assets of a new environment (e.g., a teacher who has a good relationship with the child). In the session, the facilitator can ask the parents where and with whom they expect their child to have problems, and then help them rehearse how to handle these problems if they arise.

Address Parental and Family Risk Factors

As described in chapter 8 (Comprehensive Evaluation of the Problem section), families may have risk factors that, if not addressed, will hinder the progression of the family program. For instance, parents may experience depression or other mental health problems. Parents may have problems with alcohol or drug dependency that require medical attention. Parents who have not completed high school may be intimidated by going to school because of their own bad experiences in school and they may lack the skills to support their child's academic progress. Parents may hold beliefs that do not support the peaceful resolution of conflicts or the pursuit of academic excellence. The school counselor or family facilitator needs to assess the family risk factors and determine the best action to follow (e.g., identify community resources that address their needs, address the problem during the family sessions).

CORE SKILLS FOR WORKING WITH FAMILIES

The person who leads parenting or family sessions designed to help families resolve their children's aggression and bullying problems may be a counselor, psychologist, social worker, family therapist, or other mental health worker with specific knowledge for leading family groups. To simplify the reading, we use the labels *facilitator* or *counselor*, regardless of the professional degree. We also use the generic term *parenting or family programs* to encompass counseling, therapy, and educational programs.

Before intervening with families, all facilitators should be specially trained in leading family groups. Working with families requires knowledge of family dynamics and family systems that can only be gained through special training. Counselors must recognize that families bring a history and a future with them, in addition to their current situation. Parents have an extensive history with their child and with other family members that influences the family's status quo.

In addition to general knowledge and skills related to parenting programs, facilitators need specific training to work with the families of bullies. Facilitating sessions with these families requires a strong theoretical background in how families develop and maintain coercive family systems. Although not all bullies come from families that are highly coercive, the offspring of highly coercive parents are usually aggressive (Patterson, 1982). When bullies come from noncoercive families, the family is often more amenable to cooperating with the facilitator to change the child's aggressive behavior because coercion and aggression are not a central conflict for these families.

In addition to theory, the counselor needs to develop good relationship skills to engage the family in working to reduce the bullying problem (Horne,

2000). Family therapy literature on how to develop a therapeutic alliance is abundant, but we emphasize 10 skills that are particularly helpful for working with families of persistent bullies in two major categories: skills for connecting with the family and skills for structuring sessions and interventions.

Skills for Connecting With the Family

1. *Engage the family.* Helping families become aware of their need for assistance with bullying problems requires considerable sensitivity. Most parents are resistant to being told they have a problem child. Even if they do accept that their child is aggressive, many parents may still define the problem as belonging to the child and reject any involvement in solving the problem. Thus, the facilitator needs to possess considerable ability in communicating the rationale for, and importance of, their engagement in solving the problem. Obviously, having the parents develop the skills and resources to work with the child on a daily basis would be more effective than having the child spend 1 hour a week with the facilitator; certainly the time factor can and should be a major part of the rationale offered.

2. *Communicate empathy.* The facilitator should recognize parents' difficulty in seeking help and in attempting to make major changes in how the family functions. In aggressive and coercive families, most family members are victims because they all experience pain and emotional conflict at some point. Thus, the facilitator can also recognize and support other family members' feelings as appropriate. The facilitator should use language, including acceptable colloquialisms, with which the family is comfortable.

3. *Communicate reassurance, and help to normalize the family's request for help or their willingness to participate in counseling.* Seeking help is not easy; often families fear that seeking help implies that the family is abnormal. The facilitator should reassure the family that parenting is a difficult occupation and that many families experience conflict. Bolstering the family's decision to seek professional support and helping the family to understand that professional counseling is an appropriate avenue for changing their child's bullying behavior is an important skill for counselors to possess. Comparisons to other assisted activities (e.g., tax preparation and medical advice) may alleviate parents' embarrassment or cognitive dissonance (i.e., self-doubts about their decision to seek professional help). Parents need to understand that it is imperative to change

the child's bullying behavior, but counselors need to high-light the universality of parenting problems to assure parents that requesting assistance is not atypical.

4. *Understand and accept parental frustration.* Parents are usually frustrated and angry with their child and need support to manage these emotions. The facilitator may assist the family with this frustration and anger by redefining all the members of the family as victims of the bullying problem. No one is happy when aggression and coercion reign in the family, and all family members can move toward a happier family life if the bullying is eliminated.

5. *Emphasize positive expectations for improvement.* The family will need reassurance and support. Although a facilitator cannot and should not promise positive changes, it is important to communicate that previous efforts have helped other parents with similar concerns.

Skills for Structuring the Sessions and Intervening

1. *Provide an agenda and structure.* Counselors should provide an overview of the treatment plan before beginning a family pro-gram. Parents need to know the expected duration of the treat-ment program, the agenda for individual sessions, and antici-pated benefits of the program. This overview of the treatment facilitates parental commitment to the change process, be-cause it helps them understand the rationale behind each step in the process.

2. *Gather information about the family and, in the process, explain why the information is important.* Families are often not used to or comfortable with parenting programs and may not under-stand why personal information is sought or how it will be used. Thus, providing reassurance that all information dis-closed will be used to reduce the bullying problem and de-scribing how it will be used will lessen the resistance to shar-ing information and making family changes.

3. *Make sure the family is with you.* Check the parents' compre-hension of the process and intervention strategies frequently. The information may seem facile and straightforward to the facilitator, but it may be new and foreign to family members. Moving too quickly through unfamiliar material may produce resistance. To gauge the family's understanding of the pro-gram and acquisition of new skills, the counselor needs to engage members in frequent conversations about the nature of the problem, about the application of new strategies to re-

solve the problem, and about the occurrence of expected changes.

4. *Expect resistance*. What is being asked of the parents is difficult; if it were not difficult, they would not need professional help. Resistant parents may avoid participation, refuse to complete assignments, and blame others for their problems. Resistance can be addressed by assuring the parents that they are not being blamed for the problem, explaining why the program is appropriate for their family, and verifying that the parents understand the material and can apply it.

5. *Follow the core elements of effective parenting*. Finally, facilitators must apply the core elements of effective parenting programs: Focus the intervention on parents; focus on prosocial behavior; teach parents to understand, identify, and track behavior; teach parents social learning principles; teach new parenting skills; transfer skills to new settings; and address parental and family risk factors.

WORKING WITH CHILDREN WHO BULLY AND THEIR FAMILIES

Working with families of bullies may be different from working with other types of families, particularly when planning the intervention. The process usually starts when teachers or other school personnel refer the family to the counselor, who then evaluates the nature and extent of the child's bullying. Even though parents are participating in the family program because of the child's problems at school, the facilitator may refrain from immediately addressing specific school behavior problems. Instead, the facilitator may ask the teacher of the bullying child to continue managing the inappropriate bullying behavior as usual for the next month or so. This delaying tactic allows the facilitator time to work with the family before introducing the school component. The rationale behind a delayed approach is that most parents of persistent bullies have limited control over their child's behavior at home. Because these parents have even less control over the child's behavior at school, helping parents develop more effective parenting skills at home is the first step in many parenting programs. Only when parents have some level of authority over the child's behavior in the home will they be able to promote changes in his or her behavior at school. Typically, educators have been supportive of this delayed approach because they recognize that positive behavior changes in the home environment will translate into improved school conduct.

Parent programs designed to reduce school bullying may be administered in a variety of settings, but wherever the program is offered, it is important to promote a strong connection between the child's school and the agency or facilitator. Helping parents with a child who has bullying problems is difficult under the best of circumstances, and a collaborative relationship between the two organizations will facilitate parents' acknowledgment of their child's bullying problem. Counselors and facilitators can also collaborate with teachers to help explain to parents that the school is not against their child or trying to single out their child. Rather, the emphasis should be that the school personnel are legitimately concerned about their child. Ideally, then, teachers will be seen as active and willing participants in the process of helping the child learn positive social skills.

A parenting program can be conducted with one family or with groups of families having similar problems. When working with groups of families referred by schools (e.g., Smith et al., 2004), the power and dynamics of the group can enhance the opportunities for change and growth for all the families. Sometimes working with the entire family is not feasible or indicated, or a counselor may decide to involve the parents only on a limited basis. Family programs can also vary with regard to the depth of the change they are designed to create, ranging from psychoeducational (i.e., teaching new knowledge and skills) to therapeutic (i.e., changing family processes, rules, and limits).

The remainder of this section has six components: helping families understand the problem of bullying, setting up for success, family monitoring, applying consequences appropriately, being in control of oneself, and using outside resources. All of these components are important for a successful intervention with families of persistent bullies.

Helping Families Understand the Problem of Persistent Bullying

The term *bullying* is not especially well understood by the parents of bullies. They must first learn to recognize the existence of different types of bullies (aggressive, follower, relational) and associated bullying behaviors (physical, verbal, relational, and sexual harassment). By working with families of bullies, the facilitator can choose from a number of activities that are designed to help parents understand the concept of bullying. The following are pertinent examples of such activities:

1. *Define your own childhood bully.* Ask parents to describe what thoughts arise when they hear the word *bullying* and to provide examples of bullying from their childhood or their present lives. How do they feel when they think of these bullies? If the parents admit that they were the bullies when they were younger, ask them if they now wish they could have interacted with their peers in a more positive and less threatening manner.

2. *Define the types of bullies.* With the aid of a handout, discuss the three common types of bullies (aggressive, follower, rela-

tional) with parents, and ask them to give examples of these different types of bullies from movies, their own childhood, their children's reports, or others' stories. Connecting the formal definitions from the handout with real examples will help parents understand that some behaviors attributed to "just being a kid" or excused by "not meaning anything by it" may, in fact, be a serious concern. In addition to the examples, counselors should provide parents with information about possible outcomes or long-term consequences of bullying: injuries, school truancy, delinquency, and substance abuse. Counselors can also discuss the developmental trajectory of violence, discussed in chapter 3.

3. *Discuss the rewards of bullying.* Talk with parents about why children bully their peers, and assist them in understanding that these behaviors are maintained by consequences or payoffs. Examine whether the positive consequences of bullying could be achieved by other means (e.g., gaining attention from peers by being in a leadership role) and why negative payoffs may not be strong enough to stop the bullying behaviors. Using the A-to-E Process of Thought and Action may help parents and their child to understand the sequence of behaviors from the trigger event to the final outcome.

4. *Review the making of a bully.* Using a handout of the ecological model (adapted from Figure 3.2), explain the various sources that influence the development of aggressive behaviors (see Table 2.1 for risk and protective factors at each level of the model), taking care not to present risk factors as direct causes, but rather as elements that increase the probability of bullying. Making this distinction safeguards against parents refuting the legitimacy of a risk factor by finding an example of a person who has the risk factor but does not exhibit aggressive behavior: "Johnny has really bad grades at school, but he would not hurt a fly."

5. *Discuss how bullying starts.* Help parents understand that children generally learn to bully from two distinct sources: they observe other children who bully and who are then rewarded for their behavior; and they perform the behavior themselves and are also rewarded for it. This discussion may lead parents and their children to scrutinize positive and negative role models in real life and in the media. How much television do children watch? Do parents need to limit the amount and quality of exposure to TV? Are other, more positive forms of entertainment available? What kind of influence do their children's friends exert?

6. *Develop a goal sheet.* Parents can use a goal sheet to define their current problems and their goals for the parenting sessions (Exhibit 9.1). Filling out a goal sheet helps teach the parents and the child to identify clear and measurable goals. Parents can also identify rewards for achieving acceptable levels of behavior change. Sample goal sheets are included in a number of parenting texts (Christophersen & Mortweet, 2003; Fleischman, Horne, & Arthur, 1983; Forehand & Long, 2002; Patterson & Forgatch, 1987).

Setting Up for Success

The adage "An ounce of prevention is worth a pound of cure" applies to families. Many problems with children can be prevented. With parents, the concept of setting up for success is used to focus them on bullying prevention. In other words, we emphasize positive activities and behaviors that the family is already doing so parents can continue performing them, and we discuss new strategies to avoid repeating past mistakes. Activities related to setting up for success are discussed in the following sections.

Family Council for Defining Bullying

A *family council* refers to regularly scheduled family meetings to discuss family issues. These meetings may focus primarily on problems, but usually council time includes family decision making on both positive and negative events. For example, the family may meet every Saturday morning for a 45-minute discussion to make weekend plans, including both pleasant activities and chores to accomplish. Parents can take this time to discuss family rules and set expectations, to resolve ongoing conflicts, and to ask family members to share their "prouds" and "sorries" (i.e., what they liked about the family this week and suggestions for how family experiences could be improved). The goal of a family council meeting is to facilitate a democratic and engaging discussion among family members.

To ensure positive progress, families may find it helpful to practice several of these family council meetings in the presence of the counselor before beginning to hold meetings on their own. In one of the first family council meetings, a handout with definitions and examples of different types of bullies should be given to and discussed with the children. In this way, every family member will have a common nomenclature to assign to different bullying personas and behaviors, thereby minimizing miscommunication in the future. Finally, the family should also discuss why it is important to bar all forms of bullying from family interactions.

EXHIBIT 9.1
Example of a Goal-Setting Sheet: Kevin

Concerns	Sister	Neighbor friend	Chores	School reports
Desired behavior	Spends pleasant time with sister (no fights)	Has friend over and plays cooperatively	Does chores without reminding or complaints	Has good experiences at school
Current level	Fights or yells at sister at least twice a day	Starts out well but then gets into a conflict and fights or yells	Does not start any chore until nagged to do so	Parent receives frequent reports of problem behavior in school
Acceptable change	Yells or fights no more than twice a week	Has friend over; fights less than once a week	Starts chores without a reminder 3 days a week	Parent receives no more than one report of poor behavior per week
More than expected	Yells or fights no more than once a week	Does not fight with friend	Starts chores without a reminder 5 days a week	Parent receives no reports of poor behavior

Family Council Rules

One of the first rules that the family council should address is the importance of acting appropriately and treating others with respect (i.e., "no bullying"), both at home and outside of home. The family council can also establish the consequences for breaking a family rule. Parents may need help developing specific rules and should practice how to explain new rules to their children. The counselor can review the newly developed rules and consequences with the parents to ensure that they are reasonable and attainable.

"Changing the World" Activity

Bullying almost always occurs in a context that is predictable and avoidable. In the "Changing the World" activity, family members can discuss the circumstances that precede bullying and the steps they can take to avoid a conflict from happening. For example, Rodney's parents were concerned about his behavior before dinner. Rodney, who was generally well behaved when he came home from school, became increasingly aggressive with his sister as the evening progressed. His parents made two simple changes that increased predictability and stability in their home and significantly reduced Rodney's aggression toward his sister: They provided a snack for Rodney when he came home from school, and they established a regular schedule for dinner at 6:00 p.m.

Communicating With Children

Often parents need assistance to learn more effective ways to talk with their children. Effective communication includes talking without threats, using clear and polite language, and having well-understood expectations about acceptable and unacceptable behaviors. Body language that accompanies good verbal communication includes moving closer to the child, establishing eye contact, and using the child's name in the conversation. When parents want their child to perform a particular behavior, they should communicate in a voice that is firm but polite, telling the child exactly what is expected of him or her, how the task it is to be done, and when they want it completed. Parents also need to confirm that the child understands the message, as in the following example (Box 9.4 provides additional examples):

> *Parent:* Leo, you have been having a problem with bullying, and it must stop. Last week we talked at our family council about what bullying is. We have all agreed on what it is and on our desire for it to stop. Leo, you have continued to tease your brother. I want you to apologize to your brother now for teasing him. Leo, you must stop the teasing, and if you do not, we will establish consequences for your behavior. I hope we do not have to do that. Is this understood? Tell me what you are going to do now.

Improving Cooperation Between Parents

A difficulty frequently encountered in all families, especially those with persistent bullies, is that one parent is more lenient than the other or has different behavioral expectations for the child. Separation or divorce often magnify differences in parenting styles. Parents must be willing to work as a team to address their children's problems. Such teamwork involves communicating with each other, sharing responsibilities, and being supportive of one another—behaviors that may be stressful for a separated or divorced couple.

Modeling Appropriate Behavior

Helping parents learn more effective problem-solving skills provides them with the opportunity to be good models for their children. Parents also need to encourage their children to solve conflicts without fighting. Parents who encourage their children to "get even" or to be the ones who do not start the fight "but certainly finish it" will promote aggression as a solution to conflict. It is better to teach children to address conflict with effective communication or to avoid conflict completely by walking away.

Family Monitoring

A prime predictor of bullying and aggression in children is unmonitored time. In schools, unsupervised locations such as bathrooms, hallways, and playgrounds are prime places for bullying. Similarly, within the home, children have an increased opportunity to bully whenever and wherever supervision is low or altogether absent. The opportunity for engaging in aggression diminishes in the presence of a responsible adult. To increase monitoring, parents can enroll their children in supervised after-school activities, such as Boys and Girls Clubs, or they can ask other family members for help in a "monitoring campaign." If the parents are home, they may require that the children do their homework in their presence. Being together with the child not only provides supervision but also increases parental involvement with the child's schoolwork and other activities.

An additional aspect of family monitoring includes getting to know a child's friends. By spending time with the child and his or her peers, parents can fairly determine the circle of friends with whom their child will be allowed to associate after school and on weekends. It is especially important that parents identify troublesome friends among the child's peers. By meeting the parents of the child's friends and by talking with teachers, parents can become more aware of problematic peers and, if necessary, prohibit or discourage their child from interacting with them.

Applying Consequences Appropriately

Persistent bullies expect to be able to get away with their behavior; otherwise, they would not do it. In most cases, they are successful in their attempts to bully other children without receiving punishment for their misbehavior. Because bullies learn early that the benefits of their actions generally outweigh the costs, it is important that parents establish relevant consequences that will influence their children's behavior in a positive manner. Fortunately, excellent resources are available to help parents in setting effective consequences for bullying (the annotated bibliography at the end of this chapter lists some of these resources), particularly the book *Parenting That Works* (Christophersen & Mortweet, 2003). The most important guidelines that parents should use when applying consequences are consistency, fairness, and clear communication.

Consistency

In interviews with bullies, they identify a prominent theme across their behaviors: Consistent negative consequences for what they do seldom exist; most often, they are not punished for bullying. This lack of consequences frequently occurs because adults are not available for supervision or because parents choose to ignore small incidents, hoping that they will not escalate. When parents begin a program to reduce bullying, it is important for them to learn the value of consistently providing consequences, regardless of the severity and scale of the bullying incidents. Examples of effective punishments include the use of time-outs, removal of privileges, apology to a victim, and restitution of destroyed property.

Fairness

Children are quick to point out relationships or activities that they think are inequitable. Fairness, however, does not mean that everyone receives the same but, rather, that everyone receives according to their needs and circumstances, such as age, ability, and previous experiences. During family council meetings, parents need to explain this meaning of fairness because children tend to equate fairness with equal distribution. Thus, the family will need to discuss the different needs that each family member has and agree, as a family, on what is reasonable and just.

Clear Communication

Telling their children to "behave," "cut it out," or "stop being a bully" may not clearly communicate a parent's expected behavior. A counselor can help parents develop effective verbal communication skills such as giving specific directions about what to do, how to do it, why it should be done, and a time frame within which it should be completed. Effective communication does not include the use of put-downs, sarcasm, blame, or expressions of hopelessness.

Communication can also be unintentional. Parents' nonverbal communication—being distracted, being visibly anxious, glancing away—may convey passiveness or disinterest. A parent communicating interest and concern must be close by; maintain strong eye contact; provide undivided attention; smile; and appear relaxed, open, spontaneous, warm, and gentle. Children should feel free to ask about any aspect of the communication they do not understand, either verbal or nonverbal, particularly when they are receiving conflicting messages.

Just as it is important for children to learn to ask questions for clarification of parental expectations, it is also important for parents to learn to recognize when their child is asking for help with situations involving unfair treatment or bullying. The core distinction between tattling and asking for help rests in the child's intention. The tattler seeks to inflict trouble on other children, whereas the help seeker attempts to reduce bullying. Furthermore, distinguishing between when a child is trying to get another child in trouble and when a child is legitimately asking for help will assist parents in establishing an open and respectful relationship with the child. (Box 10.3 in chap. 10 clarifies the difference between tattling and reporting.)

Being in Control

Frequently, children who bully lack self-control; that is, they act without thinking about the consequences of their actions. Key self-control skills that parents and children should learn include relaxation techniques, self-talk, and a step-by-step problem-solving model. Often, children who lack effective self-control skills have parents who lack them as well. Thus, if the counselor expects parents to model self-control and to help their child solve problems without aggression, the counselor may need to teach the parents how to manage their own emotions. Once a counselor has coached the parents on how to use these skills, the parents can pass on their knowledge by instruction and example. Taking responsibility for teaching social skills to their children will reinforce their own aptitude.

Relaxation Techniques

Remaining calm when responding to a tense situation is the first step a parent can take in achieving self-control. The facilitator can help parents master their own anxiety and excitement in a number of ways, ranging from teaching simple breathing techniques, such as slowing down one's breathing and taking deep breaths, to more sophisticated relaxation training methods or meditation. The facilitator's choice should take into consideration the parent's interests and abilities. Skills that are difficult to use or explain serve little purpose for adults or children. Thus, simple breathing and "counting to 10"–type activities may be more applicable than complicated relaxation techniques. It is important that the facilitator practice the skill with the parents, require them to demonstrate how they will use it, and discuss with them their plans to teach it to their children.

Self-Talk

The facilitator can help parents listen to what they say to themselves, which has been called *self-talk, inner talk,* or *internal dialogue* and was described in chapter 5 (Purkey, 2000). Particularly important is what they say to themselves about the child's behavior. If a parent is engaging in self-talk that generates emotional distress (e.g., "He will never learn to behave" or "I am no good at teaching her to quit bullying"), the facilitator can teach the parent how to replace upsetting self-talk with solution-focused statements, such as the examples presented in Exhibit 9.2.

Working with families to examine self-talk is enlightening and encouraging. Many parents have never examined how their thoughts affect the quality of their interactions with their children. It is encouraging to watch how parents respond to the process. For many parents, it becomes an "aha" experience, because they have never realized that their own thoughts may actually contradict their parenting goals.

EXHIBIT 9.2
Examples of Upsetting and Solution-Focused Self-Talk

Upsetting self-talk	Solution-focused self-talk
I can't stand it when he acts like that.	I don't like it when he acts like that, but with time, I can teach him more effective ways of playing with other children. The first step is to stay calm, stay goal focused, and talk with him about alternatives.
She's a horrible bully, a monster.	She's a child who's trying to get her own way; my goal is to teach her more effective ways of interacting with others.
There's no hope.	There are lots of things I can do. He has learned to bully to solve problems, and he can learn better ways of getting along.

Problem Solving

A step-by-step problem-solving model helps parents develop and refine their self-control skills. To facilitate the teaching of self-control, the counselor may choose to use the same conflict resolution model that the school is teaching to students. Frequently, classroom models use some child-friendly variation of conflict resolution (like STOPP, outlined in Box 5.6). The five-step model detailed in chapter 5 is exemplified in the following paragraphs.

Step 1: Define the Problem and the Goal. As a starting point, parents define their problem and what they would like to see changed. More specifically, parents are asked to identify a specific incident, define the problem that occurred during that incident, and suggest a specific resolution (goal). In some cases, problem and goal definition may be the focal point of a parenting program that seeks to help family members understand why the family needs counseling, as in the following example:

- *Problem:* Chuck is constantly bullying (pushing, hitting, teasing) his younger brother.
- *Parents' response:* "Chucky, stop it now!"
- *Goal:* Stop Chuck from bullying his brother.
- *Parents' description:* "The problem is that Chuck is constantly harassing Barry to the point of tears. Last night, for example, Chuck walked through the kitchen where Barry was doing his homework and shoved Barry's arm, causing him to mess up the page he was working on. Barry yelled at Chuck and then started crying because he had to start the page all over again."

The objective of walking parents through the process of defining the problem and its reciprocal goal is to prevent hasty conclusions and to examine the problem in a more detached and objective manner rather than respond on impulse. Examining the problem and desired resolutions may help parents identify parenting skills they need to learn and practice. In the example, if Chuck's parents had slowed down to analyze the problem, they might have concluded, without the aid of a facilitator, that they need to learn to stop, take a deep breath, calm down, and then clearly define the solution to Chuck's problem. A facilitator could help these parents understand how their behavior has the potential to help solve or aggravate the problem. In losing their tempers and yelling at Chuck to stop his behavior, the parents have not modeled the behaviors that they want their children to learn.

Steps 2 and 3: Generate Solutions and Examine Their Consequences. Often parents develop habitual responses to problems that prove to be unproductive. Developing solutions to problems can be performed as a family activity during a family council meeting. Parents can coordinate a discussion about problems encountered between family members, and everyone can participate in brainstorming possible solutions. The list of possible solutions should be discussed in light of their consequences, such as those provided for Chuck's example in Exhibit 9.3.

Analyzing possible consequences can be a difficult task, likely requiring leadership from the facilitator during the parents' first few attempts. The facilitator may ask the parents to describe situations in which they felt inadequate or unprepared to manage their child's bullying, and then talk the parents through the alternatives courses of action. Reviewing specific examples of alternative responses may help widen the parents' scope of thinking. For example, the facilitator might provide examples of how to use various disciplinary techniques, such as time out, logical consequences for inappropriate behavior, and talk time (a strategy in which parents talk with their child about the bullying behavior and encourage their child to suggest other, more appropriate behaviors). Part of examining consequences involves exploring whether the proposed solutions will promote a positive home and family climate.

In deciding on an appropriate response to a bullying act, it is important that parents try to objectively analyze whether their child's aggressive behavior was instrumental (i.e., pay-off bullying) or reactive (i.e., learned emotional response to a perceived offense). Whenever the behavior is instrumental, the parents' solution must be strong enough to overpower the payoff. When the behavior is reactive, the parents' solution must be designed to help the child learn more adaptive ways of responding to the perceived offense. Thus, it is important to ensure that the solution parents choose, and its related consequences, are appropriate responses to their child's bullying. This will enable the parents to reach their ultimate goal—solving the child's behavior problems.

Step 4: Choose a Solution and Implement It. The parents' next step is to select an appropriate disciplinary response and implement it. It is important that parents, when enacting an effective response, consistently implement

EXHIBIT 9.3
Examples of Possible Solutions and Consequences for Chuck's Bullying Behavior

Possible solutions (parental reactions)	Possible consequences
Ignoring the problem	Chuck learns that he can get away with his bullying, and his negative behavior escalates as he attempts to see how far he can "push the envelope" without getting into trouble.
Hitting or spanking Chuck	Hitting or spanking Chuck may have an immediate impact but teaches Chuck (a) to use force to settle problems, (b) to hit people smaller than himself, and (c) to avoid interaction with adults out of fear of being hit.
Having Chuck work with Barry to fix the homework that was ruined	This cooperative effort may be a viable choice. Chuck has to help fix the problem he caused, and he and Barry may learn to work together effectively. If they continue to argue and squabble about the problem, however, this approach may be a less effective intervention.
Having Chuck apologize, then take on several of Barry's tasks	An apology may be another viable option. Chuck learns that there are consequences to his behavior and that he has to rectify his mistake. However, this option may backfire if Chuck builds up a level of anger or resentment and later seeks revenge for having been forced to apologize and do extra work.
Using time out with Chuck	Time out is a very powerful and effective intervention for children who misbehave, and it may be a very viable option as a consequence of Chuck's behavior. However, using time out does require that family members receive some training and supervision in using it. Furthermore, parents will need to be consistent in their application of this strategy.
Having Chuck come to a family council meeting during which the whole family discusses the problem	Family council discussions are very effective interventions, because they involve everyone in the family.

similar solutions and consequences across similar incidents. Almost without exception, children will "push the limits" to test their parents' resolve to provide consequences for bullying. Whenever parents fail to follow through, they have, in fact, reinforced their child's bullying behavior. When parents react to the problem and implement a solution, it is critical that the action occur swiftly. Parents must react consistently from one incident to the next, and they must impart impartial, firm, and appropriate consequences.

Step 5: Evaluate the Results. The parents' last step in the cognitive process of problem solving is to examine whether the solution they chose was effective. Did it move the parents closer to their goals? Because children will challenge their parents' resolve, counselors should encourage parents to continue applying these problem resolution skills and strategies.

Using Outside Resources

Parents endure multiple daily stresses: earning a living, managing a household, and balancing family demands. Schools can help parents by compiling and recommending available resources and services in the community (e.g., public services such as health care, housing, food, and mental health counseling). Likewise, churches and other private service organizations frequently offer support and mentoring to families in conflict or in need of additional help. As indicated in chapter 2, parents often have little time, leaving them unavailable to monitor their children's activities and behaviors. After-school and weekend support programs—Big Brother and Big Sister programs, YMCA and YWCA programs, Foster Grandparents programs, and Boys and Girls Clubs—may provide additional opportunities for children to socially interact with their peers in a monitored environment. Obviously, interaction in this type of monitored setting yields greater opportunity for children to develop appropriate social skills than in their empty house after school.

School staff and community agency members often blame families for their children's problems. Much of the blame is justified because families are the strongest risk and protective factor in a child's life. However, these family critics are often "blaming the victim"—in this case, the family—for not having adequate resources to provide the warm, nurturing environment their children need and deserve. The vast majority of families want their children to be healthy and successful, but frequently parents lack sufficient resources to provide adequate care. Some parents are forced to work multiple jobs to feed the family and, thus, have fewer opportunities to supervise and interact with their children. Some families live in substandard housing and in neighborhoods in which children are exposed to high levels of crime. Many parents, because of their own low academic skills, can provide only limited help to their children with schoolwork and may feel intimidated by schools.

When families do not have adequate resources to provide the parenting and support children need, we believe that it is the community's responsibility to take a social justice stand. While school professionals work with individual children and their families, they should also agitate at the community, regional, and national levels to achieve adequate support for these families. Parents need, at a minimum, a safe house to live in, an income that allows them to feed and clothe their children, a secure and safe job, and access to health care and education. The motto "Think globally, act locally" requires adults to take action in the classrooms and within their communities but, at the same time, to continually push for an agenda of social support for all children and families.

ANNOTATED BIBLIOGRAPHY

- *Antisocial Behavior in Children and Adolescents: A Developmental Analysis and Model for Intervention* (Reid et al., 2002): This book, written by researchers from the Oregon Social Learning Center, discusses childhood development and ways to reduce aggressive behaviors in children age 3 to 18 years across a variety of family contexts, including traditional two-parent families, single-parent families, step-parent families, and foster homes.
- Bullying Prevention Program (Limber, 2004; Olweus, 1993b): This program, which is focused on the school, includes training materials that provide guidance for parents of bullies and victims and suggests ways in which teachers may approach parents to elicit cooperation with a schoolwide bullying prevention program.
- *Bullyproofing Your Child: A Parent's Guide* (Bonds & Stoker, 2000; Garrity, Jens, Porter, Sager, & Short-Camilli, 2004): This booklet was prepared specifically for parents and families as part of a larger and more comprehensive bullying prevention program for the entire school.
- *Parent–Child Interaction Therapy* (Hembree-Kigin & McNeil, 1995): This very readable and practical guide was developed for mental health professionals who work with children age 2 to 7 years. It focuses on disruptive behavior patterns in children and methods parents can use to address these problems.
- *Parenting That Works: Building Skills That Last a Lifetime* (Christophersen & Mortweet, 2003): This book takes a strong skill-building approach to helping children learn effective, lifelong social competencies. This approach may be applied to bullying problems.
- *Parenting the Strong-Willed Child* (Forehand & Long, 2002b): This book, based on over two decades of research, focuses on helping families reduce aggression.
- *The Parent's Book About Bullying: Changing the Course of Your Child's Life* (Voors, 2000): This bullying prevention book was written specifically for parents. On the basis of clinical experience and research conducted with families of aggressive children, it provides information to help parents understand the problem of bullying and offers specific suggestions for managing situations in which a child is a bully or a victim.
- *Troubled Families* (Fleischman et al., 1983): This book offers intervention suggestions for parents faced with a child who behaves in a disruptive manner. It includes specific recommen-

dations for reducing inappropriate behaviors and for increasing prosocial behaviors.

- *When Your Child Is Difficult* (Silberman, 1995): This book provides parents with specific steps to reduce acting out and aggressive behavior problems in children in a family context.
- *Working With Parents of Aggressive Children: A Practitioner's Guide* (Cavell, 2000): This book takes research in behavioral parent training from the last two decades and integrates it with a relationship enhancement model. It offers mental health professionals a powerful model for working with parents to address a child's aggression.

10

HELPING CHILDREN WHO
ARE THE TARGETS OF BULLYING

Every night I cry myself to sleep. I dread going to school because of those bullies.

—Eighth grader

This chapter examines the problem of children who are the targets of bullying, often called *victims*, and what adults can do to help them. The first section discusses the problem of victim blaming and what maintains victimization. The second section provides an array of strategies that can help victims handle bullying, and the last section discusses how adults can help children who are the targets of bullying. The chapter ends with some brief concluding words.

WHAT BEHAVIORS ENCOURAGE BULLYING?

When dealing with bullying and victimization, it is more important to stop the bullying from happening than to try to alter the victim's behavior. Mindful of this principle, however, educators and parents may be able to help the target of the bullying evaluate the problem and rehearse skills to resolve it. To do so, concerned adults must address the problem of victim blaming, as well as the factors that maintain victimization.

Blaming the Victim

It is the role of educators to make sure that the bullying stops and that bullies and the targets of the bullying learn new strategies to reduce the conflict. Although it is the responsibility of adults to assist victims of bullying, it is essential that, in the process, these children are not blamed for being victimized. Some people ask the question "Why does Maggie allow herself to be picked on and harassed?" or "Why is Rafael bullying him?" These questions parallel those asked when intimate partner violence occurs—"Why doesn't she leave him?" and "Why is he abusing her?" Actually, it really does not matter why an abused spouse does not leave. The abuser is breaking the law by beating the spouse; the spouse is not breaking the law by staying at home. People who are abused by their intimate partners do not leave for many reasons: They do not have anywhere to go, they do not have friends to ask for help, they do not have the resources to move, they are too depressed to take action, and frequently they want only the abuse to end, not the relationship. Similarly, many children who are the victims of bullying cannot leave. Children generally cannot choose the school that they attend. Victims of bullying are frequently picked on because they have few friends and fewer social skills than other children, making it difficult for them to resist or respond to the bullying. Children want to come to school to study and have friends, and those who are the targets of bullying would simply like the bullying to stop, and they deserve to have that happen.

In both intimate partner violence and bullying, the reasons why the abuse occurs are basically irrelevant; abuse is never justifiable or acceptable. People abuse their partners because of real or imagined provocation—the food was not ready on time, or it looked like he or she was flirting with another person. Bullies abuse their victims because they are too fat or too skinny, too smart or too dumb. The parallels between intimate partner violence and school bullying constitute an imperfect analogy at best, however, because intimate partner relationships are far more complex than school bullying interactions. The former involves the dissolution of a once-deep emotional involvement between partners, the possible presence of children whose well-being needs to be safeguarded, and the sharing of material belongings.

Nevertheless, bullies do possess a trait in common with spousal abusers: They frequently blame their own actions on their victims. In truth, many victims blame themselves for the abuse as well, furthering their depression and sense of powerlessness. Instead of concentrating on what the victim in an abusive relationship might have done to provoke the abuse, people should ask, "Why doesn't the abuser stop?" and "What can we (educators, police, family members, neighbors, community) do to stop the abuse?" Box 10.1 provides an anecdote illustrating the need to focus on bullies, not victims.

Thus, the first step in dealing with bully–victim problems should always be to stop the bullying from happening. Unfortunately, educators do not always know about the abuse. Teachers need to inform children about the importance of reporting bullying and to assure them that their reports will be taken seriously. Equally important, however, educators need to teach victims safe strategies to reduce bullying, empowering them to solve the problem on their own. And, finally, it is important to understand the reciprocal relationship between the bully and victim and to help the child who is the target of bullying to learn ways to limit any contributions to the problem. For example, not all overweight kids become victims. Thus, understanding why some overweight children become victims and others do not may help to clarify the contributions to the bullying problem of bullies and victims in a specific situation.

Understanding What Maintains the Behavior

Chapter 1 explained the differences among passive, relational, and provocative victims. Each type of victimization may be maintained by different factors, and understanding these factors will lead to a more thorough evaluation of the problem and subsequently a better intervention.

Passive victims are the targets of the bully's aggression without having done anything to provoke the bully (Box 10.2 provides the example of Ramsey, who was the target of bullying). Victims may be targeted because of characteristics that are immutable, such as size, gender, race, ethnicity, vision problems, or medical disorders. In addition, characteristics of these children's personalities or mannerisms might set them apart from the mainstream: being effeminate, liking books rather than sports, living a lifestyle that eschews materialism, or having religious or spiritual beliefs that set them apart from others in the school (Espelage & Asidao, 2001). None of these reasons justify a bully targeting these children; all are basically irrelevant.

Passive victims continue in their role for two reasons. First, they do not see any alternatives. In our interviews with victims of bullying, they frequently explained that they tolerated the bullying because they saw no other option. They did not know whom to ask for help or what they could do to stop the behavior. These children may be very depressed, and their depression may lead to further inaction. Victims are frequently perceived as easy targets (Espelage & Asidao, 2001). Second, victims stay in their role because they are scared; they may have been threatened by the bullies not to report the harassment.

BOX 10.2. SHOULD RAMSEY HAVE TO CHANGE HIS BEHAVIOR?

Ramsey entered a new school, and other students immediately tagged him as "different." He did not laugh or even smile much and seemed to prefer his own company to the company of other students. He was easy to pick out of a crowd because he wore a tie, rather than the standard student attire—a T-shirt and blue jeans. He brought his lunch from home rather than buying a meal in the school cafeteria, and the lunch he brought was vegetarian. He was small in stature, and others soon learned he did not play sports. His family did not belong to a church, and when asked about his beliefs, he refused to talk about them. He even refused to salute the flag. It was not long before other boys in the classroom began to tease him and call him names, and this behavior escalated to pushing, shoving, and hitting.

Some students may say that Ramsey became a victim of bullying because of his own actions. Should Ramsey have to change? Should an individual have to conform to the standards of the peer group—to eat meat, play sports, and salute the flag—to be safe and free from harassment? No—it is the responsibility of the school to provide a safe environment for Ramsey to just be Ramsey.

Relational victims are harassed by being ostracized from peer groups, threatened with removal of friendship, or attacked in false rumors. Most frequently, other children who have formed a clique or gang harass relational victims. Similar to passive victims, relational victims may lack the skills to handle their interpersonal relationship problems and may be unwilling to communicate with an adult. Adults can help relational victims by clarifying what a true friend is, because relational victims frequently need to be encouraged to let go of relationships that are damaging. Some victims may also need help in learning how to develop a good friendship.

The provocative victim, however, incites the bully's aggression. Fortunately, children who provoke others are usually the minority among victims. Their behavior may be maintained by external rewards (e.g., extra attention) or feelings of power (e.g., making others react to their own bullying). These children are at especially high risk of depression and rejection and may require special individual and family interventions. Because these victims have a component of bullying built into their victimization patterns, they may benefit from counseling strategies as described in chapter 8 and family interventions described in chapter 9. They do need to change their behavior, and they need help to do so.

Some children who are provocative victims are rejected by most peers and have no close relationships. Peers may define them as being intrusive, immature, insensitive, or obnoxious. Rejected children are not likely to follow the rules in class or while playing sports, and they lack the necessary social skills for developing positive relationships and friendships (e.g., praising others, maintaining a conversation, cooperating in groups). Their high risk for antisocial behaviors and truancy should be a concern for school counselors and teachers. Despite the seriousness of their problems, some of these children who participated in a structured program to increase these social skills experienced success in improving their behaviors (Frankel, Cantwell, & Myatt, 1996).

SKILLS TO HANDLE BULLYING

The first and most important skill for all children is the ability to differentiate between "dangerous" bullying and "annoying" bullying. *Dangerous bullying* refers to acts for which adults would be prosecuted but for which some bullies never get punished: stealing money, threatening to hit or injure, and physically assaulting others with or without a weapon. These behaviors may put the victim's life at risk. *Annoying bullying*, however, refers to physically, verbally, relationally, and sexually aggressive behaviors that can range from being fairly innocuous to being very cruel. However, they do not put the victim in danger of physical harm. There are strategies for handling both types of bullying.

Strategies for Handling Dangerous Bullying

All students need to have a clear understanding of the difference between dangerous and annoying bullying. Teachers can explain the difference, provide clear examples, and discuss the guidelines to follow when handling dangerous bullying.

The first guideline in handling dangerous bullies is never to risk one's life. If a child feels in danger when confronted by bullies who are bigger or stronger, the victim should first consider his or her own safety. Running away from or screaming at the bully to attract help are reasonable courses of action. If the bully demands money or possessions, the victim should not hesitate to give up these items.

The second guideline is to report what happened. The best way to ensure that students report school bullying episodes is to establish a schoolwide policy encouraging all children, including victims and bystanders, to report bullying when they see it. Having such a policy removes the full burden of reporting from the victim. As expressed in several chapters, bullying thrives in silence. To accurately report bullying, all children need to know the difference between tattling and reporting (Box 10.3 lists the differences). Teachers may need to give examples and restate these differences in various ways so that students can understand them. In interviews we have conducted with elementary school students, children as young as third grade were confused about what tattling is and what reporting is; only very young children were willing to tell the teacher everything they had seen. Victims are afraid of being called a tattletale, and bullies promote this fear (Espelage & Asidao, 2001).

BOX 10.3. *REPORTING IS NOT TATTLING*

Tattling

- Students want to get someone in trouble.
- Students want to look good in someone else's eyes.
- Students want attention.

Reporting

- Students want protection for themselves or someone else.
- Students want protection for their property or someone else's.
- Students are scared.
- Students are in danger.

Reporting also increases when the school policy establishes effective procedures to handle bullying and delineates clear consequence for inappropriate behavior; students will then feel encouraged and supported to report. A big concern of students is the ineffective handling of bullying problems by school administrators and teachers: Without a clear policy, students fear that nothing will happen or that teachers will only make the problem worse (Espelage & Asidao, 2001; Glover, Gough, Johnson, & Cartwright, 2000).

Strategies for Handling Annoying Bullying

Research on the most effective ways to react to annoying bullying is limited; thus, researchers' recommendations about how to respond are grounded in common sense and in their experiences working with children and teachers. Two general rules apply: First, victims should not get annoyed themselves (or, at least, should not show that they are annoyed), and second, victims should not respond with aggression. Much of the bullying stops when victims keep cool and nonchalant, whereas responding with aggression or helplessness may increase the bullying (Salmivalli, Karhunen, & Lagerspetz, 1996). Students who are harassed more frequently tend to use ineffective strategies, like wishing that the problem would go away (Hunter & Boyle, 2004). The bullies' goal is to make their victims react with embarrassment, anger, or fear, and when bullies get this response, their behavior is reinforced. Thus, assertive, funny, and unexpected responses are the best comebacks against annoying bulling. We are not asserting that bullying should be taken lightly or passively; rather, victims should decide what is the most effective response, try it out, and evaluate how it is working. Teachers may encourage students to try to solve annoying bullying by themselves, but students should also be assured that when their strategies do not work, it is good to ask for help.

Victims sometimes do not know how to handle the contradiction between their negative feelings about an incident and the bullies' nonchalant reply. The bully's claim—"We were just joking; we were having fun together"—reveals a very different interpretation of the same incident. Students should know the difference between bullying and rough playing (outlined in Box 1.2) and remember that "if it hurts, it must stop." Teachers need to draw a line of demarcation between positive and negative humor in their classrooms and make sure students recognize the difference. Positive humor invites people in, brings people closer, reduces anxiety, and enhances communication. Negative humor uses sarcasm, humiliation, and teasing to exclude and hurt people and to create stress. It is frequently based on stereotypes and prejudice, and it targets unwilling victims. In positive humor, people laugh together and with others; in negative humor, people laugh at others (Hageseth, 1988).

This section highlights a number of strategies that victims may choose to use to manage bullies' aggressive behaviors. There is no one best strategy; selecting the best way to respond depends on the situation and the characteristics of the bully and the victim. More ideas for handling bullies can be found in Ross's (2003) *Childhood Bullying, Teasing and Violence*; Hazler's (1996) *Breaking the Cycle of Violence: Interventions for Bullying and Victimization*, and McCoy's (1997) *What To Do . . . When Kids Are Mean to Your Child*. In his book for children *Why Is Everybody Always Picking on Me: A Guide to Handling Bullies*, Webster-Doyle (1991) combined his knowledge of psychology with strategies from the martial arts. The following strategies may be useful:

- *Make fun of the tease, not the bully*. Although the automatic response to a put-down or name-calling is to respond in kind against the bully, it is more effective and less provocative to make fun of the tease.

    Bully: Look at your shoes, did you get them in the dump?

    Victim: You mean this isn't the latest style?

    *   *   *

    Bully: Here comes Miss Pizza Face . . .

    Victim: Old, old, old—can you find something new to say?

- *Give the bully permission to tease*. Giving permission to tease removes the power from the bully and gives it to the victim. A variation of this strategy is to remind the bully of previous teasing, and then give permission.

    Victim: Here comes Jack. I give you permission to tease.

    *   *   *

    Victim: Jack, yesterday you were teasing me about my clothes and my hair. Is there anything new today? You have my permission to tease me, but please try to have something new to say.

- *Accept or agree and move on*. A victim should accept some forms of teasing, particularly when the teasing is about a true personal characteristic (e.g., being overweight, having freckles, wearing glasses, being afraid).

    Bully: Are you afraid to fight?

    Victim: Yes, I am. Do you have any other questions?

- *Reframe to a positive*. Most personal characteristics have a bright side, and victims can point this out.

    Bully: Hi, Shorty!

    Victim: Well, as my mamma used to say, good things come in small packages.

- *Ask for the behavior to stop; be assertive*. Not all bullies will stop if they are asked to stop their negative behavior, but it does work in many situations, and it is worth trying.

    Bully: [*Pinches a female classmate on the buttocks*]

    Victim: Stop it; that is wrong! Pinching is sexual harassment. It is against school policy, and I have to tell the teacher.

> *Bully:* What are you, a tattletale?
>
> *Victim:* I think that you need to learn the difference between tattling and reporting.

*   *   *

> *Bully:* [*Pulls the hair of the girl sitting in front of him*]
>
> *Victim:* Don't pull my hair again. I don't like it.

- *Talk about the behavior.* Rather than reacting to what the bully said or did, the victim can talk about the behavior.

> *Bully:* Sorry, you cannot join us in this class project.
>
> *Victim:* You can't exclude someone from a work group! That is called relational aggression, and is against school policies.

*   *   *

> *Bully:* [*Pushes the student from behind while he is standing in the cafeteria lunch line*]
>
> *Bystander:* You must be new at this school. We don't push kids around in our school. Pushing is against the school rules.

- *Say something positive about the bully, then talk about the behavior.* Every person, even a bully, has some qualities the victim can capitalize on (e.g., a quick wit, athleticism, or good looks). Mentioning those qualities at the start of a conversation can change its whole tone. Then, the victim can talk to the bully about his or her behaviors and may try acting puzzled or feigning confusion about the behaviors.

> *Victim:* I don't understand. Yesterday, you were really friendly in class. Today, you are acting like a mean bully. I like you a lot better when you are friendly.
>
> *Victim:* This is strange. You are smart; otherwise you wouldn't have gotten a B in class. I don't get it. Why would a smart person waste her time trying to hurt others?

- *Keep a journal.* Reporting a bullying incident to the school's administration can be greatly improved by keeping a log of important details about the bullying events. Victims should document who said or did what to whom, where and when the incidents happened, and the identities of bystanders and their reactions to the bully. Depending on the situation, the victim can also tell the bully that he or she is keeping a journal.

> *Bully:* [*Knocks the books of a classmate to the floor*]

> *Victim:* Oh good, I needed another example of your bullying for my journal. I'm preparing to take it to the school principal.

- *Ignore it.* Ignoring minor problems may be effective, especially if the victim explicitly states that he or she is ignoring the aggressive behavior. However, this strategy has two inherent risks. First, the victim may, consciously or unconsciously, carry a grudge, and the accumulation effect after several bullying incidents may result in an explosion of anger. Second, in some cases, ignoring the behavior can lead to an escalation of the bullying to provoke a reaction.

> *Bully:* Good morning, Miss Smarty Pants.
>
> *Victim:* Good morning. I will ignore your belittling comment for now.

- *Talk it out.* Talking about the problem is a more complex skill, but a very important one when students want to maintain a friendship. The STOPP (**S**top, **T**hink, **O**ptions, **P**lan, **P**lan working?) model described in chapter 5 (Box 5.6) can be useful when talking about a problem or having a disagreement with a friend.
- *Stay with your friends.* Staying in a group does not solve the problem but generally reduces the possibility of bullying. Bullies like easy prey, and it is much more difficult to prey on a group than on a lone individual. However, if a student feels so scared at school that he or she always needs to be with friends to avoid victimization, he or she should ask for help.
- *Ask for help.* Students have different levels of problem-solving ability, and some may need help to develop these skills. Asking an adult to intervene best solves some problems, particularly dangerous bullying and persistent annoying bullying. Children may feel uncomfortable asking for help if they do not know the difference between tattling and reporting or between dangerous and annoying bullying. Environments in which adults emphasize that children should stand up for themselves make it difficult for children to admit they need help. Other children may be too depressed to ask for help and blame themselves for being victimized. Adults must remain a source of support for these children.

HOW ADULTS CAN HELP

Adults have a crucial role in providing a safe and positive environment for children. This section discusses specific actions that educators, parents, and caregivers can take to help children who are the targets of bullying.

Educators

To help children who are the targets of bullying, the teachers and the school counselor need to be aware of the problem. Clear school policies about reporting, as well as maintaining an open-door policy, will help to increase communication with the children who have difficulty asking for help. Being aware of the warning signs of victimization (listed in Box 10.4) can also help educators identify children who are victimized but who remain silent.

> ## BOX 10.4. *WARNING SIGNS OF VICTIMIZATION*
>
> - The child has no friends at school.
> - The child comments that nobody likes him or her.
> - The child is afraid to go to school.
> - The child feels nervous or anxious about going to school or fears encounters with particular peers.
> - The child shows anxiety symptoms (e.g., crying, nervousness, bedwetting).
> - The child has unexplained emotional outbursts.
> - The child uses unexplained aches and symptoms to avoid going to school.
> - The child has unexplained bruises, cuts, torn clothes, or missing books.
> - The child is very hungry because he or she "lost" the lunch money.
> - The child has to run to the bathroom as soon as he or she gets home (i.e., is afraid to go to the bathroom at school).
> - The child's mood changes suddenly after a phone call (other students may be harassing).
> - The child is very quiet and does not communicate with parents.

Once an adult is aware that a student is the target of bullying, a good assessment of the problem should guide the choice of the best available intervention and its implementation. In some situations, the obvious solution is to work with the bully to stop the harassment without involving the victim. In other situations, the victim and the educator may decide to brainstorm solutions with the aid of the STOPP problem-solving model (outlined in Box 5.6). Part of the plan to solve the problem may require that the victim acquire new skills. The rehearsal of these skills is a key component of success, as the victim must feel confident about using them before confronting the bully. In other situations, the counselor may decide to talk with the victim and the bully using a counseling method like Promoting Issues in Common

(Hazler, 1996), presented in chapter 8. The same counseling principles discussed in chapter 8 for working with persistent bullies apply to working with victims: Use a solution-focused approach, establish an invitational relationship, focus on developing skills and behavior change, promote academic success, and involve teachers and parents as necessary.

Parents and Caregivers

Like educators, parents need to first be aware of the problems their children are facing to provide any effective help. Positive parent–child relationships and open communication about bullying both increase the likelihood that children will inform their parents about school problems. Parents should recognize the victimization warning signals described in Box 10.4. Armed with an accurate knowledge of what constitutes bullying, parents should communicate their concerns to teachers and counselors. If parents' suspicions are confirmed, they should take immediate action to solve the problem, remembering that schools are required to provide a safe environment for every child.

Exhibit 10.1 suggests actions parents can take when their child has been the target of bullying. Parents, like school counselors, can help their children brainstorm strategies to solve bullying problems and can rehearse these behavioral strategies at home before their children test them at school. For example, Ray, a fifth grader, told his mother that he was being teased by a boy at school. The teasing had started a few weeks before and was not triggered by anything Ray had done. After discussing the problem, the mother commented, "Maybe he is jealous of you." She recommended that Ray question the bully about his behavior and worked with Ray to practice how he would ask the bully about his motivations. The next day, after the first tease, Ray asked, "Why are you teasing me? Are you jealous of me?" The bully was so surprised by the question and by being confronted about his behavior that he stopped teasing Ray.

Of special concern to parents are children who have special needs. Children who are developmentally delayed, physically disabled, or visually or hearing impaired sometimes experience almost unbearable levels of bullying. Thus, these parents often require special support to help their children manage the bullying. Maintaining open communication with their children is essential; without it, parents do no know when they should step in to alleviate the situation. Just as with any other student, children with special needs can learn effective responses to teasing and other inappropriate behaviors. If the bullying occurs in a way that the child cannot handle, the parents need to take immediate action to work with the school or agency to stop the bullying.

Most important, parents need to be proactive in working with the schools (or any other organization the child attends) to accommodate the special

EXHIBIT 10.1
Suggestions for Parents of a Child Who Is the Target of Bullying

Strategy	Tactics
Talk about bullying	Have an open door or invitational relationship with your child to let him or her know that you are open to talking about bullying. Inform your child that if there are problems at home, in the neighborhood, or at school, you are there to help him or her.
	Convey to your child the idea that bullying is wrong and that all the reasons bullies may give to support their bullying behavior are irrelevant.
	Do not encourage your child to fight back. Children should not be bullied at school, and it is the responsibility of the adults in their lives, not the victim, to make sure that it stops. Most frequently, fighting makes the problem worse.
	Do not promise that you will keep bullying a secret.
	Help your child identify strategies that will help to reduce or eliminate the problem of bullying, such as developing effective skills to make friends or talk out a problem. Practice those skills with the child.
	Increase awareness of bullying among all family members, including siblings, parents, grandparents, and cousins. Indicate that bullying will not be tolerated in the family.
Document the problem	Take pictures of any physical evidence of bullying (e.g., bruises, cuts, damaged books, torn clothes). Use this documentation to insist on a safe environment for children.
	Keep a written record of all the incidents that have happened, that describes who, where, when, and how. Also, find out who witnessed the bullying and how they responded.
	Find out what your child has done to prevent and stop bullying and what the consequences of those actions have been for the bullies and for your child. Ask your child how he or she thinks that the problem could and should be solved.
	If safe and easy measures did stop the bullying (e.g., sitting at a different table at lunch time), encourage your child to continue with them and monitor the situation. If your child has to resort to unsafe measures (e.g., avoiding use of a bathroom all day) or is scared to go to school, take immediate action by requesting a meeting with the school principal.
Work with the school	Be calm.
	Be informed about the nature of bullying and its typical manifestations among children and adolescents. Know your child's rights. No child should be bullied at school. It is your child's right to study and learn in a safe place. The term *bullying* should not be used as a euphemism for illegal behaviors such as theft, assault, and harassment.
	Remember that bullying thrives in silence; you should not keep it a secret. You will need to talk with the school principal, teachers, and possibly the parents of the bully.
	Meet with the school principal and develop a plan to solve the problem. Monitor how the plan is being implemented and its results. Make sure that the plan is specific: Who will do what, by when. The school should be accountable for implementing the plan.
	Keep a written record of all the actions you have taken to stop the bullying, such as talking with the principal, teacher, and parents of the bully.
	Be involved with the school and with any programs to reduce bullying and promote prosocial skills.
	Work cooperatively with other parents to stop bullying in the school and the community.

needs of these children. For example, parents may request that a teacher or counselor talk with the rest of the class about how each child is unique. A teacher's examples of individuals' differences can do a great deal to ease tensions in a classroom, where some children mistake accommodation of special needs as preferential treatment. Some children need a very quiet spot to concentrate, others need a special class for math, and others need to sit in the front of the class and wear glasses. Talking with students about how to relate to a student with a disability or special needs is altogether appropriate. Some teachers may go a step further, asking the class to identify what kind of help they can offer a peer who is blind or in a wheelchair. It is essential to remind students that rules about bullying apply to everyone; thus, no child—including children with special needs—should be ostracized or picked on.

A number of bully prevention programs have specific materials for parents of children who are victimized. For example, the Olweus Bully Prevention Program actively involves parents in schoolwide and class-level meetings on bullying and includes one or more parents on the coordinating committee that guides the program at each school (Limber, 2003). Other programs with useful information for parents are Bullyproofing (Garrity, Baris, & Porter, 2000) and Bully Busters (Horne, Bartolomucci, & Newman-Carlson, 2003; Newman, Horne, & Bartolomucci, 2000).

CONCLUSION

Bullying has no place in schools or in any community. The duty of adults, no matter what role they play in children's lives, is to provide a safe environment for learning to take place. As educators, psychologists, mental health providers, caregivers, researchers, policy makers, and concerned citizens, adults must be conscious that their actions can and do affect the safety of children. We hope that each chapter of this book has provided answers to the many questions about bullying and direction on how to take a stand against this problem. Further, we hope you have a much clearer understanding of the answers to the following questions:

- How do you define bullying? How has your understanding of bullying changed since you were a child, since you began working with children, or since you read this book? Think about the school environments that surround the children in your life or in your community. Is bullying occurring there? What is the magnitude of the problem?
- What are the causes of bullying? What makes some systems and organizations more susceptible to bullying problems? Many individuals and corporate bodies have unspoken theories about the causes of aggressive behavior. What opportunities to un-

cover the roots of bullying are most appropriate and accessible to you in your work or community?

- What is your role in developing a positive, caring environment and teaching social competence to children? Do you model social competence by using alternatives to aggression to resolve conflict? Many people have personal contact with children every day, whereas others influence children indirectly through their work, through their voting and social advocacy decisions, or simply through their behavior in public places.

- How can you facilitate schools' efforts to adopt models such as the School Social Competence and Bullying Prevention Model? Implementing such models will necessarily influence—and will probably need to be tailored to—curriculums, staff training procedures, and discipline structures already in place.

- When undertaking a school needs assessment, implementing an antibullying program, or conducting a program evaluation, collaboration with other professionals is often called for. Do the schools in your area have healthy working relationships with each other and with higher levels of administration? Can you identify some strategic contacts your school may be able to take advantage of for help in these efforts? Think about school accreditation boards, university academicians, government or private research organizations, or other professionals who can serve as consultants. Evaluation is also very time-consuming. How can time and resources be allocated and redistributed to make room for evaluation? Are there opportunities for volunteers to contribute their time and talents to evaluation?

- Even when universal prevention programs drastically improve the safety of the school environment and children's social competence skills, some children will continue to bully others. Can you identify persistent bullying behaviors and victim behaviors that seem to be immune to universal interventions? What signs tell you that a more individualized counseling intervention may be needed? Take stock of your own skills in controlling your own aggression or in repelling others' aggression. How can you share these skills with children? How can you help children who are the targets of bullies?

In the appendix we provide additional resources for psychologists, counselors, educators, parents and caregivers, children, researchers, and the media. We hope that this book helps you to think critically about the problem of bullying and ways in which it can be prevented or minimized. We hope that you will take action!

APPENDIX: RESOURCES FOR BULLYING PREVENTION

AMERICAN PSYCHOLOGICAL ASSOCIATION

American Psychological Association Online (http://www.apa.org/topics/topicbully.html) provides numerous resources, research articles, and brochures specifically about what bullying is and how to prevent it. Press releases and articles from the *Monitor on Psychology* are available. The *Warning Signs of Teen Violence* are available at http://www.apahelpcenter.org/featuredtopics/.

BAM! BODY AND MIND

The Centers for Disease Control and Prevention developed Bam! Body and Mind specifically for children 9 to 13 years of age (http://www.bam.gov). The Web site, using kid-friendly lingo, provides games, quizzes, and other interactive features. The Web site also serves as an aid to teachers, providing them with interactive, educational, and fun activities that are linked to the national education standards for science and health. The section "Str8 Talk" addresses bullying and getting along, and the section "Head Strong" addresses stress management.

BULLY ONLINE

Bully Online, a site maintained by Tim Field from the United Kingdom, provides a comprehensive revision of bullying-related issues (http://www.bullyonline.org/). The site includes information on school, workplace, and family bullying (such as the impact of bullying on health), monthly news about bullying and related issues, practical advice for tackling bullying, legal advice, guidance for employers' human resources and personnel officers to deal with bullying at work, case studies, and a list of books on bullying and related subjects.

CALIFORNIA DEPARTMENT OF EDUCATION

The California Department of Education provides numerous resources on bullying prevention, hate-motivated crime, and classroom management (http://www.cde.ca.gov/ls/ss/se/). The site offers examples of school policies, documents that can be downloaded, and links to other resources.

Resources for Bullying Prevention

Resource	Audience						
	Psychologists, counselors	Educators	Children, adolescents	Activities for children	Family, parents	Researchers	Media
American Psychological Association	✓	✓			✓	✓	✓
BAM! Body and Mind	✓	✓	✓		✓		✓
Bully Online	✓	✓		✓			
California Department of Education	✓	✓					
Center for Effective Collaboration and Practice	✓	✓				✓	
Centers for Disease Control and Prevention	✓	✓	✓	✓			✓
Cyber Bullying	✓	✓	✓		✓	✓	
Family Guide to Keeping Youth Mentally Healthy and Drug Free	✓				✓	✓	
Hamilton Fish Institute	✓	✓	✓	✓	✓	✓	✓
I–Safe America	✓	✓			✓	✓	
Kids Count	✓					✓	
Minnesota Center Against Violence and Abuse	✓	✓				✓	
National Center for Education Statistics	✓					✓	
National Center for Victims of Crime	✓					✓	
National Criminal Justice Reference Service	✓		✓				
National Education Association	✓	✓	✓	✓			
National Mental Health and Education Center	✓	✓	✓		✓		
National Parent–Teacher Association	✓	✓	✓		✓		
National Youth Violence Prevention Resource Center	✓	✓	✓	✓	✓		
Stay Alert . . . Stay Safe	✓	✓	✓	✓	✓	✓	✓
Take a Stand. Lend a Hand. Stop Bullying Now!	✓	✓	✓	✓	✓		✓

CENTER FOR EFFECTIVE COLLABORATION AND PRACTICE

The Center for Effective Collaboration and Practice is part of the American Institutes for Research and is funded by the U.S. Department of Education and the U.S. Department of Health and Human Services (http://cecp.air.org/). The School Violence Prevention and Intervention page includes numerous resources for schools and researchers to use in developing and carrying out violence prevention plans. The site does not address bullying specifically, but rather school violence in general.

CENTERS FOR DISEASE CONTROL AND PREVENTION

The Centers for Disease Control and Prevention is the leading federal agency for protecting the health and safety of people in the United States (http://www.cdc.gov/). The Web site provides credible information about health, including violence and injury-related problems, indicating prevalence, risk factors, and prevention strategies. No information is specific to bullying. Publications, media releases, data, and funding opportunities are available. The National Center for Injury Prevention and Control (http://www.cdc.gov/ncipc/) provides information about different types of violence. A number of free publications are available, including a compendium of scales to measure violence. This site also provides up-to-date homicide and suicide statistics (http://www.cdc.gov/ncipc/wisqars/) by state and by demographic characteristics of the victims. The Division of Adolescent and School Health (http://www.cdc.gov/HealthyYouth/) provides resources for schools to improve children's and adolescents' health, including the Coordinated School Health Program model and the School Health Index, a school self-assessment and planning tool.

CYBER BULLYING

The Cyber Bully Web site is provided by the Center for Safe and Responsible Internet Use (http://cyberbully.org/). This site defines *cyberbullying* and provides resources for educators, parents, and children to combat Internet bullying. The site also provides links to media coverage of Internet bullying.

FAMILY GUIDE TO KEEPING YOUTH MENTALLY HEALTHY AND DRUG FREE

This Family Guide Web site is sponsored by the Substance Abuse and Mental Health Services Administration (SAMHSA) of the U.S. Department of Health and Human Services (http://www.family.samhsa.gov). SAMHSA's mission is to strengthen the nation's health care capacity to prevent, diagnose, and treat substance abuse and mental illnesses. The Web site was developed to support the efforts of parents and other caring adults to promote mental health and prevent the use of alcohol, tobacco, and illegal drugs by children and adolescents. The site provides some information specific to bullying.

HAMILTON FISH INSTITUTE

The Hamilton Fish Institute is administered by the School of Education and Human Development at George Washington University and funded by the Office of Juvenile Justice and Delinquency Prevention at the U.S. Department of Justice (http://www.hamfish.org). The institute is a national resource for research on and development of school violence prevention strategies. Services include providing the most current information about the levels of and trends in school violence in the nation; providing comprehensive literature reviews, research papers, and a searchable database for resources on violence prevention topics; consulting on effective strategies and promising model programs for violence prevention; assisting schools in assessing their needs for violence prevention and in implementing interventions; and providing assistance to policy-makers at the local, state, and national levels. Specific bullying prevention information is available.

I–SAFE AMERICA

Sponsored by the U.S. Department of Justice, i–Safe America provides Internet safety information to kids and teens, educators, parents, law enforcement agents, and the media (http://www.isafe.org/). The site includes newsletters, videos, a monitored chat room for teens, media releases, and links to relevant sites.

KIDS COUNT

Kids Count, a project of the Annie E. Casey Foundation, is a national and state-by-state effort to track the status of children in the United States (http://www.aecf.org/kidscount/). The site provides researchers and policymakers with detailed statistics about child well-being. The information is not specific to bullying.

MINNESOTA CENTER AGAINST VIOLENCE AND ABUSE

Minnesota Center Against Violence and Abuse is an electronic clearinghouse that provides access to more than 3,000 resources related to all forms of violence and abuse (http://www.mincava.umn.edu). The site includes publications, training resources, multimedia, bibliographies, service providers, experts, courses, research centers, job opportunities, event calendars, and funding. Some resources are specific to bullying.

NATIONAL CENTER FOR EDUCATION STATISTICS

The National Center for Education Statistics (NCES), part of the U.S. Department of Education, collects and analyzes data about education in the United States (http://nces.ed.gov). The NCES also reviews and reports on education activities internationally. The site provides education-related statistics for researchers; an educational, non-bullying-related home page for kids (http://nces.ed.gov/nceskids/); and information for schools; and multiple resources and links. The NCES publishes a yearly report, *Indicators of School Crime and Safety*, that provides some statistics about bullying (available online).

NATIONAL CENTER FOR VICTIMS OF CRIME

The National Center for Victims of Crime is the nation's leading resource and advocacy organization for crime victims (http://www.ncvc.org/). This not-for-profit organization maintains a toll-free help line (1-800-FYI-CALL) for victims of violence. Through collaboration with local, state, and federal partners, this organization provides direct services and resources, advocates for passage of laws and public policies for the protection of crime victims, and provides training and technical assistance. The Teen Victim Project (http:// www.ncvc.org/tvp/) provides specific information about bullying.

NATIONAL CRIMINAL JUSTICE REFERENCE SERVICE

The National Criminal Justice Reference Service, which is administered by the Office of Justice Programs at the U.S. Department of Justice, is a federally funded resource offering justice-related and substance abuse information to support research, policy, and program development (http://www.ncjrs.org/). A search of the library abstracts and full-text publications can lead to numerous bullying-related articles.

NATIONAL EDUCATION ASSOCIATION

The National Education Association (NEA) is a large professional employee organization committed to advancing the cause of public education (http://www.nea.org/schoolsafety/). NEA's 2.7 million members work in educational settings from preschools to university graduate programs. The site provides specific information about bullying and harassment for educators, parents, and children.

NATIONAL MENTAL HEALTH AND EDUCATION CENTER

The National Mental Health and Education Center, a public service of the National Association of School Psychologists, is an information and action network to foster best practices in education and mental health for children and families (http://www.naspcenter.org). Resources and information are available for educators, parents, children, and teens. Worksheets, activity handouts, and publications can be downloaded. Several documents are specific about bullying. Some resources are available in Spanish.

NATIONAL PARENT–TEACHER ASSOCIATION

The National Parent–Teacher Association is a volunteer, not-for-profit child advocacy organization (http://www.pta.org/bullying/). Its more than 6 million members include parents, students, educators, and citizens who are active in the schools and communities. The site provides specific information about bullying.

NATIONAL YOUTH VIOLENCE PREVENTION RESOURCE CENTER

The National Youth Violence Prevention Resource Center is sponsored by the Centers for Disease Control and Prevention and numerous other federal partners (http://www.safeyouth.org/). The center was established as a central source of information on prevention, intervention programs, publications, research, and statistics on violence committed by and against children and teens. The Web site is a user-friendly, single point of access to federal information on youth violence prevention and suicide. Numerous resources are specific to bullying.

STAY ALERT . . . STAY SAFE

Stay Alert . . . Stay Safe is a Canadian Web site sponsored by Curriculum Services Canada, the Canadian Association of Chiefs of Police, and the Ontario Trillium Foundation (http://www.sass.ca). The site offers "street-proofing" games and activities that teach knowledge about street safety to children 7 to 10 years old.

TAKE A STAND. LEND A HAND. STOP BULLYING NOW!

The Take a Stand. Lend a Hand. Stop Bullying Now! campaign Web site is sponsored by the Health Resources and Services Administration at the

U.S. Department of Health and Human Services (http://www.stopbullyingnow. hrsa.gov/). The site offers information about bullying for children, parents, educators, and the media. For children and young adolescents (most of the characters are 12 years old), the site provides games and activities using kid-friendly lingo and characters designed to increase understanding of what bullying is and how to prevent it. For parents and educators, the site provides information and activities. A free bullying prevention kit can be ordered online. For the media, the site provides news archives and ready-to-use public service announcements.

REFERENCES

Achenbach, T. M. (1991). *Manual for the Child Behavior Checklist, 4–18 and 1991 Profile*. Burlington: University of Vermont, Department of Psychiatry.

Ainsworth, M. D. S., & Bowlby, J. (1991). An ethological approach to personality development. *American Psychologist, 46*, 333–341.

Alder, N. (2000). Part III: Creating multicultural classrooms. *Multicultural Perspectives, 2*, 28–31.

American Association of University Women. (2001). *Hostile hallways: Bullying, teasing, and sexual harassment in school*. Washington, DC: Author.

American Federation of Teachers. (2001). *Building on the best, learning from what works: Five promising discipline and violence prevention programs*. Retrieved June 8, 2005, from http://www.aft.org/pubs-reports/downloads/teachers/wwdiscipline.pdf

American Psychological Association, Council of Representatives. (1999). *Violence in mass media*. Retrieved May 12, 2005, from http://www.apa.org/pi/cyf/cyfres.html#media

Anderson, C. A., Berkowitz, L., Donnerstein, E., Huesmann, L. R., Johnson, J. D., Linz, D., et al. (2003). The influence of media violence on youth. *Psychological Science in the Public Interest, 4*, 81–110.

Andrews, D. A., Zinger, I., Hoge, R. D., Bonta, J., Gendreau, P., & Cullen, F. T. (1990). A clinically relevant and psychologically informed meta-analysis. *Criminology, 28*, 369–387.

Arbuthnot, J. B., & Faust, D. (1981). *Teaching moral reasoning: Theory and practice*. New York: Harper & Row.

Arsenio, W. F., & Lemerise, E. A. (2001). Varieties of childhood bullying: Values, emotion processes, and social competence. *Social Development, 10*, 59–78.

Aspy, D. N., & Roebuck, F. N. (1977). *Kids don't learn from people they don't like*. Amherst, MA: Human Resource Development Press.

Atlas, R. S., & Pepler, D. J. (1998). Observations of bullying in the classroom. *Journal of Educational Research, 92*, 86–99.

Baldry, A. C. (2003). Bullying in schools and exposure to domestic violence. *Child Abuse & Neglect, 27*, 713–732.

Baldry, A. C., & Farrington, D. P. (1998). Parenting influences on bullying and victimization. *Criminal and Legal Psychology, 3*, 237–254.

Bandura, A. (1973). *Aggression: A social learning analysis*. Englewood Cliffs, NJ: Prentice Hall.

Bandura, A. (1986). *Social foundations of thought and action: A social cognitive theory*. Englewood Cliffs, NJ: Prentice Hall.

Bartholomew, L. K., Parcel, G. S., Kok, G., & Gottlieb, N. H. (2001). *Intervention mapping: Designing theory- and evidence-based health promotion programs*. Mountain View, CA: Mayfield Publishing.

Bear, G. G. (1998). School discipline in the United States: Prevention, correction, and long-term social development. *School Psychology Review, 27,* 14–32.

Beck, A. T. (1972). *Depression: Causes and treatment.* Philadelphia: University of Pennsylvania Press.

Berthold, K. A., & Hoover, J. H. (2000). Correlates of bullying and victimization among intermediate students in the Midwestern USA. *School Psychology International, 21,* 65–78.

Biglan, A., Duncan, T. E., Ary, D. V., & Smolkowski, K. (1995). Peer and parental influences on adolescent tobacco use. *Journal of Behavioral Medicine, 18,* 315–330.

Blechman, E. (1998). Parent training in moral context: Prosocial family therapy. In J. M. Briesmeister & C. E. Schaefer (Eds.), *Handbook of parent training: Parents as co-therapists for children's behavior problems* (2nd ed., pp. 508–548). New York: Wiley.

Bogenschneider, K., Wu, M. Y., Raffaelli, M., & Tsay, J. C. (1998). Parent influences on adolescent peer orientation and substance use: The interface of parenting practices and values. *Child Development, 69,* 1672–1688.

Bohlin, K. E., Farmer, D., & Ryan, K. (2001). *Building character in schools: Resource guide.* San Francisco: Jossey-Bass.

Bonds, M., & Stoker, S. (2000). *Bully-proofing your middle school.* Longmont: Sopris West.

Bosworth, K. (2000). *Protective schools: Linking drug abuse prevention with student success.* Tucson: University of Arizona, College of Education. Retrieved February 20, 2005, from http://www.drugstats.org

Bosworth, K., Espelage, D. L., & Simon, T. R. (1999). Factors associated with bullying behavior in middle school students. *Journal of Early Adolescence, 19,* 341–362.

Botvin, G. J., Mahalic, S. F., & Grotpeter, J. K. (1998). *Life skills training* (Book 5, Blueprints for Violence Prevention). Boulder: Center for the Study and Prevention of Violence, Institute of Behavioral Science, University of Colorado at Boulder.

Boulton, M. J., & Smith, P. K. (1994). Bully victim problems in middle-school children: Stability, self-perceived competence, peer perceptions and peer acceptance. *British Journal of Developmental Psychology, 12,* 315–329.

Boulton, M. J., & Underwood, K. (1992). Bully/victim problems among middle school children. *British Journal of Educational Psychology, 62,* 73–87.

Bowen, M. (1985). *Family therapy in clinical practice.* New York: Jason Aronson.

Bowlby, J. (1982). *Attachment and loss* (2nd ed., Vol. 1). New York: Basic Books.

Brame, B., Nagin, D. S., & Tremblay, R. E. (2001). Developmental trajectories of physical aggression from school entry to late adolescence. *Journal of Child Psychology and Psychiatry and Allied Disciplines, 42,* 503–512.

Brener, N. D., Krug, E. G., Dahlberg, L. L., & Powell, K. E. (1997). Nurses' logs as an evaluation tool for school-based violence prevention programs. *Journal of School Health, 67,* 171–174.

Broidy, L. M., Nagin, D. S., Tremblay, R. E., Bates, J. E., Brame, B., & Dodge, K. A. (2003). Developmental trajectories of childhood disruptive behaviors and adolescent delinquency: A six-site, cross-national study. *Developmental Psychology, 39*, 222–245.

Brown, B. B., Mounts, N., Lamborn, S. D., & Steinberg, L. (1993). Parenting practices and peer group affiliation in adolescence. *Child Development, 64*, 467–482.

Buka, S., & Earls, F. (1993). Early determinants of delinquency and violence. *Health Affairs, 12*, 46–64.

Busch, K. G., Zagar, R., Hughes, J. R., Arbit, J., & Bussell, R. E. (1990). Adolescents who kill. *Journal of Clinical Psychology, 46*, 472–485.

Calhoun, G. B., Glaser, B. A., & Bartolomucci, C. L. (2001). The juvenile counseling and assessment model and program: A conceptualization and intervention for juvenile delinquency. *Journal of Counseling and Development, 79*, 131–141.

Caprara, G. V., Barbaranelli, C., Pastorelli, C., Bandura, A., & Zimbardo, P. G. (2000). Prosocial foundations of children's academic achievement. *Psychological Science, 11*, 302–306.

Carr, R. A. (1988). The city-wide peer counseling program. *Children and Youth Services Review, 10*, 217–232.

Cavell, T. A. (2000). *Working with parents of aggressive children: A practitioner's guide*. Washington, DC: American Psychological Association.

Center for the Study and Prevention of Violence. (n.d.). *Blueprints for violence prevention*. Boulder: Institute for Behavioral Sciences at the University of Colorado, Center for the Study and Prevention of Violence. Retrieved June 8, 2005, from http://www.colorado.edu/cspv/blueprints/

Centers for Disease Control and Prevention. (2003). *Overweight and obesity: Frequently asked questions*. Retrieved June 8, 2005, from http://www.cdc.gov/nccdphp/dnpa/obesity/faq.htm

Chambless, D. L., & Hollon, S. D. (1998). Defining empirically supported therapies. *Journal of Consulting and Clinical Psychology, 66*, 7–18.

Chavez, E. R., Edwards, R., & Oetting, E. R. (1989). Mexican American and white American school dropouts' drug use, health status, and involvement in violence. *Public Health Reports, 104*, 594–604.

Christophersen, E. R., & Mortweet, S. L. (2001). *Treatments that work with children: Empirically supported strategies for managing childhood problems*. Washington, DC: American Psychological Association.

Christophersen, E. R., & Mortweet, S. L. (2003). *Parenting that works: Building skills that last a lifetime*. Washington, DC: American Psychological Association.

Cohen, D. A., Farley, T. A., Taylor, S. N., Martin, D. H., & Schuster, M. A. (2002). When and where do youths have sex? The potential role of adult supervision. *Pediatrics, 110*, e66.

Coie, J. D., & Dodge, K. A. (1983). Continuities and changes in children's social status: A 5-year longitudinal study. *Merrill–Palmer Quarterly—Journal of Developmental Psychology, 29*, 261–282.

Coie, J. D., & Dodge, K. A. (1988). Multiple sources of data on social behavior and social status in the school: A cross-age comparison. *Child Development, 59,* 815–829.

Conduct Problems Prevention Research Group. (1992). A developmental and clinical model for the prevention of conduct disorders: The FAST Track program. *Development and Psychopathology, 4,* 509–527.

Cowie, H. (1999). Peers helping peers: Interventions, initiatives and insights. *Journal of Adolescence, 22,* 433–436.

Crick, N. R., & Bigbee, M. A. (1998). Relational and overt forms of peer victimization: A multi-informant approach. *Journal of Consulting and Clinical Psychology, 66,* 337–347.

Crick, N. R., Casas, J. F., & Ku, H. C. (1999). Relational and physical forms of peer victimization in preschool. *Developmental Psychology, 35,* 376–385.

Crick, N. R., & Dodge, K. A. (1994). A review and reformulation of social information-processing mechanisms in children's social adjustment. *Psychological Bulletin, 115,* 74–101.

Crick, N. R., & Grotpeter, J. K. (1995). Relational aggression, gender, and social psychological adjustment. *Child Development, 66,* 710–722.

Curwin, R. L., & Mendler, A. N. (1997). *As tough as necessary: Countering violence, aggression, and hostility in our schools.* Alexandria, VA: Association for Supervision and Curriculum Development.

Curwin, R. L., & Mendler, A. N. (1999). *Discipline with dignity.* Alexandria, VA: Association for Supervision and Curriculum Development.

Dadds, M. (1995). *Families, children, and the development of dysfunction.* Thousand Oaks, CA: Sage.

Dagley, J. C. (2000). Adlerian family therapy. In A. M. Horne & J. L. Passmore (Eds.), *Family counseling and therapy* (3rd ed., pp. 366–419). Itasca, IL: F. E. Peacock Publishers.

Dahlberg, L. L., Toal, S. B., Swahn, M., & Behrens, C. B. (2005). *Measuring violence-related attitudes, behaviors, and influences among youths: A compendium of assessment tools* (2nd ed.). Atlanta, GA: Centers for Disease Control and Prevention, National Center for Injury Prevention and Control.

Development Services Group. (n.d.). *Model programs guide and database.* Retrieved June 8, 2005, from http://www.dsgonline.com/

DeVoe, J. F., Peter, K., Kaufman, P., Ruddy, S. A., Miller, A. K., Planty, M. G., et al. (2002). *Indicators of school crime and safety: 2002.* Washington, DC: U.S. Department of Education, U. S. Department of Justice.

Dishion, T. J., McCord, J., & Poulin, F. (1999). When interventions harm—Peer groups and problem behavior. *American Psychologist, 54,* 755–764.

Dodge, K. A. (1980). Social cognition and children's aggressive behavior. *Child Development, 51,* 162–170.

Dodge, K. A., & Coie, J. D. (1987). Social-information-processing factors in reactive and proactive aggression in children's peer groups. *Journal of Personality and Social Psychology, 53,* 1146–1158.

Dodge, K. A., & Frame, C. L. (1982). Social cognitive biases and deficits in aggressive boys. *Child Development, 53,* 620–635.

Dodge, K. A., & Newman, J. P. (1981). Biased decision-making processes in aggressive boys. *Journal of Abnormal Psychology, 90,* 375–379.

Dodge, K. A., Price, J. M., Bachorowski, J. A., & Newman, J. P. (1990). Hostile attributional biases in severely aggressive adolescents. *Journal of Abnormal Psychology, 99,* 385–392.

Donnerstein, E., Slaby, R. G., & Eron, L. D. (1996). The mass media and youth aggression. In L. D. Eron, J. H. Gentry, & P. Schlegel (Eds.), *Reason to hope: A psychosocial perspective on violence and youth* (2nd ed., pp. 219–250). Washington, DC: American Psychological Association.

Dubow, E. F., Huesmann, R., & Eron, L. D. (1987). Mitigating aggression and promoting prosocial behavior in aggressive elementary schoolboys. *Behaviour Research and Therapy, 25,* 527–531.

Dwyer, K., Osher, D., & Warger, C. (1998). *Early warning, timely response: A guide to safe schools.* Washington, DC: U.S. Department of Education.

Eagly, A. H., & Steffen, V. J. (1986). Gender and aggressive behavior: A meta-analytic review of the social psychological literature. *Psychological Bulletin, 100,* 303–330.

Eddy, J. M., Reid, J. B., & Fetrow, R. A. (2000). An elementary school-based prevention program targeting modifiable antecedents of youth delinquency and violence: Linking the Interests of Families and Teachers (LIFT). *Journal of Emotional and Behavioral Disorders, 8,* 165–176.

Eden, D. (1990). *Pygmalion in management: Productivity as a self-fulfilling prophecy.* Lexington, MA: Heath.

Eisenberg, M. E., Neumark-Sztainer, D., & Perry, C. L. (2003). Peer harassment, school connectedness, and academic achievement. *Journal of School Health, 73,* 311–316.

Ellis, A. (1962). *Reason and emotion in psychotherapy* (2nd ed.). New York: Lyle Stuart.

Embry, D. D. (2002). The Good Behavior Game: A best practice candidate as a universal behavioral vaccine. *Clinical Child and Family Psychology Review, 5,* 273–297.

Eron, L. D. (1987). The development of aggressive behavior from the perspective of developing behaviorism. *American Psychologist, 42,* 435–442.

Espelage, D. L. (2004). Preventing bullying among school-age children. *The Prevention Researcher, 11,* 3–6.

Espelage, D. L., & Asidao, C. S. (2001). Conversations with middle school students about bullying and victimization: Should we be concerned? *Journal of Emotional Abuse, 2,* 49–62.

Espelage, D. L., Bosworth, K., & Simon, T. R. (2000). Examining the social context of bullying behaviors in early adolescence. *Journal of Counseling and Development, 78,* 326–333.

Espelage, D. L., Bosworth, K., & Simon, T. R. (2001). Short-term stability and prospective correlates of bullying in middle-school students: An examination of potential demographic, psychosocial, and environmental influences. *Violence and Victims, 16,* 411–426.

Espelage, D. L., & Holt, M. K. (2001). Bullying and victimization during early adolescence: Peer influences and psychosocial correlates. *Journal of Emotional Abuse, 2,* 123–142.

Espelage, D. L., Mebane, S., & Adams, R. (2004). Empathy and the bully–victim continuum. In D. L. Espelage & S. M. Swearer (Eds.), *Bullying in American schools: A social ecological perspective on prevention and intervention* (pp. 37–61). Mahwah, NJ: Erlbaum.

Espelage, D. L., & Swearer, S. M. (Eds.). (2004). *Bullying in American schools: A social–ecological perspective on prevention and intervention.* Mahwah, NJ: Erlbaum.

Eyberg, S. (1992). Parent and teacher behavior inventories for the assessment of conduct problem behaviors in children. In L. VandeCreek & S. Knapp (Eds.), *Innovations in clinical practice: A source book* (Vol. 11, pp. 261–270). Sarasota, FL: Professional Resource Press/Professional Resource Exchange.

Faber, A., & Mazlish, E. (1995). *How to talk so kids can learn at home and at school.* New York: Fireside.

Farrington, D. P. (1989). Early predictors of adolescent aggression and adult violence. *Violence and Victims, 4,* 79–100.

Federal Bureau of Investigation. (n.d.). *A parent's guide to Internet safety.* Retrieved February 20, 2005, from http://www.fbi.gov/publications/pguide/guidee.htm

Feindler, E. L., & Ecton, R. B. (1986). *Adolescent anger control: Cognitive–behavioral techniques.* New York: Pergamon Press.

Fergusson, D. M., & Horwood, L. J. (1995). Early disruptive behavior, IQ, and later school achievement and delinquent behavior. *Journal of Abnormal Child Psychology, 23,* 183–199.

Fergusson, D. M., & Horwood, L. J. (2002). Male and female offending trajectories. *Development and Psychopathology, 14,* 159–177.

Feshbach, S. (1971). Dynamics and morality of violence and aggression: Some psychological considerations. *American Psychologist, 26,* 281–292.

Festinger, L. (1962). Cognitive dissonance. *Scientific American, 107,* 99–113.

Flannery, D. J., Vazsonyi, A. T., Liau, A. K., Guo, S. Y., Powell, K. E., Atha, H., et al. (2003). Initial behavior outcomes for the PeaceBuilders universal school-based violence prevention program. *Developmental Psychology, 39,* 292–308.

Flay, B. R. (2002). Positive youth development requires comprehensive health promotion programs. *American Journal of Health Behavior, 26,* 407–424.

Flay, B. R., & Allred, C. G. (2003). Long-term effects of the Positive Action program. *American Journal of Health Behavior, 27,* S6–S21.

Fleischman, M., Horne, A. M., & Arthur, J. (1983). *Troubled families.* Champaign, IL: Research Press.

Forehand, R., Kotchick, B., Shaffer, A., & Dorsey, S. (2002, June). *Behavioral parent training: Accomplishments, challenges, and promises.* Paper presented at the Third

International Conference on Child and Adolescent Mental Health, Brisbane, Australia.

Forehand, R., & Long, N. (2002). *Parenting the strong-willed child: The clinically proven five-week program for parents of two- to six-year-olds* (2nd ed.). Chicago: Contemporary Books.

Fors, S. W., Crepaz, N., & Hayes, D. M. (1999). Key factors that protect against health risks in youth: Further evidence. *American Journal of Health Behavior, 23,* 368–380.

Frankel, F., Cantwell, D. P., & Myatt, R. (1996). Helping ostracized children: Social skills training and parent support for socially rejected children. In E. D. Hibbs & P. S. Jensen (Eds.), *Psychosocial treatments for child and adolescents disorders: Empirically based strategies for clinical practice* (pp. 595–617). Washington, DC: American Psychological Association.

Fry, P. S. (1983). Process measures of problem and non-problem children's classroom behaviour: The influence of teacher behaviour variables. *British Journal of Educational Psychology, 53,* 79–88.

Funk, J., Elliott, R., Bechtoldt, H., Pasold, T., & Tsavoussis, A. (2003). The Attitudes Toward Violence Scale—Child Version. *Journal of Interpersonal Violence, 18,* 186–196.

Garmezy, N. (1993). Children in poverty—Resilience despite risk. *Psychiatry—Interpersonal and Biological Processes, 56,* 127–136.

Garrity, C., Baris, M., & Porter, W. (2000). *Bully-proofing your child—A parent's guide.* Longmont, CO: Sopris West.

Garrity, C., Jens, K., Porter, W., Sager, N., & Short-Camilli, C. (2004). *Bully-proofing your elementary school: Working with victims and bullies.* Longmont, CO: Sopris West.

Glover, D., Gough, G., Johnson, M., & Cartwright, N. (2000). Bullying in 25 secondary schools: Incidence, impact, and intervention. *Educational Research, 42,* 141–156.

Goldstein, A. P., Glick, B., & Gibbs, J. C. (1998). *Aggression Replacement Training: A comprehensive intervention for aggressive youth.* Champaign, IL: Research Press.

Goldstein, A. P., McGinnis, E., Sprafkin, R. P., Gershaw, N. J., & Klein, P. (1997). *Skillstreaming the adolescent: New strategies and perspectives for teaching social skills.* Champaign, IL: Research Press.

Goldstein, A. P., Sprafkin, R. P., Gershaw, N. J., & Klein, P. (1980). *Skillstreaming the adolescent: A structured learning approach to teaching prosocial skills.* Champaign, IL: Research Press.

Goleman, D. (1995). *Emotional intelligence.* New York: Bantam Books.

Gottfredson, D. C., & Gottfredson, G. D. (2002). Quality of school-based prevention programs: Results from a national survey. *Journal of Research in Crime and Delinquency, 39,* 3–35.

Gottfredson, D. C., Gottfredson, G. D., & Skroban, S. (1998). Can prevention work where it is needed most? *Evaluation Review, 22,* 315–340.

Greenberg, M. T., Kusche, C. A., & Mihalic, S. (1998). *Promoting alternative thinking strategies (PATHS;* Book 10, Blueprints for Violence Prevention). Boulder: Center for the Study and Prevention of Violence, Institute of Behavioral Science, University of Colorado at Boulder.

Greenberg, M. T., Speltz, M. L., & DeKlyen, M. (1993). The role of attachment in the early development of disruptive behavior problems. *Development and Psychopathology, 5,* 191–213.

Greenberg, M. T., Weissberg, R. P., O'Brien, M. U., Zins, J. E., Fredericks, L., Resnik, H., et al. (2003). Enhancing school-based prevention and youth development through coordinated social, emotional, and academic learning. *American Psychologist, 58,* 466–474.

Greene, M. B. (2003). Counseling and climate change as treatment modalities for bullying in school. *International Journal for the Advancement of Counselling, 25,* 293–302.

Grossman, D. C., Neckerman, H. J., Koepsell, T. D., Liu, P. Y., Asher, K. N., Beland, K., et al. (1997). Effectiveness of a violence prevention curriculum among children in elementary school: A randomized controlled trial. *Journal of the American Medical Association, 277,* 1605–1611.

Gruber, K. J., Wiley, S. D., Broughman, S. P., Strizek, G. A., & Burian-Fitzgerald, M. (2002). *School and staffing survey, 1999–2000: Overview of the data for public, private, public charter, and Bureau of Indian Affairs elementary and secondary schools* (Publication No. NCES 2002-313). Washington, DC: U.S. Department of Education, National Center for Education Statistics.

Grunbaum, J. A., Kann, L., Kinchen, S., Ross, J., Hawkins, J., Lowry, R., et al. (2004). Youth Risk Behavior Surveillance—United States, 2003. *Morbidity and Mortality Weekly Report, 53*(SS-2), 1–96.

Guerra, N. G., & Slaby, R. G. (1989). Evaluative factors in social problem solving by aggressive boys. *Journal of Abnormal Child Psychology, 17,* 277–289.

Hageseth, C. (1988). *A laughing place: The art and psychology of positive humor in love and adversity.* Fort Collins, CO: Berwick Publishing.

Hawker, D. S., & Boulton, M. J. (2000). Twenty years' research on peer victimization and psychosocial maladjustment: A meta-analytic review of cross-sectional studies. *Journal of Child Psychology and Psychiatry, 41,* 441–455.

Hazler, R. J. (1996). *Breaking the cycle of violence: Interventions for bullying and victimization.* Washington, DC: Accelerated Development.

Hein, K. (2004). Preventing aggression in the classroom: A case study of extraordinary teachers (Doctoral dissertation, University of Georgia).

Hembree-Kigin, T. L., & McNeil, C. B. (1995). *Parent-child interaction therapy.* New York: Plenum.

Henderson, N., & Milstein, M. M. (2003). *Resiliency in schools: Making it happen for students and educators.* Thousand Oaks, CA: Corwin Press.

Herrenkohl, T. I., Guo, H., Kosterman, R., Hawkins, J. D., Catalano, R. F., & Smith, B. H. (2001). Early adolescent predictors of youth violence as mediators of childhood risks. *Journal of Early Adolescence, 21,* 447–469.

Hewitt, J. D., Huizinga, D., Elliot, D. S., Corley, R., Grotpeter, J. K., Smolen, A., et al. (2003, November). *The National Youth Survey Family Study: A multigenerational, multidisciplinary, longitudinal design*. Paper presented at the Annual Conference of the American Society of Criminology. Retrieved June 8, 2005, from http://www.asc41.com/www/2003/absqt037.htm

Hill, C. E. (2001). *Helping skills: The empirical foundation*. Washington, DC: American Psychological Association.

Hoover, J. H., Oliver, R., & Hazler, R. J. (1992). Bullying: Perceptions of adolescent victims in the Midwestern USA. *School Psychology International, 13*, 5–16.

Horne, A. M. (1991). Social learning family therapy. In A. M. Horne & J. L. Passmore (Eds.), *Family counseling and therapy* (2nd ed., pp. 461–496). Itasca, IL: F. E. Peacock Publishers.

Horne, A. M. (2000). *Family counseling and therapy* (3rd ed.). Itasca, IL: F. E. Peacock Publishers.

Horne, A. M., Bartolomucci, C. L., & Newman-Carlson, D. (2003). *Bully busters: A teacher's manual for helping bullies, victims, and bystanders (grades K–5)*. Champaign, IL: Research Press.

Horne, A. M., Orpinas, P., Newman-Carlson, D., & Bartolomucci, C. (2004). Elementary school Bully Busters program: Understanding why children bully and what to do about it. In D. L. Espelage & S. M. Swearer (Eds.), *Bullying in American schools: A social–ecological perspective on prevention and intervention* (pp. 297–325). Mahwah, NJ: Erlbaum.

Horne, A. M., & Sayger, T. V. (1990). *Treating conduct and oppositional defiant disorders in children*. New York: Pergamon Press.

Horne, A. M., & Sayger, T. V. (2000). Behavioral approaches to couple and family therapy. In A. M. Horne (Ed.), *Family counseling and therapy* (3rd ed., pp. 454–488). Itasca, IL: F. E. Peacock Publishers.

Howes, C., & Eldredge, R. (1985). Responses of abused, neglected, and non-maltreated children to the behavior of their peers. *Journal of Applied and Developmental Psychology, 6*, 261–270.

Huesmann, L. R., & Eron, L. D. (1984). Cognitive processes and the persistence of aggressive behavior. *Aggressive Behavior, 10*, 243–251.

Huesmann, L. R., & Guerra, N. G. (1997). Children's normative beliefs about aggression and aggressive behavior. *Journal of Personality and Social Psychology, 72*, 408–419.

Huesmann, L. R., & Malamuth, N. M. (1986). Media violence and antisocial behavior—An overview. *Journal of Social Issues, 42*, 1–6.

Hughes, J. N. (2003). Commentary: Participatory action research leads to sustainable school and community improvement. *School Psychology Review, 32*, 38–43.

Hunter, S. C., & Boyle, J. M. E. (2004). Appraisal and coping strategy use in victims of school bullying. *British Journal of Educational Psychology, 74*, 83–107.

Hyde, J. S. (1984). How large are gender differences in aggression? A developmental meta-analysis. *Developmental Psychology, 20*, 722–736.

Hyman, I. A., & Perone, D. C. (1998). The other side of school violence: Educator policies and practices that may contribute to student misbehavior. *Journal of School Psychology, 36*, 7–27.

Ialongo, N., Poduska, J., Werthamer, L., & Kellam, S. (2001). The distal impact of two first-grade preventive interventions on conduct problems and disorder in early adolescence. *Journal of Emotional and Behavioral Disorders, 9*, 146–160.

Ialongo, N. S., Werthamer, L., Kellam, S., Brown, C. H., Wang, S., & Lin, Y. (1999). Proximal impact of two first-grade preventive interventions on the early risk behaviors for later substance abuse, depression, and antisocial behavior. *American Journal of Community Psychology, 27*, 599–641.

Ingoldsby, E. M., Shaw, D. S., & Garcia, M. M. (2001). Intrafamily conflict in relation to boys' adjustment at school. *Development and Psychopathology, 13*, 35–52.

Joffe, R. D., Dobson, K. S., Fine, S., Marriage, K., & Haley, G. (1990). Social problem-solving in depressed, conduct-disordered, and normal adolescents. *Journal of Abnormal Child Psychology, 18*, 565–575.

Johnson, S. (1988). *The history of Rasselas, Prince of Abissinia.* New York: Oxford University Press. (Original work published 1759)

Kamphaus, R. W., Huberty, C. J., DiStefano, C., & Petoskey, M. D. (1997). A typology of teacher-rated child behavior for a national U.S. sample. *Journal of Abnormal Child Psychology, 25*, 453–463.

Kasen, S., Berenson, K., Cohen, P., & Johnson, J. G. (2004). The effects of school climate on changes in aggressive and other behaviors related to bullying. In D. L. Espelage & S. M. Swearer (Eds.), *Bullying in American schools: A social–ecological perspective on prevention and intervention* (pp. 187–210). Mahwah, NJ: Erlbaum.

Kashani, J. H., Deuser, W., & Reid, J. C. (1991). Aggression and anxiety: A new look at an old notion. *Journal of the American Academy of Child and Adolescent Psychiatry, 30*, 218–223.

Kashani, J. H., & Shepperd, J. A. (1990). Aggression in adolescents: The role of social support and personality. *Canadian Journal of Psychiatry, 35*, 311–315.

Kazdin, A. E. (1987). Treatment of antisocial behavior in children: Current status and future directions. *Psychological Bulletin, 102*, 187–203.

Kazdin, A. E., & Weisz, J. R. (1998). Identifying and developing empirically supported child and adolescent treatments. *Journal of Consulting and Clinical Psychology, 66*, 19–36.

Kazdin, A., & Weisz, J. R. (2003). *Evidence based psychotherapies for children and adolescents.* New York: Guilford Press.

Kelley, B. T., Loeber, R., Keenan, K., & DeLamatre, M. (1997). *Developmental pathways in boys' disruptive and delinquent behavior* (Publication No. NCJRS 165152). Washington, DC: U.S. Department of Justice, Office of Juvenile Justice and Delinquency Prevention.

Kelley, B. T., Thornberry, T. P., & Smith, C. A. (1997). *In the wake of childhood maltreatment* (Publication No. NCJ 165257, pp. 1–16). Washington, DC: U.S. Department of Justice, Office of Juvenile Justice and Delinquency Prevention.

Kochenderfer, B. J., & Ladd, G. W. (1996). Peer victimization: Manifestations and relations to school adjustment in kindergarten. *Journal of School Psychology, 34,* 267–283.

Kohlberg, L. (1984). *Essays on moral development: The psychology of moral development.* San Francisco: Harper & Row.

Kolb, K., & Jussim, L. (1994). Teacher expectations and underachieving gifted children. *Roeper Review, 17,* 26–31.

Kotchick, B., Shaffer, A., Dorsey, S., & Forehand, R. (2004). Parenting antisocial children and adolescents. In M. Hoghughi & N. Long (Eds.), *Handbook of parenting: Theory and research for practice* (pp. 256–275). Thousand Oaks, CA: Sage.

Krug, E. G., Mercy, J. A., Dahlberg, L. L., & Zwi, A. B. (2002). The world report on violence and health. *Lancet, 360,* 1083–1088.

Lacourse, E., Nagin, D., Tremblay, R. E., Vitaro, F., & Claes, M. (2003). Developmental trajectories of boys' delinquent group membership and facilitation of violent behaviors during adolescence. *Development and Psychopathology, 15,* 183–197.

Ladd, G. H. (1992). Themes and theories: Perspectives on processes in family–peer relationships. In R. D. Park & G. W. Ladd (Eds.), *Family–peer relationships: Modes of linkage* (pp. 3–34). Hillsdale, NJ: Erlbaum.

Larson, R., & Richards, M. H. (1991). Daily companionship in late childhood and early adolescence—Changing developmental contexts. *Child Development, 62,* 284–300.

Ledoux, S., Miller, P., Choquet, M., & Plant, M. (2002). Family structure, parent–child relationships, and alcohol and other drug use among teenagers in France and the United Kingdom. *Alcohol and Alcoholism, 37,* 52–60.

Leff, S. S., Kupersmidt, J. B., Patterson, C. J., & Power, T. J. (1999). Factors influencing teacher identification of peer bullies and victims. *School Psychology Review, 28,* 505–517.

Leff, S. S., Power, T. J., & Goldstein, A. B. (2004). Outcome measures to assess the effectiveness of bully-prevention programs in the schools. In D. L. Espelage & S. M. Swearer (Eds.), *Bullying in American schools: A social–ecological perspective on prevention and intervention* (pp. 269–293). Mahwah, NJ: Erlbaum.

Leff, S. S., Power, T. J., Manz, P. H., Costigan, T. E., & Nabors, L. A. (2001). School-based aggression prevention programs for young children: Current status and implications for violence prevention. *School Psychology Review, 30,* 344–362.

Lewin, K. (1951). *Field theory in social science: Selected theoretical papers.* New York: Harper & Row.

Lewis, T. J., Sugai, G., & Colvin, G. (1998). Reducing problem behavior through a school-wide system of effective behavioral support: Investigation of a school-wide social skills training program and contextual interventions. *School Psychology Review, 27,* 446–459.

Lickona, T. (1991). *Educating for character: How our schools can teach respect and responsibility.* New York: Bantam Books.

Lieberman, M., Doyle, A. B., & Markiewicz, D. (1999). Developmental patterns in security of attachment to mother and father in late childhood and early adolescence: Associations with peer relations. *Child Development, 70*, 202–213.

Limber, S. P. (2003). Efforts to address bullying in U. S. Schools. *American Journal of Health Education, 34*, 23–29.

Limber, S. P. (2004). Implementation of the Olweus bullying prevention program in American schools: Lessons learned from the field. In D. L. Espelage & S. M. Swearer (Eds.), *Bullying in American schools: A social–ecological perspective on prevention and intervention* (pp. 351–363). Mahwah, NJ: Erlbaum.

Limber, S. P., & Small, M. A. (2003). State laws and policies to address bullying in schools. *School Psychology Review, 32*, 445–455.

Lipsey, M. W., & Wilson, D. B. (1998). Effective intervention for serious juvenile offenders: A synthesis of research. In R. Loeber & D. Farrington (Eds.), *Serious and violent juvenile offenders: Risk factors and successful intervention* (pp. 313–345). Thousand Oaks, CA: Sage.

Loeber, R., & Dishion, T. J. (1983). Early predictors of male delinquency: A review. *Psychological Bulletin, 94*, 68–99.

Loeber, R., Kalb, L., & Huizinga, D. (2001). *Juvenile delinquency and serious injury victimization* (Publication No. NCJ 188676, pp. 1–8). Washington, DC: U.S. Department of Justice, Office of Juvenile Justice and Delinquency Prevention.

Loeber, R., & Stouthamer-Loeber, M. (1998). Development of juvenile aggression and violence—Some common misconceptions and controversies. *American Psychologist, 53*, 242–259.

Maccoby, E. E., & Jacklin, C. N. (1974). *The psychology of sex differences.* Stanford, CA: Stanford University Press.

Magen, Z. (1998). *Exploring adolescent happiness: Commitment, purpose, and fulfillment.* Thousand Oaks, CA: Sage.

Maines, B., & Robinson, G. (1992). *Michael's story: The "No Blame Approach."* Bristol, England: Lame Duck.

Maslach, C., & Jackson, S. E. (1993). *Maslach Burnout Inventory manual* (2nd ed.). Palo Alto, CA: Consulting Psychologists Press.

Masten, A. S., & Coatsworth, J. D. (1998). The development of competence in favorable and unfavorable environments—Lessons from research on successful children. *American Psychologist, 53*, 205–220.

Maughan, B., Rowe, R., Messer, J., Goodman, R., & Meltzer, H. (2004). Conduct and oppositional defiant disorder in a national sample: Developmental epidemiology. *Journal of Child Psychology and Psychiatry, 45*, 609–621.

Maultsby, M. C. (1984). *Rational behavior therapy.* Englewood Cliffs, NJ: Prentice Hall.

May, R. (1980). *Sex and fantasy: Patterns of male and female development.* New York: Norton.

McCoy, E. (1997). *What to do . . . When kids are mean to your child.* Pleasantville, NY: Reader's Digest.

McGinnis, E., & Goldstein, A. P. (2003). *Skillstreaming in early childhood: New strategies and perspectives for teaching prosocial skills.* Champaign, IL: Research Press.

McMahon, R. J., & Wells, K. C. (1998). Conduct problems. In E. J. Mash & R. A. Barkley (Eds.), *Treatment of childhood disorders* (2nd ed., pp. 111–207). New York: Guilford Press.

Meichenbaum, D. K. (1977). *Cognitive–behavior modification: An integrative approach.* New York: Plenum Press.

Mendler, A. N. (2000). *Motivating students who don't care: Successful techniques for educators.* Bloomington, IN: National Educational Service.

Mendler, A. N., & Curwin, R. L. (1999). *Discipline with dignity for the challenging youth.* Bloomington, IN: National Educational Service.

Mercy, J. A., Rosenberg, M. L., Powell, K. E., Broome, C. V., & Roper, W. L. (1993). Public health policy for preventing violence. *Health Affairs, 12,* 7–29.

Metzler, C. W., Noell, J., Biglan, A., Ary, D. V., & Smolkowski, K. (1994). The social context for risky sexual behavior among adolescents. *Journal of Behavioral Medicine, 17,* 419–438.

Meyer, A. L., Allison, K. W., Reese, L. R. E., Gay, F. N., & Multisite Violence Prevention Project. (2004). Choosing to be violence free in middle school— The student component of the GREAT schools and families universal program. *American Journal of Preventive Medicine, 26,* 20–28.

Meyer, A. L., Farrell, A. D., Northup, W., Kung, E. M., & Plybon, L. (2000). *Promoting non-violence in early adolescence: Responding in peaceful and positive ways.* New York: Kluwer Academic/Plenum Publishers.

Moffitt, T. E. (1993). Adolescence-limited and life-course-persistent antisocial behavior—A developmental taxonomy. *Psychological Review, 100,* 674–701.

Moffitt, T. E., Caspi, A., Harrington, H., & Milne, B. J. (2002). Males on the life-course-persistent and adolescence-limited antisocial pathways: Follow-up at age 26 years. *Development and Psychopathology, 14,* 179–207.

Multisite Violence Prevention Project. (2004a). Lessons learned in the Multisite Violence Prevention Project Collaboration—Big questions require large efforts. *American Journal of Preventive Medicine, 26,* 62–71.

Multisite Violence Prevention Project. (2004b). The Multisite Violence Prevention Project—Background and overview. *American Journal of Preventive Medicine, 26,* 3–11.

Munroe, R. L., Munroe, R. H., Turner, J., Zaron, E., Potter, H. A., & Woulbroun, E. J. (1989). Sex differences in East-African dreams of aggression. *Journal of Social Psychology, 129,* 727–728.

Murphy, J. J. (1997). *Solution-focused counseling in middle and high schools.* Alexandria, VA: American Counseling Association.

Murray, N., Kelder, S., Parcel, G., & Orpinas, P. (1998). Development of an intervention map for a parent education intervention to prevent violence among Hispanic middle school students. *Journal of School Health, 68,* 46–52.

Mytton, J. A., DiGuiseppi, C., Gough, D. A., Taylor, R. S., & Logan, S. (2002). School-based violence prevention programs—Systematic review of secondary prevention trials. *Archives of Pediatrics & Adolescent Medicine, 156,* 752–762.

Nansel, T. R., Overpeck, M. D., Haynie, D. L., Ruan, W. J., & Scheidt, P. C. (2003). Relationships between bullying and violence among U.S. youth. *Archives of Pediatrics & Adolescent Medicine, 157,* 348–353.

Nansel, T. R., Overpeck, M., Pilla, R. S., Ruan, W. J., Simons-Morton, B., & Scheidt, P. (2001). Bullying behaviors among U.S. youth—Prevalence and association with psychosocial adjustment. *Journal of the American Medical Association, 285,* 2094–2100.

Nasby, W., Hayden, B., & Depaulo, B. M. (1980). Attributional bias among aggressive boys to interpret unambiguous social stimuli as displays of hostility. *Journal of Abnormal Psychology, 89,* 459–468.

Nastasi, B. K., Pluymert, K., Varjas, K., & Moore, R. B. (2002). *Exemplary mental health programs: School psychologists as mental health service providers.* Bethesda, MD: National Association of School Psychologists. Retrieved June 8, 2005, from http://www.naspcenter.org/Exemp/EMHPfront_matter.pdf

Naylor, P., & Cowie, H. (1999). The effectiveness of peer support systems in challenging school bullying: The perspectives and experiences of teachers and pupils. *Journal of Adolescence, 22,* 467–479.

Neel, R. S., Jenkins, Z. N., & Meadows, N. (1990). Social problem-solving behaviors and aggression in young children: A descriptive observational study. *Behavioral Disorders, 16,* 39–51.

Nelson, J. R., Benner, G. J., Reid, R. C., Epstein, M. H., & Currin, D. (2002). The convergent validity of office discipline referrals with the CBCL–TRF. *Journal of Emotional and Behavioral Disorders, 10,* 181–188.

Nelsen, J., Lott, L., & Glenn, H. S. (2000). *Positive discipline in the classroom: Developing mutual respect, cooperation, and responsibility in your classroom* (3rd ed.). Roseville, CA: Prima Publishing.

Newman, D. A., & Horne, A. M. (2004). Bully Busters: A psychoeducational intervention for reducing bullying behavior in middle school students. *Journal of Counseling and Development, 82,* 259–268.

Newman, D. A., Horne, A. M., & Bartolomucci, C. L. (2000). *Bully Busters: A teacher's manual for helping bullies, victims, and bystanders.* Champaign, IL: Research Press.

Ney, P., Colbert, P., Newman, B., & Young, J. (1986). Aggressive behavior and learning difficulties as symptoms of depression in children. *Child Psychiatry and Human Development, 17,* 3–13.

Novaco, R. W. (1975). *Anger control: The development and evaluation of an experimental treatment.* Lexington, MA: D. C. Heath.

Olweus, D. (1979). Stability of aggressive reaction patterns in males: A review. *Psychological Bulletin, 86,* 852–875.

Olweus, D. (1991). Bully–victim problems among school children: Basic facts and effects of a school based intervention program. In K. Rubin & D. Pepler (Eds.),

The development and treatment of childhood aggression (pp. 411–448). Hillsdale, NJ: Erlbaum.

Olweus, D. (1993a). Bullies on the playground: The role of victimization. In C. H. Hart (Ed.), *Children on playgrounds* (pp. 85–128). Albany, NY: SUNY Press.

Olweus, D. (1993b). *Bullying at school: What we know and what we can do.* Cambridge, MA: Blackwell Publishers.

Olweus, D. (1994a). Annotation: Bullying at school: Basic facts and effects of a school based intervention program. *Journal of Child Psychology and Psychiatry, 35,* 1171–1190.

Olweus, D. (1994b). Bullying at school: Long-term outcomes for the victims and an effective school-based intervention program. In L. R. Huesmann (Ed.), *Aggressive behavior: Current perspectives* (pp. 97–130). New York: Plenum Press.

Olweus, D., & Limber, S. (2002). *Bullying prevention program* (Book 9). Boulder: University of Colorado at Boulder, Center for the Study and Prevention of Violence, Institute of Behavioral Science.

O'Moore, M. (2000). Critical issues for teacher training to counter bullying and victimisation in Ireland. *Aggressive Behavior, 26,* 99–111.

O'Moore, M., & Kirkham, C. (2001). Self-esteem and its relationship to bullying behaviour. *Aggressive Behavior, 27,* 269–283.

Orpinas, P. (1999). Who is violent? Factors associated with aggressive behaviors in Latin America and Spain. *Revista Panamericana de Salud Pública, 5,* 232–244.

Orpinas, P. K., Basen-Engquist, K., Grunbaum, J. A., & Parcel, G. S. (1995). The comorbidity of violence-related behaviors with health-risk behaviors in a population of high school students. *Journal of Adolescent Health, 16,* 216–225.

Orpinas, P., & Frankowski, R. (2001). The Aggression Scale: A self-report measure of aggressive behavior for young adolescents. *Journal of Early Adolescence, 21,* 51–68.

Orpinas, P., Horne, A. M., & Multisite Violence Prevention Project. (2004). A teacher-focused approach to prevent and reduce students' aggressive behavior—The GREAT Teacher Program. *American Journal of Preventive Medicine, 26,* 29–38.

Orpinas, P., Horne, A. M., & Staniszewski, D. (2003). School bullying: Changing the problem by changing the school. *School Psychology Review, 32,* 431–444.

Orpinas, P., Kelder, S., Frankowski, R., Murray, N., Zhang, Q., & McAlister, A. (2000). Outcome evaluation of a multi-component violence-prevention program for middle schools: The Students for Peace project. *Health Education Research, 15,* 45–58.

Orpinas, P., Murray, N., & Kelder, S. (1999). Parental influences on students' aggressive behaviors and weapon carrying. *Health Education & Behavior, 26,* 774–787.

Patterson, G. R. (1982). *A social learning approach: Volume 3. Coercive family process.* Eugene, OR: Castalia Publishing.

Patterson, G. R., DeBaryshe, B. D., & Ramsey, E. (1989). A developmental perspective on antisocial behavior. *American Psychologist, 44*, 329–335.

Patterson, G. R., & Forgatch, M. (1987). *Parents and adolescents living together*. Eugene, OR: Castalia Publishing.

Patterson, G. R., Reid, J. B., Jones, R. M., & Conger, R. E. (1975). *A social learning approach to family intervention*. Eugene, OR: Castalia Publishing.

Patterson, G. R., & Stouthamer-Loeber, M. (1984). The correlation of family management practices and delinquency. *Child Development, 55*, 1299–1307.

Patton, M. (1996). *Utilization-focused evaluation*. Thousand Oaks, CA: Sage.

Pellegrini, A. D. (1996). *Observing children in their natural worlds: A methodological primer*. Mahwah, NJ: Erlbaum.

Pellegrini, A. D. (1998). Bullies and victims in school: A review and call for research. *Journal of Applied Developmental Psychology, 19*, 165–176.

Pellegrini, A. D., & Bartini, M. (2000). An empirical comparison of methods of sampling aggression and victimization in school settings. *Journal of Educational Psychology, 92*, 360–366.

Perry, D. G., Kusel, S. J., & Perry, L. C. (1988). Victims of peer aggression. *Developmental Psychology, 24*, 807–814.

Perry, D. G., Perry, L. C., & Rasmussen, P. (1986). Cognitive social learning mediators of aggression. *Child Development, 57*, 700–711.

Perry, D. G., Williard, J. C., & Perry, L. C. (1990). Peers' perceptions of the consequences that victimized children provide aggressors. *Child Development, 61*, 1310–1325.

Pettit, G. S., Bates, J. E., Dodge, K. A., & Meece, D. W. (1999). The impact of after-school peer contact on early adolescent externalizing problems is moderated by parental monitoring, perceived neighborhood safety, and prior adjustment. *Child Development, 70*, 768–778.

Pianta, R. C. (1999). *Enhancing relationships between children and teachers*. Washington, DC: American Psychological Association.

Pierce, C. (1994). Importance of classroom climate for at-risk learners. *Journal of Educational Research, 88*, 37–42.

Pikas, A. (2002). New developments of the shared concern method. *School Psychology International, 23*, 307–326.

Pollak, S., & Gilligan, C. (1982). Images of violence in Thematic Apperception Test stories. *Journal of Personality and Social Psychology, 42*, 159–167.

Porche-Burke, L., & Fulton, C. (1992). *The impact of gang violence: Strategies for prevention and intervention*. Newbury Park, CA: Sage.

Price, J. H., Merrill, E. A., & Clause, M. E. (1992). The depiction of guns on prime-time television. *Journal of School Health, 62*, 15–18.

Prinstein, M. J., Boergers, J., & Vernberg, E. M. (2001). Overt and relational aggression in adolescents: Social–psychological adjustment of aggressors and victims. *Journal of Clinical Child Psychology, 30*, 479–491.

Prinz, R. J., & Miller, G. E. (1996). Parental engagement in interventions for children at risk for conduct disorder. In R. Peters & R. J. McMahon (Eds.), *Preventing childhood disorders, substance abuse, and delinquency* (pp. 161–183). Thousand Oaks, CA: Sage.

Purkey, W. W. (2000). *What students say to themselves: Internal dialogue and school success.* Thousand Oaks, CA: Corwin Press.

Purkey, W. W., & Schmidt, J. J. (1996). *Invitational counseling: A self-concept approach to professional practice.* Pacific Grove, CA: Brooks/Cole.

Quinn, W. H. (2004). *Family solutions for youth at risk: Applications to juvenile delinquency, truancy, and behavior problems.* New York: Brunner-Routledge.

Reid, J. B. (1978). *A social learning approach to family intervention: Observation in home settings* (Vol. 2). Eugene, OR: Castalia Publishing.

Reid, J. B., Patterson, G. R., & Snyder, J. (2002). *Antisocial behavior in children and adolescents: A developmental analysis and model for intervention.* Washington, DC: American Psychological Association.

Resnick, M. D., Bearman, P. S., Blum, R. W., Bauman, K. E., Harris, K. M., Jones, J., et al. (1997). Protecting adolescents from harm—Findings from the National Longitudinal Study on Adolescent Health. *Journal of the American Medical Association, 278,* 823–832.

Reyna, C. (2000). Lazy, dumb, or industrious: When stereotypes convey attribution information in the classroom. *Educational Psychology Review, 12,* 85–110.

Reynolds, C. R., & Kamphaus, R. W. (1992). *BASC—Behavioral Assessment System for Children: Manual.* Circle Pines, MN: American Guidance Service.

Robinson, S. E., Morrow, S., Kigin, T., & Lindeman, M. (1991). Peer counselors in a high school setting: Evaluation and training impact on students. *School Counselor, 39,* 35–40.

Rohrbach, L. A., Graham, J. W., & Hansen, W. B. (1993). Diffusion of a school-based substance abuse prevention program: Predictors of program implementation. *Preventive Medicine, 22,* 237–260.

Rosenthal, R. (1994). Interpersonal expectancy effects—A 30-year perspective. *Current Directions in Psychological Science, 3,* 176–179.

Ross, D. M. (1996). *Childhood bullying and teasing: What school personnel, other professionals, and parents can do.* Alexandria, VA: American Counseling Association.

Ross, D. M. (2003). *Childhood bullying, teasing, and violence: What school personnel, other professionals, and parents can do* (2nd ed.). Alexandria, VA: American Counseling Association.

Rowlings, J. K. (1999). *Harry Potter and the chamber of secrets.* New York: Arthur A. Levine Books.

Rule, B. G., & Ferguson, T. J. (1986). The effect of media violence on attitudes, emotions, and cognitions. *Journal of Social Issues, 42,* 29–50.

Rusnak, T. (1998). *An integrated approach to character education.* Thousand Oaks, CA: Corwin Press.

Sabella, R. A., & Myrick, R. D. (1995). *Confronting sexual harassment: Learning activities for teens*. Minneapolis, MN: Educational Media Corporation.

Sallis, J. F., & Owen, N. (2002). Ecological models of health behavior. In K. Glanz, B. K. Rimer, & F. M. Lewis (Eds.), *Health behavior and health education: Theory, research, and practice* (3rd ed., pp. 462–484). San Francisco: Jossey-Bass.

Salmivalli, C. (1999). Participant role approach to school bullying: Implications for interventions. *Journal of Adolescence, 22*, 453–459.

Salmivalli, C., Karhunen, J., & Lagerspetz, K. M. J. (1996). How do the victims respond to bullying? *Aggressive Behavior, 22*, 99–109.

Salmivalli, C., Kaukiainen, A., Kaistaniemi, L., & Lagerspetz, K. M. J. (1999). Self-evaluated self-esteem, peer-evaluated self-esteem, and defensive egotism as predictors of adolescents' participation in bullying situations. *Personality and Social Psychology Bulletin, 25*, 1268–1278.

Salmivalli, C., Lappalainen, M., & Lagerspetz, K. M. (1998). Stability and change of behavior in connection with bullying in schools: A two-year follow-up. *Aggressive Behavior, 24*, 205–218.

Sayger, T. V., Horne, A. M., Walker, J. M., & Passmore, J. L. (1988). Social learning family therapy with aggressive children: Treatment outcome and maintenance. *Journal of Family Psychology, 1*, 261–285.

Scales, P., & Leffert, N. (1999). *Developmental assets*. Minneapolis, MN: Search Institute.

Schmidt, J. J. (1997). *Making and keeping friends: Ready-to-use lessons, stories, and activities for building relationships grades 4–8*. West Nyack, NY: Center for Applied Research in Education.

Schneider, M., & Robin, A. (1976). The turtle technique. In J. Krumboltz & C. Thoresen (Eds.), *Counseling methods* (pp. 157–162). New York: Holt, Rinehart & Winston.

Schwartz, D., Dodge, K. A., & Coie, J. D. (1993). The emergence of chronic peer victimization in boys' play groups. *Child Development, 64*, 1755–1772.

Schwartz, D., Dodge, K. A., Pettit, G. S., & Bates, J. E. (1997). The early socialization of aggressive victims of bullying. *Child Development, 68*, 665–675.

Seligman, M. E. P., Reivich, K., Jaycox, L., & Gillham, J. (1995). *The optimistic child: A proven program to safeguard children against depression and build lifelong resiliency*. New York: HarperPerennial.

Sessions, P., Fanolis, V., Corwin, M., & Miller, J. (2003). Partners for success: A collaborative approach. In J. Miller, I. Martin, & G. Schamess (Eds.), *School violence and children in crisis: Community and school interventions for social workers and counselors* (pp. 241–254). Denver, CO: Love Publishing.

Shapiro, E. S., Dupaul, G. J., Bradley, K. L., & Bailey, L. T. (1996). A school-based consultation program for service delivery to middle school students with attention-deficit/hyperactivity disorder. *Journal of Emotional and Behavioral Disorders, 4*, 73–81.

Shaw, D. S., & Bell, R. Q. (1993). Developmental theories of parental contributors to antisocial behavior. *Journal of Abnormal Child Psychology, 21*, 493–518.

Shure, M. B. (2001). *I can problem solve: An interpersonal cognitive problem-solving program. Kindergarten and primary grades.* Champaign, IL: Research Press.

Silberman, M. L. (1995). *When your child is difficult: Solve your toughest child-raising problems with a four-step plan that works.* Champaign, IL: Research Press.

Silvernail, D. L., Thompson, A. M., Yang, Z., & Kopp, H. J. P. (2000). *A survey of bullying behavior among Maine third graders.* Retrieved February 20, 2005, from http://lincoln.midcoast.com/~wps/against/bullying.html

Simonoff, E., Pickles, A., Meyer, J. M., Silberg, J. L., Maes, H. H., Loeber, R., et al. (1997). The Virginia Twin Study of adolescent behavioral development—Influences of age, sex, and impairment on rates of disorder. *Archives of General Psychiatry, 54,* 801–808.

Skiba, R. J. (2000). *Zero tolerance, zero evidence: An analysis of school disciplinary practice* (Publication No. SRS2). Bloomington: Indiana Education Policy Center.

Skroban, S. B., Gottfredson, D. C., & Gottfredson, G. D. (1999). A school-based social competency promotion demonstration. *Evaluation Review, 23,* 3–27.

Slaby, R. G., & Guerra, N. G. (1988). Cognitive mediators of aggression in adolescent offenders: 1. Assessment. *Developmental Psychology, 24,* 580–588.

Slaby, R. G., Wilson-Brewer, R., & Dash, K. (1994). *Aggressors, victims, and bystanders: Thinking and acting to prevent violence.* Newton, MA: Education Development Center.

Smith, E. P., Connell, C. M., Wright, G., Sizer, M., & Norman, J. M. (1997). An ecological model of home, school, and community partnerships: Implications for research and practice. *Journal of Educational and Psychological Consultation, 8,* 339–360.

Smith, E. P., Gorman-Smith, D., Quinn, W. H., Rabiner, D. L., Tolan, P. H., Winn, D. M., et al. (2004). Community-based multiple family groups to prevent and reduce violent and aggressive behavior—The GREAT Families Program. *American Journal of Preventive Medicine, 26,* 39–47.

Smylie, M. A. (1989). Teachers' views of the effectiveness of sources of learning to teach. *Elementary School Journal, 89,* 543–558.

Solomon, D., Battistich, V., Watson, M., Schaps, E., & Lewis, C. (2000). A six-district study of educational change: Direct and mediating effects of the Child Development Project. *Social Psychology of Education, 4,* 3–51.

Somersalo, H., Solantaus, T., & Almqvist, F. (2002). Classroom climate and the mental health of primary school children. *Nordic Journal of Psychiatry, 56,* 285–290.

Staub, E. (1999). Aggression and self-esteem. *APA Monitor Online, 30.* Retrieved June 8, 2005, from http://www.apa.org/monitor/jan99/pcp.html

Stein, N., Gaberman, E., & Sjostrom, L. (1996). *Bullyproof: A teacher's guide on teasing and bullying for use with fourth and fifth grade students.* Wellesley, MA: Wellesley College Center for Research on Women.

Steinberg, L., Fletcher, A., & Darling, N. (1994). Parental monitoring and peer influences on adolescent substance use. *Pediatrics, 93,* 1060–1064.

Steinberg, L., & Morris, A. S. (2001). Adolescent development. *Annual Review of Psychology, 52,* 83–110.

Steinberg, M. S., & Dodge, K. A. (1983). Attributional bias in aggressive adolescent boys and girls. *Journal of Social and Clinical Psychology, 1,* 312–321.

Stockdale, M. S., Hangaduambo, S., Duys, D., Larson, K., & Sarvela, P. D. (2002). Rural elementary students', parents', and teachers' perceptions of bullying. *American Journal of Health Behavior, 26,* 266–277.

Stokols, D. (1996). Translating social ecological theory into guidelines for community health promotion. *American Journal of Health Promotion, 10,* 282–298.

Straus, M. A. (1994). *Beating the devil out of them: Corporal punishment in American families.* New York: Cambridge University Press.

Straus, M. A., Sugarman, D. B., & GilesSims, J. (1997). Spanking by parents and subsequent antisocial behavior of children. *Archives of Pediatrics & Adolescent Medicine, 151,* 761–767.

Substance Abuse and Mental Health Services Administration [SAMHSA], & U. S. Department of Health and Human Services. (2005). *SAMHSA model programs: Effective substance abuse and mental health programs for every community.* Retrieved June 8, 2005, from http://modelprograms.samhsa.gov/

Sugai, G., & Horner, R. (2002). The evolution of discipline practices: School-wide positive behavior supports. *Child & Family Behavior Therapy, 24,* 23–50.

Sullivan, K. (2000). *The anti-bullying handbook.* Auckland, New Zealand: Oxford University Press.

Sutton, J., Smith, P. K., & Swettenham, J. (1999a). Bullying and "theory of mind": A critique of the "social skills deficit" view of anti-social behaviour. *Social Development, 8,* 117–127.

Sutton, J., Smith, P. K., & Swettenham, J. (1999b). Social cognition and bullying: Social inadequacy or skilled manipulation? *British Journal of Developmental Psychology, 17,* 435–450.

Swearer, S. M., & Espelage, D. L. (2004). Introduction: A social–ecological framework of bullying among youth. In D. L. Espelage & S. M. Swearer (Eds.), *Bullying in American schools: A social ecological perspective on prevention and intervention* (pp. 1–12). Mahwah, NJ: Erlbaum.

Swearer, S. M., Song, S. Y., Cary, P. T., Eagle, J. W., & Mickelson, W. T. (2001). Psychosocial correlates in bullying and victimization: The relationship between depression, anxiety, and bully/victim status. *Journal of Emotional Abuse, 2,* 95–122.

Terry, R. (2000). Recent advances in measurement theory and the use of sociometric techniques. In A. Cillessen & W. Bukowski (Eds.), *Recent advances in measurement of acceptance and rejection in the peer system: New directions in child and adolescent development* (pp. 27–53). San Fransisco: Jossey-Bass.

Thomas, M. H., Horton, R. W., Lippincott, E. C., & Drabman, R. S. (1977). Desensitization to portrayals of real-life aggression as a function of exposure to television violence. *Journal of Personality and Social Psychology, 35,* 450–458.

Thompson, N. J., & McClintock, H. O. (2000). *Demonstrating your program's worth: A primer on evaluation for programs to prevent unintentional injury* (rev. ed.). Atlanta, GA: Centers for Disease Control and Prevention, National Center for Injury Prevention and Control.

Tomada, G., & Schneider, B. H. (1997). Relational aggression, gender, and peer acceptance: Invariance across culture, stability over time, and concordance among informants. *Developmental Psychology, 33*, 601–609.

Tripp, G., & Alsop, B. (1999). Sensitivity to reward frequency in boys with attention deficit hyperactivity disorder. *Journal of Clinical Child Psychology, 28*, 366–375.

Tripp, G., & Alsop, B. (2001). Sensitivity to reward delay in children with attention deficit hyperactivity disorder (ADHD). *Journal of Child Psychology and Psychiatry and Allied Disciplines, 42*, 691–698.

Trouilloud, D. O., Sarrazin, P. G., Martinek, T. J., & Guillet, E. (2002). The influence of teacher expectations on student achievement in physical education classes: Pygmalion revisited. *European Journal of Social Psychology, 32*, 591–607.

Troy, M., & Sroufe, L. A. (1987). Victimization among preschoolers: Role of attachment relationship history. *Journal of the American Academy of Child and Adolescent Psychiatry, 63*, 166–172.

Twemlow, S. W., Fonagy, P., Sacco, F. C., Gies, M. L., Evans, R., & Ewbank, R. (2001). Creating a peaceful school learning environment: A controlled study of an elementary school intervention to reduce violence. *American Journal of Psychiatry, 158*, 808–810.

U.S. Department of Education, & Safe, Disciplined, and Drug-Free Schools Expert Panel. (2002). *Exemplary and promising: Safe, disciplined, and drug-free schools programs-2001.* Retrieved June 8, 2005, from http://www.ed.gov/admins/lead/safety/exemplary01/exemplary01.pdf

U.S. Department of Health and Human Services. (2001). *Youth violence: A report of the Surgeon General.* Rockville, MD: U.S. Department of Health and Human Services; Centers for Disease Control and Prevention, National Center for Injury Prevention; Substance Abuse and Mental Health Services Administration, Center for Mental Health Services; and National Institutes of Health, National Institute of Mental Health.

Van Evra, J. (1990). *Television and child development.* Hillsdale, NJ: Erlbaum.

Vessels, G. G. (1998). *Character and community development: A school planning and teacher training handbook.* Westport, CT: Praeger.

Virginia Commonwealth University, Center for the Study and Prevention of Youth Violence, & Virginia Department of Education. (n.d.). *Virginia best practices in school-based violence prevention.* Retrieved June 8, 2005, from http://www.pubinfo.vcu.edu/vabp/

Volling, B. L., & Belsky, J. (1992). The contribution of mother–child and father–child relationships to the quality of sibling interaction: A longitudinal study. *Child Development, 63*, 1209–1222.

Voors, W. (2000). *Bullying: Changing the course of your child's life*. Center City, MN: Hazelden.

Vossekuil, B., Fein, R., Reddy, M., Borum, R., & Modzeleski, W. (2002). *The final report and findings of the safe school initiative: Implications for the prevention of school attacks in the United States*. Washington, DC: U.S. Department of Education, Office of Elementary and Secondary Education, Safe and Drug-Free Schools Program, and U.S. Secret Service, National Threat Assessment Center.

Walker, E. A., Gelfand, A., Katon, W. J., Koss, M. P., Von Korff, M., Bernstein, D., et al. (1999). Adult health status of women with histories of childhood abuse and neglect. *American Journal of Medicine, 107,* 332–339.

Webster-Doyle, T. (1991). *Why is everybody always picking on me: A guide to handling bullies*. Middlebury, VT: Atrium Society.

Welsh, M., Parke, R., Widaman, K., & O'Neil, R. (2001). Linkages between children's social and academic competence: A longitudinal analysis. *Journal of School Psychology, 39,* 463–482.

Weltmann, R., & Center for Applied Research in Education. (1996). *Ready-to-use social skills lessons and activities for grades 7–12*. New York: Society for Prevention of Violence.

Werner, E. E. (1989). High-risk children in young adulthood—A longitudinal study from birth to 32 years. *American Journal of Orthopsychiatry, 59,* 72–81.

Whitaker, T. (1999). *Dealing with difficult teachers*. Larchmont, NY: Eye on Education.

Widom, C. S. (1989a). The cycle of violence. *Science, 244,* 160–166.

Widom, C. S. (1989b). Does violence beget violence? A critical examination of the literature. *Psychological Bulletin, 106,* 3–28.

Williams, K., Chamgers, M., Logan, S., & Robinson, D. (1996). Association of common health symptoms with bullying in primary school children. *British Medical Journal, 313,* 17–19.

Wilson, D. B., Gottfredson, D. C., & Najaka, S. S. (2001). School-based prevention of problem behaviors: A meta-analysis. *Journal of Quantitative Criminology, 17,* 247–272.

Wolke, D., Woods, S., Bloomfield, L., & Karstadt, L. (2001). Bullying involvement in primary school and common health problems. *Archives of Disease in Childhood, 85,* 197–201.

INDEX

Instrumental aggression, 23–25, 184
    and parents' response, 227
    seeking attention and power as, 187
Integrated Approach to Character Education, An
    (Rusnak), 132
Intention(s)
    and aggressive attributional bias, 60–61
    in definitions of violence, aggression
        and bullying, 15
    imagined as aggressive, 41
Internal dialogue, 122, 225
Internet, 51, 52–53. *See also* Web sites
Internet bullying, 251
Interpersonal skills. *See* Social competence
Interpersonal theories, 59, 60. *See also* At-
    tachment theory; Social–cognitive
    theory
Interpersonal violence, 13
Interpretation, by bullies vs. victims, 239
Intervention programs
    and dysfunctional family, 71
    in public health model, 36
    targeted, 147 (*see also* Persistent bullies)
        indicated, 147
        selective, 147
    and theory, 55–59
    universal, 7, 147, 165 (*see also* Evalua-
        tion of problems and programs; Pre-
        vention programs; School environ-
        ment, positive; Social competence)
Interviews, in evaluation process, 161
Intimate partner violence, 234
Intrapersonal risk and protective factors, 37–
    43
Intrapersonal theories and models, 59, 60. *See
    also* Attribution theories; Social in-
    formation-processing model
Intrapersonal violence, 13. *See also* Suicide
Invitational approach, 193, 196
I-Safe America, 250, 252

Johnson, Samuel, on character education,
    131
Journal, of bullying events, 241, 245
Justification of reprehensible conduct, 66-69

Kauai Study, 73
Kids Count project, 250, 252
King, Martin Luther, quoted, 8

Labeling, 67
Language, negative, 213

Learning, commitment to, 42
Learning abilities, 136
Lewin, Kurt, on practicality of theory, 6, 55,
    58
Life Skills Training, 176
Linking the Interests of Families and Teach-
    ers program, 176
Listening skills, 135
Log, of bullying events, 241, 245

Macro theories and models, 59, 60. *See also*
    Ecological model
*Making and Keeping Friends: Ready-to-Use
    Lessons, Stories, and Activities for
    Building Relationships Grades 4–8*
    (Schmidt), 136
Maslach Burnout Inventory, 163
*Measuring Violence-Related Attitudes, Behav-
    iors, and Influences Among Youths: A
    Compendium of Assessment Tools*
    (Dahlberg, Toal, Swahn, and
    Behrens), 161
Media, risk and protective factors in, 39, 51–
    53
Mental health, 136
Meta-analyses, 7, 166–167
Minnesota Center Against Violence and
    Abuse, 250, 252–253
Modeling
    of appropriate behavior, 170, 197, 222
    of respect, 95–96
    of social competence, 247
Model Programs Guide and Database, 168
Models (theoretical), 58–59
Monitoring
    family, 223
    or program execution, 142
Moral development, in ART program, 200.
    See also Character development
Moral justification, 67
Motivating Students Who Don't Care
    (Mendler), 83
Multimodal approach, and school counsel-
    ing, 197
Multiple risk factors, 6
Myths. *See also* Erroneous beliefs
    about bullying and victimization, 87, 88
    about program evaluation, 140–141

National Association of School Psycholo-
    gists, *Exemplary Mental Health Pro-
    grams*, 168

World Health Organization (WHO), violence defined by, 13, 16

Youth development, and positive school climate, 80
Youth Risk Behavior Survey, Center for Disease Control and Prevention, 37

Youth violence
early vs. late onset of, 73–74
Surgeon General on, 197, 201

Zero tolerance policies, 48

ABOUT THE AUTHORS

Pamela Orpinas, PhD, MPH, is an associate professor in the Department of Health Promotion and Behavior, College of Public Health, at the University of Georgia. She studied psychology at the Catholic University of Chile. Before coming to the United States, she worked in Santiago for 10 years conducting research and treatment programs related to individual and family violence. She received a master's degree in public health from the University of California, Los Angeles, and a PhD from the School of Public Health, University of Texas Health Science Center at Houston, and the focus of her studies switched from treatment to prevention. For over a decade, Dr. Orpinas has worked in several research projects specifically related to the prevention of violence among children and adolescents, including the Multisite Violence Prevention Project, Students for Peace, the I–CARE project, and the ACTIVA project. She has been a consultant in the area of violence prevention in several countries and has worked with national and international agencies to prevent violence. She has published and presented at conferences extensively on this topic.

Arthur (Andy) M. Horne, PhD, is Distinguished Research Professor of Counseling Psychology, College of Education, at the University of Georgia. He has been involved in research and treatment programs addressing child and family aggression and violence for more than two decades. During the past years, he has been a principal investigator for the Multisite Violence Prevention Project—GREAT Schools and Families—funded by the Centers for Disease Control and Prevention (1999–present). He has also been a principal investigator for ACT Early, a program funded by the U.S. Department of Education that examines risk and protective factors affecting children's academic, behavioral, and emotional development; the I–CARE program, funded by the Arthur M. Blank Family Foundation to examine effective character development and aggression reduction programs in elementary schools; and the Bully Busters program, developed to evaluate bully reduction programs in elementary and middle schools.